D0152759

Speech Genres and Other Late Essays

University of Texas Press Slavic Series, No. 8

Speech Genres and Other Late Essays

M. M. BAKHTIN

Translated by Vern W. McGee

Edited by Caryl Emerson

and Michael Holquist

UNIVERSITY OF TEXAS PRESS, AUSTIN

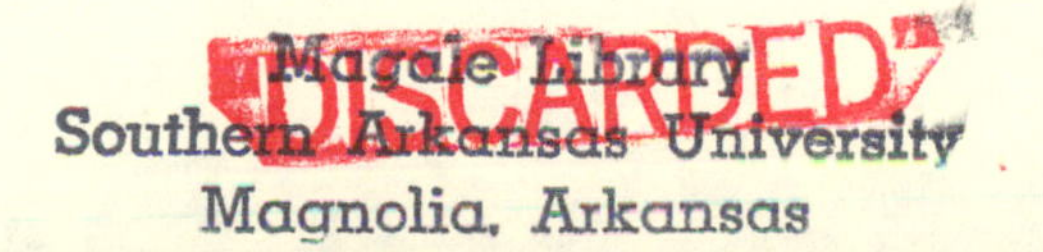

Printed in the United States of America
First Edition, 1986

Library of Congress Cataloging-in-Publication Data
Bakhtin, M. M. (Mikhail Mikhaĭlovich), 1895–1975.
Speech genres and other late essays.

(University of Texas Press Slavic series ; no. 8)
Translation of: Éstetika slovesnogo tvorchestva.
Includes bibliographies and index.
1. Philology. I. Holquist, Michael, 1935–
II. Emerson, Caryl. III. Title. IV. Series.
P49.B2813 1986 410 86-11399
ISBN 0-292-72046-7
ISBN 0-292-72560-1 (pbk.)

Contents

Note on Translation

This translation has benefited a great deal from being among the last rather than the first translations of Bakhtin's work. I have been able to take advantage of the careful consideration previous translators have given to many of the problematic terms and concepts that are so plentiful in Bakhtin's theory. In most cases I have borrowed the terms used in previous translations in the Slavic Series, such as "heteroglossia" (*raznorechie*), "speech" (*rech*), and "discourse" (*slovo*), among others, not only for the sake of consistency throughout the series but because I believe they are good choices.

The essays offered in this volume also contain many of their own perplexing words and concepts, such as "outsideness" (*vnenakhodimost*), which have never before appeared in translation—or in Russian for that matter. On these I have consulted with both native Russian speakers and recognized Bakhtin scholars. In each case the options were weighed carefully, and the one most appropriate in style and tone as well as the closest in meaning was chosen.

With respect to style, I believe these essays show Bakhtin at his most Bakhtinian. The rough, unfinished quality that comes through in his previously translated work is even more in evidence here, because most of these essays were not actually prepared by Bakhtin for publication. They show more the process of his thought than the final product. I have attempted to convey this quality in the translation.

The transliteration system is a modification of the International Phonetic Alphabet: those letters requiring a hachek have been changed to the variants that use the letter "h"—"zh," "ch," "sh," "shch"; the IPA "c" is rendered as "ts" and the "x" as "kh." Proper names are rendered as they ordinarily are or would be spelled in English (e.g., Tolstoy, Dostoevsky).

V. W. McG.

Introduction

"To strive at higher mathematical formulas for linguistic meaning while knowing nothing correctly of the shirt-sleeve rudiments of language is to court disaster."
Benjamin Lee Whorf, "Linguistics as an Exact Science," 1941

". . . there can be neither a first nor a last meaning; [anything that can be understood] always exists among other meanings as a link in the chain of meaning, which in its totality is the only thing that can be real. In historical life this chain continues infinitely, and therefore each individual link in it is renewed again and again, as though it were being reborn."
M. M. Bakhtin, "From Notes Made in 1970–71"

The first recognition in the United States of Bakhtin's status as a major thinker came in 1968, when he was included among a group of internationally known theoreticians contributing to a volume of *Yale French Studies* on the topic "Game, Play, Literature."[1] The identification of Bakhtin provided in the notes on contributors has an unmistakable diffidence about it: "M. Bakhtin . . . is reaching the end of a long career, but only recently have the boldness of his speculation and the breadth of his ideas been appreciated outside the restricted circle of his Russian friends and colleagues." Less than a mere two decades later, Bakhtin is being hailed as "the most important Soviet thinker in the human sciences and the greatest theoretician of literature in the twentieth century."[2] And in March 1985, the executive director of the Modern Language Association announced a "trend-spotting contest to *PMLA* readers . . . I will offer [a prize] to the first reader to locate the earliest mention in *PMLA* of any of the following: Bakhtin, Barthes, Derrida, Freud, Lévi-Strauss, and Karl Marx."[3] In the great marketplace of ideas, Bakhtin has obviously risen very high.

It is, however, a curious fact that of all the names listed in *PMLA*'s roster of trends, Bakhtin is surely still the least known, if only in the sense that much of his work is still unavailable in English translation. Although deceased, he is similar to the still living figures with whom his name is so often conjoined, for in his case as in theirs we lack a complete canon of finished works. He is a figure very much still in the process of becoming who he will be. There can be no question, then, of "introducing" Bakhtin at this point in his unfolding. But before describing each of these essays individually, we may briefly ponder the effect they may have as they appear in English for the first time.

In Bakhtin's thought the place from which we speak plays an important role in determining what we say. A little uneasy, then, about the place from which I myself speak, I suggest that Bakhtin has achieved the degree of eminence at which those who invoke his name can be divided into a number of different camps or schools. There are those who have responded to him primarily as a literary critic; others have seen him as social thinker; still others value him as a philosopher of language (and, of course, these shadings tend to blend into each other in any specific appropriation of Bakhtin). But increasingly a suspicion is beginning to dawn that his work may best (or at least most comprehensively) be thought of as philosophy of another kind, a philosophy across the boards: he is being perceived as belonging to a tradition of systematic philosophy of a sort that did not automatically equate "system" with "method" as we do now. Since the time of Kant, we have with ever increasing insistence perceived system as a closed order rather than as an open-ended series of connections. System for Kant meant not only the rigorous application of a fully worked out and absolutely coherent set of categories. System also implied that no major question should be treated in isolation: thus, any consideration of reason had to answer demands not only of logic or epistemology, but of ethics and aesthetics as well. It is in this latter sense *only* that Bakhtin's thought might be labeled systematic: the sense he seeks to invoke when he calls—as in these pages he so frequently does—for an "open unity." These essays, then, will provide new confirmation and questions for each of the rapidly emerging Bakhtinian tendencies. But since most of the essays come from very late in Bakhtin's activity, at a point when he was again meditating the global questions that had sparked lively debate during the "philosophical evenings" of his youth, they will deepen awareness of Bakhtin's status as a thinker. For these essays are all attempts to think various specific topics in light of the more comprehensive categories we usually associate with philosophy.

The collection of Bakhtin's essays in this book first appeared together in a volume called *Estetika slovesnogo tvorchestva* (Aesthetics of verbal creativity) published in Moscow in 1979. The book was edited by two highly respected scholars: Sergey Averintsev (born 1937), a philosopher and historian admired by Bakhtin; and Sergey Bocharov (born 1927), a literary critic who was particularly close to Bakhtin during the last years of his life.

The 1979 anthology was similar to a collection of Bakhtin's essays that had been published in 1975 (translated into English as *The Dialogic Imagination*);[4] in both, the pieces included came from different periods in the author's long life; and in neither were the essays organized around any single, unified theme. The reason for such apparently casual editing was in both cases the same: the editors, aware of how quickly publishing conditions can change in the Soviet Union, were eager to get as much of Bakhtin into print as they could while they could. *Aesthetics of Verbal Creativity*, then, contained pieces written in Bakhtin's first phase and in his last. It included the first essay Bakhtin ever published, "Art and Answerability," which appeared in 1919 when he was a young man of twenty-four, but it also contained what is probably the last thing he wrote before his death in 1975, "Toward a Methodology for the Human Sciences." The later, less patently philosophical pieces here are mostly devoted to questions of what linguists now call "pragmatics," including excerpts from unpublished manuscripts devoted to literature and essays on the distinctiveness of the human sciences among other forms of knowledge. This translation does not contain everything that was published in 1979 as *Aesthetics of Verbal Creativity*, but *does* include most of the literary essays, and all those on pragmatics and the human sciences from that volume.[5] The essays in this edition have been arranged once again according to the degree of their complexity (not necessarily of their importance) with the literary essays first, followed by the essay on speech genres (pragmatics), concluding with three essays on the larger implications of conceiving dialogue as the root condition of human being.

This volume opens with a transcript of Bakhtin's remarks to a reporter from *Novy Mir*, the "liberal" monthly journal read by most Soviet intellectuals. We begin with this piece because it presents some of Bakhtin's most fundamental assumptions in their most economical and uncomplicated expression. He had been asked what he thought of the state of literary scholarship in 1970, and he used the opportunity not only to point out some inadequacies, but to suggest a positive program of improvement. Not surprisingly, Bakhtin's program for other critics is essentially the program that had organized his own work for over fifty years. Thus, although the title this piece was given by the editors of

Novy Mir when it appeared in November 1970 ("Use Opportunities More Boldly!") sounds rather silly, it fairly captures the aspect of Bakhtin's message that would have been of most immediate consequence to other intellectuals at the time: despite some of the unique difficulties literary scholars have to confront in a society like the Soviet Union, there is no excuse for not doing more serious work. This was a message he above all had the right to convey, for, as everyone knew, the profoundest and most unorthodox of his own works had been written under external conditions far worse than those that existed in 1970.

Bakhtin does not shy away from praising specific critics or, by exclusion, attacking others. Those he honors among the living, such as the great Orientalist Konrad, the medievalist Likhachev, or Yury Lotman, leader of the so-called Tartu School of Semiotics, are all very different from each other in their specific methodologies. They nevertheless all share the habit of stitching whatever text they analyze into a deeply realized cultural context. The other figures Bakhtin mentions with approval—the founder of the great Kharkov School of philologists, Potebnya; Veselovsky, the founder of comparative literature in Russia and a scholar with encyclopedic knowledge of Italian culture; and the Formalist Tynyanov—all insist on the central role the history of culture must play in any analysis of a literary text.[6]

The specific way Bakhtin chooses to discuss culture in this essay dramatizes the extraordinary continuity in his long life, while making clear as well the variety and diversity of the different stages that constitute his career. For instance, the emphasis on openness, on unfinishedness (*nezavershennost*) that is so much a feature of his earliest work is still evident here in his opposition to Spengler's habit of treating cultural units as closed monads, *finished* systems.

But unfinishedness is only one of the key concepts from Bakhtin's early period that is invoked in these remarks made fifty years after their first appearance in his notebooks: others are outsidedness (*vnenakhodimost*) and the distinctive use he makes of the word "body," as when he talks about "material bearers of meaning" in terms of "*bodies* of meaning." The terms and their relation to each other are the same as those found in texts from the early 1920s, but the level at which they operate is different: in "Author and Hero in Aesthetic Activity," he discusses relations between writers and the characters they create; in 1970, he discusses the relation between one's own society and other cultures that are foreign to it in space or time. But in the case of both relationships the analytical model is the same: he stresses the need first to use one's understanding to penetrate the other person or the other culture as deeply as possible; but then, having done this, he stresses in both cases the no less urgent need to *return* to the perspective provided by our native self or our native culture. Circa 1920, he writes, "a pure projection of myself into the other, a move involving the loss of my own unique place outside the other, is, on the whole, hardly possible; in any event it is quite fruitless. . . . Aesthetic activity proper actually begins at the point when we return into ourselves and to our own place outside the [other] person. . . .";[7] in 1970, he says, "a certain entry as a living being into a foreign culture, the possibility of seeing the world through its eyes, is a necessary part of the process of understanding it; but if this were the only aspect of this understanding, it would merely be duplication and would not entail anything new or enriching. . . . In order to understand, it is immensely important for the person who understands to be *located outside* the object of his or her creative understanding—in time, in space, in culture" ("Response to a Question from the *Novy Mir* Editorial Staff").

The essay on the *Bildungsroman* is actually a fragment from one of Bakhtin's several lost books. In this case, nonpublication cannot be blamed on insensitive censors. Its nonappearance resulted, rather, from effects that grew out of the Second World War, one of the three great historical moments Bakhtin lived through (the other two being the Bolshevik Revolution and the Stalinist purges). Sovetsky pisatel (Soviet Writer), the publishing house that was to bring out Bakhtin's book *The Novel of Education and Its Significance in the History of Realism*, was blown up in the early months of the German invasion, with the loss of the manuscript on which he had worked for at least two years (1936–38). Bakhtin retained only certain preparatory materials and a prospectus of the book; due to the paper shortage, he had torn them up page by page during the war to make wrappers for his endless chain of cigarettes. He began smoking pages from the conclusion of the manuscript, so what we have is a small portion of its opening section, primarily about Goethe.[8]

Goethe is a major figure in Bakhtin's personal pantheon for reasons that are apparent in the fragment here translated. Rabelais and Dostoevsky had in their turn permitted him to write a history of large-scale cultural transformations (similar to what the Annales School of French historians have called transformations of *mentalités*). Such novelists enabled Bakhtin to use a literary genre to focus data from a number of different areas that—without such a prism—would be hopelessly diffused. Goethe, too, serves as a center around which Bakhtin can lay open a whole age. We see in this fragment why Bakhtin thought of himself less as a literary critic than as a "philosophical anthropologist," for the questions he seeks to answer in his study are less those that occupy other historians of literature than questions about the nature of human consciousness under particular cultural and historical conditions. Bakhtin was throughout his life obsessed by Kant (eighteenth-century Germany constitutes a kind of Golden Age in his thought); we see Bakhtin here once again posing the question with which Kant always opened his course on anthropology—"What is Man?"—where the answer depends on specific shadings of the temporal and spatial categories used to organize the world at different historical moments.

This fragment also manifests a tendency in Bakhtin's work methods that characterized him early and late: the tendency to think through a central problem by coming at it in a number of different texts, each of which has its own particular way of bringing out nuances less apparent or even missing in the others. Bakhtin's first years as a mature thinker are marked by different versions (some possibly of book length) of his phenomenology of self/other relations; in the twenties, there are different books devoted to the linguistic and societal implications of such a phenomenology; and in the thirties we see at least six texts devoted to the novel as a genre,[9] of which the book on the *Bildungsroman* is one. It is not surprising, then, that it shares many of the concerns, and even some of the locutions, of other works in the thirties. Like the others, it attempts to distinguish a period's most deeply held cultural values through analysis of the formal constructions by which the age's greatest artist manifested time/space perception in the novel. Yet again we are given an account of chronotopes as they are present in adventure novels, biographical novels, and the novel of ordeal, a catalog of types also found in "Discourse in the Novel" (1934–35) and in the monograph on Bakhtin's concept of the chronotope (1937–38). But all of this has a different resonance in the specific context made available by Goethe, who calls up associations with new works or whole genres not treated in other essays of the 1930s.

Of course, what is chiefly remarkable about this fragment is the view of Goethe it provides. There are suggestive similarities with the vision of Goethe we get in Emil Staiger's monumental three-volume study.[10] But this fragment is notable for the inventiveness with which Bakhtin documents that quality of *wholeness*, which he sees as the distinctive feature of everything Goethe did, as a man, a scientist, a poet, or a novelist—even as a town planner.[11] There are many reasons to deplore the loss of the total manuscript of which only this fragment remains, perhaps not least that it would have provided a counterweight to the overly exuberant appropriations recently made of carnival as Bakhtin bodied it forth in his Rabelais book dating from this same period: the concept of education, of self-formation, that was at the heart of the larger book shows us a Bakhtin honoring such apparently conventional values (even if, as in Goethe's case, taken to an unconventional extreme) as measure, balance, and civic rectitude. Carnival as we have it in Rabelais (or at least in Bakhtin's book on Rabelais) calls out for the dialogic context that education, *Erziehung*, provides in Goethe (or at least in Bakhtin's Goethe fragment). This essay manifests, then, a stoic sense of external constraint common to all the pieces included in the present anthology.

"The Problem of Speech Genres," the piece giving this anthology its title, is extremely dense because it takes up within relatively small compass a topic to which Bakhtin planned to devote a large book during the last twenty years of his life (*The Genres of Speech*). The essay as it is presented here was written in 1952–53, while Bakhtin was still teaching at the Mordvinian State University in Saransk, but shows evidence of Bakhtin's own editing that makes it more organized and cohesive than some of the others here included. It will fit better, too, into the expectations of those who value Bakhtin primarily as a philosopher of language, the Bakhtin of *Marxism and the Philosophy of Language*, for it takes up once again the difference between Saussurean linguistics and language conceived as living dialogue (or, as Bakhtin sometimes called it, meta- or translinguistics).

Perhaps the most important aspect of this essay is the light it sheds on Bakhtin's understanding of the differences between literary and everyday language—that bugbear of the Russian Formalists (and their heirs)—as graduated rather than as absolute. He begins by pointing to the irony that genres have been studied only in the areas of rhetoric and literature, whereas the enormous ocean of extraliterary genres from which those two disciplines have drawn their forms has remained unexplored. Yet it is from that ocean that they get their life: there are primary genres that legislate permissible locutions in lived life, and secondary genres made up out of these that constitute not only literary but all other text types (legal, scientific, journalistic) as well. In fact, what distinguishes one human undertaking from another, one science from another, is the roster of genres each has appropriated as its own. Secondary genres may be more complex, but they are still part of the spectrum of possible genre types that includes at its other pole the most banal expressions we use every day at work, with our friends, and so forth. What ensures the connectedness of all genres, from the most highly wrought experimental novel to the simple salutations with which we greet our families when returning home from work, is the fact that they are all constructed out of the same material: words.

But genres are constructed with words not as they exist in the system Bakhtin here calls mere language, but rather as they are present in communication. The distinction between the two is not, as is sometimes assumed, merely a reformulation of the difference between *langue* and *parole,* general system and particular performance. "Communication" as Bakhtin uses the term does indeed cover many of the aspects of Saussure's *parole,* for it is concerned with what happens when real people in all the contingency of their myriad lives actually speak to each other. But Saussure conceived the individual language user to be an absolutely free agent with the ability to choose any words to implement a particular intention. Saussure concluded, not surprisingly, that language as used by heterogeneous millions of such willful subjects was unstudiable, a chaotic jungle beyond the capacity of science to domesticate.

Bakhtin, on the other hand, begins by assuming that individual speakers do not have the kind of freedom *parole* assumes they have: the basic unit for the study of actual speech practice is the "utterance," which, "with all its individuality and creativity, can in no way be regarded as a *completely free combination* of forms of language, as is supposed, for example, by Saussure . . . who juxtaposed the utterance (*la parole*) as a purely individual act, to the system of language as a phenomenon that is purely social and mandatory for the individuum" ("The Problem of Speech Genres"). The problem here is that the great Genevan linguist overlooks the fact that "in addition to the forms of language there are also *forms of combinations* of these forms" (ibid.). These forms of combinations of forms are what Bakhtin calls speech genres. And although he recognizes their enormous variety, he is able to conclude, unlike Saussure, that the immediate reality of living speech *can* be studied, for although "each separate utterance is individual . . . each sphere in which language is used develops its own *relatively stable types* of these utterances" (ibid.).

This essay, then, not only outlines what such stable types are, but suggests implications for the study of linguistics, literature, and other human sciences. Since this essay is one of Bakhtin's most pellucid, I shall not dwell on these, but remark only that, for those concerned with the thought of Bakhtin himself, this piece holds great interest as a further contribution not only to his translinguistics, but to his conception of the subject. Given its emphasis on normative restraints that control even our most intimate speech, the essay should at the very least sound a cautionary note for those who wish to invoke Bakhtin in the service of a boundless libertarianism.

"The Problem of the Text" is typical of most works from Bakhtin's last years in that it is not so much an essay as a series of entries from the notebooks in which Bakhtin jotted down his thoughts. Keeping such notebooks was a habit he had developed in his youth and one he maintained throughout his career. This lifelong dialogue with himself accounts for many of the features that characterize Bakhtin's style (or, more accurately, *one* of Bakhtin's styles): the allusive structure of his remarks and the repetitiveness that so often bothers readers trained to value more economical and forensic presentation. Anyone expecting a finished, consecutively prosecuted argument in these pieces that have been torn out of the notebooks is bound to be frustrated. But the suspension of such expectations reveals a style that has its own rewards: not the pleasure we derive from an author who compels us to believe his logic is ineluctable, but the excitement that comes from seeing a mind at work *while* it is at work.

Such a style diminishes the capacity of titles to name a text's subject, for it is a style that never focuses on any *single* topic. Most of the titles for these late pieces have been assigned by Bakhtin's editors; they have done an excellent job, but it is in the nature of Bakhtin's modus operandi that in many cases these titles could just as well be applied to other texts from the same period. Thus, while this particular piece has been called "The Problem of the Text," and while, indeed, it is a meditation most concentrated on that topic, it also contains long sections devoted to related but different topics announced in titles of other pieces, such as speech genres, the status of the author, or the distinctiveness of the human sciences.

This piece is of particular importance because, in worrying the problem of how a text relates to its context, the essay has a good deal to say about the general topic of dialogue, the central category in Bakhtin's thought and yet the most misunderstood aspect of his work.

Bakhtin himself must bear part of the responsibility for the widespread confusion that characterizes appropriations of "dialogism." For while dialogue is a frequently invoked concept in most of what he wrote, there are relatively few places where he concentrates on the subject in any detail, as he does here. The cloud of binaries at the beginning of the piece (repeatable/nonrepeatable, natural science/human science, thing/meaning, etc.) is later resolved into a set of relations that are revealed to be not binary, but tertiary: "The word is a drama in which three characters participate (it is not a duet, but a trio)" ("The Problem of the Text"). Working as always with a specular subject (a self derived from the other), he makes it clear that speakers always shape an utterance not only according to the object of discourse (*what* they are talking *about*) and their immediate addressee (*whom* they are speaking *to*), but also according to the particular image in which they model the belief they will be understood, a belief that is the *a priori* of all speech. Thus, each speaker authors an utterance not only with an audience-addressee, but a *superaddressee* in mind: ". . . in addition to [the immediate addressee] the author of the utterance, with a greater or lesser awareness, presupposes a higher *superaddressee* (third), whose absolutely just and responsive understanding is presumed, either in some metaphysical distance or in distant historical time. . . . In various ages and with various understandings of the world, this superaddressee and his ideally true responsive understanding assume various ideological expressions (God, absolute truth, the court of dispassionate human conscience, the people, the court of history, science, and so forth)" (ibid.).

If there is something like a God concept in Bakhtin, it is surely the superaddressee, for without faith that we will be understood somehow, sometime, by *somebody*, we would not speak at all. Or if we did, it would be babbling. And babble, as Dostoevsky shows in his short story "Bobok," is the language of the dead.

Dostoevsky was very much on Bakhtin's mind—as usual—during 1970 and 1971, as we can see in the fragments printed here from the notebook he kept in those years. Although seventy-six years old and a transient moving between hospitals and homes for the aged, he was energized by the excitement his republished works had aroused and his head was full of new projects. These included several extremely ambitious studies, among others a big book on sentimentalism and a major article for *Questions of Philosophy*, the leading Soviet philosophical journal, that was to be a manifesto showing how both the natural and human sciences could be reconceived in light of his dialogism. But in the winter of 1971, Bakhtin's deeply loved wife and his truest other, Elena Aleksandrovna, died, and he was cast into a deep depression that kept him from realizing most of his writing plans.

The notebook entries included here, however, were jotted down before his wife's death, when Bakhtin was still full of energy. They reflect a figure of great intelligence, erudition, and life experience at the height of his powers. A common theme running throughout is the need to exceed boundaries, while still recognizing that only through awareness of the very real restraints at work in mental and social life can we do so. The tone here is hortatory as he encourages others to conceive more expansive borders between utterances ("There can be no such thing as an isolated utterance" ["From Notes Made in 1970–71"]), at one level, and between whole modes of knowledge, at another ("The distinction between the human and natural sciences. The rejection of the idea of an insurmountable barrier between them" [ibid.]). He celebrates the infinite possibility of interpretation,[12] deploring at the same time the way "we have narrowed it terribly by selecting and by modernizing what has been selected. We impoverish the past and do not enrich ourselves. We are suffocating in the captivity of narrow and homogeneous interpretations" (ibid.).

A note of caution is in order here: Bakhtin's call to liberation is everywhere informed by a stern awareness of necessity's central place in the biological limits of our perception, the structure of language, and the laws of society. Our very status as the subjects of our own lives depends on the necessary presence of other subjects. Thus, when Bakhtin says "we are suffocating in the captivity of narrow and homogeneous interpretations," he is not suggesting there is some freedom *beyond* interpretation. All understanding is constrained by borders: freedom consists in knowing insofar as possible—for our ability to know is controlled by contextual factors larger than mere individual intention—what those borders are, so that they may be substituted by, translated into different borders. Speech genres provide a good example of this *relative* degree of freedom: the better we know possible variants of the genres that are appropriate to a given situation, the more choice we have among them. Up to a point we may play with speech genres, but we cannot avoid being generic. There is no pure spontaneity, for breaking frames depends on the existence of frames.

Bakhtin had serious differences with Gestalt theorists such as Koffka, but the central concept in their psychology he maintained with even greater vigor than they in his translinguistics: there is no figure without a ground. Even dialogue needs monologue.

These notebook entries are a useful corrective, then, to the carnivalistic image of Bakhtin now abroad, for they come back again and again to the power of frames. There is much in these notes on such characteristic Bakhtinian topics as the situatedness of the subject, the distinctiveness of the Dostoevskian novel, and the myriad complexities concentrated in the activity we call authorship. But behind each of these separate topics there is an overarching insistence on the degree to which our lives are drenched in signs and conventions. Yet another border Bakhtin asks us here to acknowledge is that between life and ritual. Conventional wisdom holds that our everyday existence is semiotically "pure," uncontaminated by the theatrical markedness that is most obvious in ceremonies; but "pure everyday life is a fiction . . . Human life is always shaped and this shaping is always ritualistic" ("From Notes Made in 1970–71"). Thus, a major border between private and public life is here breached, as well as that between aesthetics as it is now—narrowly—understood and aesthetics as it has been understood in former ages (as in Kant's third critique). Bakhtin is arguing here that art is only one (if a fundamentally important) sphere of the larger activity of aesthetics, which encompasses as well most other aspects of life as lived by men and women who manifest their humanity by authoring utterances. Just as in the logosphere that is our home there are genres at work in all our speech, not just in art speech, so is there "everyday ritual" (ibid.), ritual not confined merely to political or religious life. The legacy of these notes is less a series of *dicta* than it is a catalog of questions open for further exploration, none more pressing, perhaps, than: "It is customary to speak about the authorial masks. But in which utterances (speech acts) is there ever a *face* and not a mask . . . ?" (ibid.).

This volume concludes with jottings from the notebook Bakhtin kept in the middle seventies, when he began work again after recovering from the grief of his wife's death. He had been encouraged to rework an unfinished piece abandoned in the late thirties or early forties that had the provisional title "On the Philosophical Bases of the Human Sciences." Beginning with the old text, Bakhtin made a number of notations in 1974 that are translated here. This was the last project on which Bakhtin worked before he died on 7 March 1975.

We conclude with this piece not only because it is Bakhtin's last, but because it picks up on many of the other concerns of this anthology with the greatest conciseness. He returns again to the obsessions of his youth—the difference between dialectic and dialogics, the world as event (*sobytie*), intonation, the difference between text and the aesthetic object, philosophy (especially German philosophy in general and Kant in particular), and the persistence of the past. He makes clear his differences with both the Formalists (once again because in his view they underestimate content and oversimplify the nature of change) and Structuralists (because even in the best of them, he feels, there is too rigid a conception of "code").

These notations made on the edge of the grave are, not surprisingly, greatly concerned with continuity in time, that "great time" in which all utterances are linked to all others, both those from the primordial past and those in the furthest reach of the future. There is a special poignancy, then, in Bakhtin's evocation of Marc Bloch's book *The Historian's Craft*. This classic apologia for remembering is invoked by Bakhtin because it so passionately articulates the need to conceive living wholes.[13] But there are other reasons as well why Bloch is an instructive instance. He was a founder of the *Annales d'histoire économique et sociale*, the review around which formed the great school that produced Febvre, Braudel, Le Goff, and many others. But after the French defeat in the Second World War, Bloch's Jewishness precluded return to his post at the Sorbonne, and he went into virtual exile in the south of France. Like Bakhtin in his exile, Bloch continued to work, using schoolboy notebooks, as Bakhtin always had. And like Bakhtin, too, Bloch was arrested. But unlike Bakhtin, the French historian was shot for his role in the underground resistance. Bakhtin remembers Bloch for remembering the French medieval peasants (in *Les caractères originaux de l'histoire rurale française*), silent for so long, who, in Bloch, found their voices again, much as the even ruder and older makers of carnival found their voice again in Bakhtin. Bloch is a very recent link in a chain that goes back into the darkest past; by remembering Bloch, Bakhtin not only forges another link, but demonstrates the truth of his own concluding words: "Nothing is absolutely dead. . . ."

These essays themselves, it is hoped, will serve to forge further links between cultures as they become available to a new generation of scholars in the West.

Notes

1. "The Role of Games in Rabelais" (a fragment from *Rabelais and His World,* which had just appeared in Helene Iswolsky's translation), *Yale French Studies,* no. 41 (September 1968), 124–32.

2. Tzvetan Todorov, *Mikhail Bakhtin: The Dialogical Principle,* tr. Wlad Godzich (Minneapolis: University of Minnesota Press, 1984; original publication in French, 1981), p. ix.

3. English Showalter, "Editor's Column," *PMLA,* vol. 100, no. 2 (March 1985), 140.

4. Ed. Michael Holquist, tr. Caryl Emerson and Michael Holquist (Austin and London: University of Texas Press, 1981).

5. Not included here are a piece made up from notes taken by the two Mirkin sisters on a lecture Bakhtin delivered in the early 1920s on the Symbolist poet Vyacheslav Ivanov and Bakhtin's notes for reworking his 1929 book on Dostoevsky for its second edition in 1963, which were published in English as an appendix to the new translation of that edition. See Mikhail Bakhtin, *Problems of Dostoevsky's Poetics,* ed. and tr. Caryl Emerson (Minneapolis: University of Minnesota Press, 1984), pp. 283–304.

6. Potebnya was a pioneer in the study of inner speech to whom not only Bakhtin but Vygotsky and Shpet are beholden. The obscurity of Potebnya and his followers in the West is simply one more example of our provincialism.

Bakhtin's praise for the Formalist Tynyanov may surprise some, but it should be remembered that Tynyanov is the least "Formalist" of the OPOJaZ circle, a scholar who was always concerned with the historical status of genres and texts. The other Formalists Bakhtin praises in this essay, after a period early in their careers of excessive insistence on the autotelic nature of the text (a tendency, however, much exaggerated by their enemies and certain historians), incorporated more and more historical and cultural factors in their work. They were, even in the early period, like the others Bakhtin here honors, original thinkers who set out new ways to conceive literary analysis.

For a fuller description of the circumstances under which Bakhtin published this essay, see Peter Seyffert, *Soviet Literary Structuralism* (Columbus, Ohio: Slavica, 1983), esp. pp. 295–297.

7. "Avtor i geroj *v estetičeskoj dejatel'nosti,*" *Estetika slovesnogo tvorchestva* (Moscow: Iskusstvo, 1979), pp. 25–26.

8. It has been reliably reported that the lost portions of the book carried "the history of realism" up to Gorky and Soviet attempts to formulate a specifically Socialist Realism; cf. S. S. Konkin, "Mixail Baxtin: Kritiko-biografičeskij očerk," in *Problemy naučnogo nasledija M. M. Baxtina,* ed. S. S. Konkin (Saransk: Mordovskij universitet, 1985), p. 14.

9. The others in order of composition are "Discourse in the Novel" (1934–35); the book on Goethe and the *Bildungsroman* (1936–38); a long monograph on the concept of chronotope (1937–38); an essay on the prehistory of the novel (1940); and the essay "Epic and Novel" (1941). In addition, he completed the manuscript of a dissertation on Rabelais during the same period.

10. The similarities with Staiger's views are not surprising, considering the impact of Husserl and (especially) Heidegger on Staiger's work. Part of the Zurich School that also included Ludwig Binswanger, Staiger constantly sought the temporal ground of a work's author as the basis for interpretation. The summa of his methodological thinking, *Grundbegriffe per Poetik* (Zurich: Atlantic Verlag, 1961), is remarkably close to Bakhtin in many of its assessments, a closeness that is also paralleled in the judgment of both thinkers that Goethe's uniqueness in large measure could be attributed to his ability to "see" space in time. But Staiger's closeness to Heidegger means that ultimately space, especially the kind of *concrete* space that obsesses Bakhtin, has a status inferior to that of time, marking a fundamental difference from the chronotope, in which time and space have equally important status.

11. Bakhtin was provided a wealth of specialist knowledge on Goethe's activity as a natural scientist by his close friend Ivan Kanaev, an eminent biologist with a lifelong passion for Goethe. He published two books on the subject: *Iogann Volfgang Gete: Ocherki iz zhizni poeta-naturalista* (Johann Wolfgang Goethe: Notes from the life of a poet-naturalist) (Leningrad: Nauka, 1962); and *Gete kak estestvoispytatel* (Goethe as a natural scientist) (Leningrad: Nauka, 1970). In the case of both books, Bakhtin wrote long letters to the publisher encouraging publication. These letters provide further witness to the major role Goethe plays in Bakhtin's thought.

12. And in so doing comes as close to Derrida as he ever does: cf. Jacques Derrida, "Signature Event Context," in *Margins of Philosophy*, tr. Alan Bass (Chicago: University of Chicago Press, 1982), pp. 307–30.

13. As when Bloch praises the—very disparate—Michelet and Fustel de Coulanges, because "these two great historians were too great to overlook the fact that a civilization, like a person, is no mechanically arranged game of solitaire; the knowledge of fragments, studied by turns, each for its own sake, will never produce the knowledge of the whole; it will not even produce that of the fragments themselves" (Marc Bloch, *The Historian's Craft*, tr. Peter Putnam [New York: Vintage Books, 1953], p. 155).

Speech Genres and Other Late Essays

Response to a Question from the *Novy Mir* Editorial Staff

The editorial staff of *Novy Mir* has asked me how I would evaluate the current state of literary scholarship.

Of course, it is difficult to answer this question categorically or with much assurance. When evaluating our own times, our own contemporaneity, we always tend to err (in one direction or another). And this must be taken into account. Nonetheless, I shall attempt a response.

Our literary scholarship holds great possibilities: we have many serious and talented literary scholars, including young ones, and we have high scholarly traditions that have developed both in the past (Potebnya, Veselovsky) and in the Soviet period (Tynyanov, Tomashevsky, Eikhenbaum, Gukovsky, and others).[1] Of course, the external conditions necessary for its development also exist (research institutes, faculties, financing, publishing possibilities, and so forth). But in spite of all this, it seems to me that our recent literary scholarship (from essentially almost all of the past decade) is, in general, neither realizing these possibilities nor satisfying our legitimate demands. There is no bold statement of general problems, no discoveries of new areas or significant individual phenomena in the boundless world of literature; there is no real, healthy struggle among scholarly trends. A certain fear of the investigatory risk, a fear of hypotheses, prevails. Literary scholarship is still essentially a young science. Its methods have not been developed and tested through experience, as have those of the natural sciences; thus, the absence of a struggle of trends and the fear of bold hypotheses inevitably lead to a predominance of truisms and stock phrases. Unfortunately, we have no shortage of them.

Such, in my view, is the *general* nature of our contemporary literary scholarship. But no general description is ever completely fair. In our day, of course, fairly good and useful books are being published (especially on the history of literature), interesting and profound articles are appearing, and there are, finally, *large* phenomena to which my general description cannot possibly extend. I have in mind Nikolay Konrad's book, *West and East,* Dmitry Likhachev's *Poetics of Ancient Russian Literature,* and *Research on Sign Systems,* in four installments so far (the school of young researchers headed by Yury M. Lotman).[2] These are the most highly gratifying phenomena of recent years. I shall perhaps touch on these works during the course of our further discussion.

Since my primary purpose is to discuss the tasks facing literary scholarship, I shall limit myself here to two tasks that are related only to the literature of past epochs, and then in the most general terms. I shall not touch at all upon the study of *modern* literature and literary criticism, although it is precisely here that we find most of the important and immediate tasks. I have selected the two problems I intend to discuss because, in my opinion, they have a certain ripeness about them; productive development of them has already begun and it must be continued.

First of all, literary scholarship should establish closer links with the history of culture. Literature is an inseparable part of culture and it cannot be understood outside the total context of the entire culture of a given epoch. It must not be severed from the rest of culture, nor, as is frequently done, can it be correlated with socioeconomic factors, as it were, behind culture's back. These factors affect culture as a whole, and only through it and in conjunction with it do they affect literature. For a fairly long period of time we have devoted special attention to questions of the specific features of literature. At one time this was, possibly, necessary and useful. One must say, however, that narrow specification is alien to the best traditions of our scholarship. Recall how very broad were the cultural horizons in the research of Potebnya and especially of Veselovsky. In our enthusiasm for specification we have ignored questions of the interconnection and interdependence of various areas of culture; we have frequently forgotten that the boundaries of these areas are not absolute, that in various epochs they have been drawn in various ways; and we have not taken into account that the most intense and productive life of culture takes place on the boundaries of its individual areas and not in places where these areas have become enclosed in their own specificity. Our historical and literary critical research usually contains characterizations of epochs to which the literary phenomena under study refer, but in the majority of cases these characterizations differ in no way from those that are given in general histories; they do not include a differentiated analysis of the areas of culture and their interaction with literature. And even the methodology of these analyses is poorly developed. The so-called literary process of the epoch, studied apart from an in-depth analysis of culture, amounts to a superficial struggle of literary schools, and in modern times (especially the nineteenth century), amounts essentially to an uproar in the newspapers and magazines, exerting no essential influence on the great and real literature of the epoch. The powerful deep currents of culture (especially the lower, popular ones), which actually determine the creativity of writers, remain undisclosed, and sometimes researchers are completely unaware of them. Such an approach does not make it possible to penetrate into the depths of great works, and literature itself begins to seem a trivial instead of a serious pursuit.

The task I am discussing and the problems related to it (the problem of the boundaries of the epoch as a cultural entity, the problem of a typology of cultures, and so forth) loom very large when one considers the question of baroque literature in Slavic countries, and especially the discussions, continuing to this day, of the Renaissance and humanism in countries of the East. The need for a deeper study of the inseparable link between the literature and culture of the epoch is manifested especially strikingly.

The outstanding works of recent literary scholarship that I have mentioned—Konrad, Likhachev, Lotman and his school—with all the diversity of their methodology are alike in that they do not separate literature from culture; they strive to understand literary phenomena in the differentiated unity of the epoch's entire culture. It should be emphasized here that literature is too complex and multifaceted a phenomenon and literary scholarship is still too young for it to be possible to speak of any one single "redeeming" method in literary scholarship. *Various* approaches are justified and are even quite necessary as long as they are serious and reveal something new in the literary phenomenon being studied, as long as they promote a deeper understanding of it.

If it is impossible to study literature apart from an epoch's entire culture, it is even more fatal to encapsulate a literary phenomenon in the single epoch of its creation, in its own contemporaneity, so to speak. We usually strive to explain a writer and his work precisely through his own time and the most recent past (usually within the epoch, as we understand it). We are afraid to remove ourselves in time from the phenomenon under investigation. Yet the artwork extends its roots into the distant past. Great literary works are prepared for by centuries, and in the epoch of their creation it is merely a matter of picking the fruit that is ripe after a lengthy and complex process of maturation. Trying to understand and explain a work solely in terms of the conditions of its epoch alone, solely in terms of the conditions of the most immediate time, will never enable us to penetrate into its semantic depths. Enclosure within the epoch also makes it impossible to understand the work's future life in subsequent centuries; this life appears as a kind of paradox. Works break through the boundaries of their own time, they live in centuries, that is, in *great time* and frequently (with great works, always) their lives there are more intense and fuller than are their lives within their own time. To put it somewhat simplistically and crudely, if the significance of any work is reduced, for example, to its role in the struggle against serfdom (as is done in our secondary schools), this work will lose all of its significance when serfdom and its remnants no longer exist in life. It is frequently the case, however, that a work gains in significance, that is, it enters *great time*. But the work cannot live in future centuries without having somehow absorbed past centuries as well. If it had belonged *entirely* to today (that is, were a product only of its own time) and not a continuation of the past or essentially related to the past, it could not live in the future. Everything that belongs only to the present dies along with the present.

It seems paradoxical that, as I have already said, great works continue to live in the distant future. In the process of their posthumous life they are enriched with new meanings, new significance: it is as though these works outgrow what they were in the epoch of their creation. We can say that neither Shakespeare himself nor his contemporaries knew that "great Shakespeare" whom we know now. There is no possibility of squeezing our Shakespeare into the Elizabethan epoch. Belinsky in his day spoke of the fact that each epoch always discovers something new in the great works of the past. But do we then attribute to Shakespeare's works something that was not there, do we modernize and distort them? Modernization and distortion, of course, have existed and will continue to exist. But that is not the reason why Shakespeare has grown. He has grown because of that which actually has been and continues to be found in his works, but which neither he himself nor his contemporaries could consciously perceive and evaluate in the context of the culture of their epoch.

Semantic phenomena can exist in concealed form, potentially, and be revealed only in semantic cultural contexts of subsequent epochs that are favorable for such disclosure. The semantic treasures Shakespeare embedded in his works were created and collected through the centuries and even millennia: they lay hidden in the language, and not only in the literary language, but also in those strata of the popular language that before Shakespeare's time had not entered literature, in the diverse genres and forms of speech communication, in the forms of a mighty national culture (primarily carnival forms) that were shaped through millennia, in theater-spectacle genres (mystery plays, farces, and so forth), in plots whose roots go back to prehistoric antiquity, and, finally, in forms of thinking. Shakespeare, like any artist, constructed his works not out of inanimate elements, not out of bricks, but out of forms that were already heavily laden with meaning, filled with it. We may note in passing that even bricks have a certain spatial form and, consequently, in the hands of the builder they express something.

Genres are of special significance. Genres (of literature and speech) throughout the centuries of their life accumulate forms of seeing and interpreting particular aspects of the world. For the writer-craftsman the genre serves as an external template, but the great artist awakens the semantic possibilities that lie within it. Shakespeare took advantage of and included in his works immense treasures of potential meaning that could not be fully revealed or recognized in his epoch. The author himself and his contemporaries see, recognize, and evaluate primarily that which is close to their own day. The author is a captive of his epoch, of his own present. Subsequent times liberate him from this captivity, and literary scholarship is called upon to assist in this liberation.

It certainly does not follow from what we have said that the writer's own epoch can somehow be ignored, that his creativity can be cast back into the past or projected into the future. One's own present retains all of its immense and, in many respects, decisive significance. Scholarly analysis can proceed only from it and must always refer to it in its subsequent development. A work of literature, as we said above, is revealed primarily in the differentiated unity of the culture of the epoch in which it was created, but it cannot be closed off in this epoch: its fullness is revealed only in *great time*.

But even the culture of an epoch, however temporally distant from us it may be, cannot be enclosed within itself as something ready-made, completely finalized, and irrevocably departed, deceased. Spengler's ideas about closed and finalized cultural worlds still exert a great influence on historians and literary scholars. But these ideas must be subjected to significant correctives. Spengler imagined the culture of an epoch as a closed circle. But the unity of a particular culture is an *open* unity.

Each such unity (for example, classical antiquity), with all its uniqueness, enters into the single (although not linear) process of the evolution of human culture. In each culture of the past lie immense semantic possibilities that have remained undisclosed, unrecognized, and unutilized throughout the entire historical life of a given culture. Antiquity itself did not know the antiquity that we know now. There used to be a school joke: the ancient Greeks did not know the main thing about themselves, that they were *ancient* Greeks, and they never called themselves that. But in fact that temporal distance that transformed the Greeks into *ancient* Greeks had an immense transformational significance: it was filled with increasing discoveries of new *semantic* values in antiquity, values of which the Greeks were in fact unaware, although they themselves created them. One must say that Spengler himself, in his great analysis of classical culture, was also able to discover new semantic depths in it. True, in some ways he supplemented it to give it more roundness and finality, but nevertheless, he, too, participated in the great cause of liberating antiquity from the captivity of time.

We must emphasize that we are speaking here about new *semantic* depths that lie embedded in the cultures of past epochs and not about the expansion of our factual, material knowledge of them—which we are constantly gaining through archeological excavations, discoveries of new texts, improvement in deciphering them, reconstructions, and so forth. In those instances we acquire new material bearers of meaning, as it were, bodies of meaning. But one cannot draw an absolute distinction between body and meaning in the area of culture:[3] culture is not made of dead elements, for even a simple brick, as we have already said, in the hands of a builder expresses something through its form. Therefore new discoveries of material bearers of meaning alter our semantic concepts, and they can also force us to restructure them radically.

There exists a very strong, but one-sided and thus untrustworthy, idea that in order better to understand a foreign culture, one must enter into it, forgetting one's own, and view the world through the eyes of this foreign culture. This idea, as I said, is one-sided. Of course, a certain entry as a living being into a foreign culture, the possibility of seeing the world through its eyes, is a necessary part of the process of understanding it; but if this were the only aspect of this understanding, it would merely be duplication and would not entail anything new or enriching. *Creative understanding* does not renounce itself, its own place in time, its own culture; and it forgets nothing. In order to understand, it is immensely important for the person who understands to be *located outside* the object of his or her creative understanding—in time, in space, in culture. For one cannot even really see one's own exterior and comprehend it as a whole, and no mirrors or photographs can help; our real exterior can be seen and understood only by other people, because they are located outside us in space and because they are *others*.

In the realm of culture, outsideness is a most powerful factor in understanding. It is only in the eyes of *another* culture that foreign culture reveals itself fully and profoundly (but not maximally fully, because there will be cultures that see and understand even more). A meaning only reveals its depths once it has encountered and come into contact with another, foreign meaning: they engage in a kind of dialogue, which surmounts the closedness and one-sidedness of these particular meanings, these cultures. We raise new questions for a foreign culture, ones that it did not raise itself; we seek answers to our own questions in it; and the foreign culture responds to us by revealing to us its new aspects and new semantic depths. Without *one's own* questions one cannot creatively understand anything other or foreign (but, of course, the questions must be serious and sincere). Such a dialogic encounter of two cultures does not result in merging or mixing. Each retains its own unity and *open* totality, but they are mutually enriched.

As concerns my own evaluation of prospects for the development of our literary scholarship, I think they are quite good in view of our immense potential. We lack only scholarly, investigatory boldness, and without this we cannot rise to the heights or descend to the depths.

Notes

1. Aleksandr Potebnya (1835–91), distinguished Russian philologist who examined the relationship among language, thought, and poetry. He was heavily influenced by the theories of Wilhelm von Humboldt (1767–1835) concerning the role of creativity in everyday language production and the relation of language to thought. Potebnya's *Thought and Language* (1862) was an influence on both Lev Vygotsky and Gustav Shpet.

Aleksandr Veselovsky (1838–1906), Russian literary historian who sought to establish the history of literature as an independent branch of history with its own aims and methods. He was attractive to Bakhtin because of his efforts to create a full-fledged historical poetics.

Yury Tynyanov (1894–1943), Russian literary theorist and novelist, probably the most important Formalist thinker (with the exception of Jakobson, with whom he worked very closely). In such works as *Problems of Verse Language* (1924; translated into English as *The Problem of Verse Language*, ed. and tr. Michael Sosa and Brent Harvey [Ann Arbor: Ardis, 1981]; there is a moving afterword by Jakobson) and *Archaizers and Innovators* (1929), Tynyanov argued for a complex, dynamic conception of literary texts and their relation to each other in history.

Boris Tomashevsky (1890–1957), professor at Leningrad University and close affiliate of the Formalists. Tomashevsky, who had training in statistics, is among the more systematic of the Formalists, as can be seen in his *Theory of Literature (Poetics)* (1925) and *The Writer and the Book: An Outline of Textology* (1928).

Boris Eikhenbaum (1886–1959), one of the very earliest Formalists who quickly became one of their most productive members and staunchest defenders. He is the author of several influential studies on Gogol, Lermontov, Tolstoy, and other Russian classics. He supervised the edition of Tolstoy's works published in the early 1930s that included two introductory essays by Bakhtin.

Grigory Gukovsky (1902–50), a close associate of the Formalists who had a prodigious knowledge of the eighteenth century, an area superficially explored before Gukovsky opened it up with a series of articles whose influence is still being felt; he founded the sector for the study of the eighteenth century in Pushkinsky Dom. He was also an expert on the nineteenth century and wrote important studies of Pushkin and Gogol.

2. Nikolay Konrad (1891–1970), Russian philologist and historian who specialized in the languages and literatures of Japan and China. He was an acquaintance of Bakhtin's in the 1920s. Konrad is one of the very few comparatists who had an encyclopedic knowledge of both Western and Oriental culture. He published on technical problems of establishing obscure texts and translated Chinese poetry.

Dmitry Likhachev (1906–), distinguished scholar of Russian medieval literature and culture. He is author or editor of several books on the period from the tenth to the seventeenth centuries, but has also published on textology, the image of the human being in old Russian culture, and the role of laughter in the medieval period.

Research on Sign Systems (*Trudy po znakvym sistemam*) is a series of works on topics in semiotic theory of art and culture published at Tartu University (formerly Dorpat) in Estonia.

Yury Lotman (1922–) is professor of Russian literature at Tartu University, where he has organized a number of conferences on the theory of art and culture that have made Tartu a world center of semiotic activity. His prodigious learning and feverish activity as a lecturer and writer make him the most important literary scholar in the Soviet Union today.

3. Bakhtin wrote a good deal about the indivisibility of "body" and "meaning" in the 1920s, polemically rejecting the "materialist aesthetics" of the Formalists on the one hand and "abstract idealism" on the other: "the meaning of art is completely inseparable from all the details of its material body. The work of art is meaningful in its entirety. The very construction of the body-sign [*telo-znak*] has primary importance in this instance. Technically auxiliary, and therefore replaceable, elements are held to a minimum. The individual reality of the object, with all the uniqueness of its features, acquires artistic significance here" (P. N. Medvedev/M. M. Bakhtin, *The Formal Method in Literary Scholarship*, tr. Albert J. Wehrle [Cambridge, Mass.: Harvard University Press, 1985], p. 12).

The *Bildungsroman* and Its Significance in the History of Realism (Toward a Historical Typology of the Novel)

The need for a historical investigation into the novel genre (one that would not be statically formal or normative). The diverse subcategories of the genre. An attempt at a historical classification of these subcategories. Classification according to how the image of the main hero is constructed: the travel novel, the novel of ordeal, the biographical (autobiographical) novel, the *Bildungsroman*. No specific historical subcategory upholds any given principle in pure form; rather, each is characterized by the prevalence of one or another principle for formulating the figure of the hero. Since all elements are mutually determined, the principle for formulating the hero figure is related to the particular type of plot, to the particular conception of the world, and to a particular composition of a given novel.

1. *The travel novel.* The hero is a point moving in space. He has no essential distinguishing characteristics, and he himself is not at the center of the novelist's artistic attention. His movement in space—wanderings and occasionally escapade-adventures (mainly of the ordeal type)—enables the artist to develop and demonstrate the spatial and static social diversity of the world (country, city, culture, nationality, various social groups and the specific conditions of their lives). This type of positioning of the hero and construction of the novel is typical of classical naturalism (Petronius, Apuleius, the wanderings of Encolpius and others, the wanderings of Lucius the Ass), and of the European picaresque novel: *Lazarillo de Tormes*, *The Life of Guzmán de Alfarache*, *Francion*, *Gil Blas*, and others.[1] And the same principle for formulating the hero prevails in an even more complex form in the adventure-picaresque novels of Defoe (*Captain Singleton*, *Moll Flanders*, and others) as well as in the adventure stories of Smollett (*Roderick Random*, *Peregrine Pickle*, and *Humphry Clinker*).[2] Finally, certain kinds of nineteenth-century adventure novels, continuing the tradition of the picaresque novel, are based on the same principle with different complications.

The travel novel typically involves a purely spatial and static conception of the world's diversity. The world is a spatial contiguity of differences and contrasts, and life is an alternation of various contrasting conditions: success/failure, happiness/unhappiness, victory/defeat, and so on.

Temporal categories are extremely poorly developed. In this type of novel, time in and of itself lacks any significance or historical coloring; even "biological time"—the hero's age, his progress from youth through maturity to old age—is either completely absent or is noted only as a matter of form. The only time developed in this type of novel is adventure time, which consists of the most immediate units—moments, hours, days—snatched at random from the temporal process. Typical temporal descriptions in this kind of novel are: "at the same moment," "the next moment," "he was an hour ahead of time," "the next day," "a second earlier, later," "he was late," "he was ahead of schedule," and so forth (when describing an encounter, a battle, a duel, a scuffle, a robbery, flight, and other adventures). "Day," "morning," and "night" as settings for adventure action. The special significance of night in adventure time, and so on.

Because of the absence of historical time, emphasis is placed only on differences and contrasts. There are almost no intrinsic ties at all, and there is no understanding of the wholeness of such sociocultural phenomena as nationalities, countries, cities, social groups, and occupations. Hence these novels typically perceive alien social groups, nations, countries, ways of life, and so forth, as "exotic," that is, they perceive bare distinctions, contrasts, and strangeness. Hence the naturalistic quality of this subcategory of the novel: the world disintegrates into individual things, phenomena, and events that are simply contiguous or alternating. The image of man in the novel—which is barely distinguishable—is quite static, as static as the world that surrounds him. This novel does not recognize human emergence and development. Even if his status changes sharply (in the picaresque novel he changes from beggar to rich man, from homeless wanderer to nobleman), he himself remains unchanged.

2. *The novel of ordeal.* The second type of novel is constructed as a series of tests of the main heroes, tests of their fidelity, valor, bravery, virtue, nobility, sanctity, and so on. This is the most widespread subcategory of the novel in European literature. It encompasses a considerable majority of all the novels produced. The world of this novel—the arena of the struggle and testing of the hero; events and

adventures—is a touchstone for the hero. The hero is always presented as complete and unchanging. All his qualities are given from the very beginning, and during the course of the novel they are only tested and verified.

The novel of ordeal also appears in the classical period, and in its two main subcategories. The first subcategory is represented by the Greek romance (*Aethiopica*, *Leucippe and Clitophon*, and others).[3] The second subcategory is represented by the early Christian hagiographies (especially of martyrs).

The first subcategory—the Greek romance—is constructed as a test of fidelity in love and the purity of the ideal hero and heroine. Almost all its adventures are organized as threats to the heroes' innocence, purity, and mutual fidelity. The static, immutable nature of their characters and their abstract ideality preclude any emergence or development;[4] nothing that takes place, nothing they see or undergo, can be utilized as life experience that alters and shapes them.

Unlike the travel novel, this type of novel provides a developed and complex image of man, one that has had an immense influence on the subsequent history of the novel. This image is essentially unitary, but its unity is specific; it is static and substantial. The Greek romance—rising out of the "Second Sophistic" and nourished on rhetorical casuistry—creates basically a rhetorical, juridical concept of man.[5] Here one already sees the image of a human being who is profoundly steeped in those judicial-rhetorical categories and concepts of guilt/innocence, judgment/vindication, accusation, crime, virtue, merits, and so forth, which have for so long hung suspended over the novel and dictated the presentation of the hero in the novel as accused or defended, transforming the novel into a kind of court of law for the hero. In the Greek romance these categories are formalistic in nature, but even here they create a unique *unity* of man as the subject of judgment, defense, or accusation, the bearer of crimes and merits. The juridical, judicial-rhetorical categories in the Greek romance are frequently cast out into the world as well, transforming events into causes, things into evidence, and so forth. All these points are developed in an analysis of the specific material of the Greek romance.

In the second subcategory of the novel of ordeal, which also arose on classical soil, there is a significant change in the ideological content both of man's image and of the idea of testing. The early Christian hagiographies of martyrs and other saints (Dion Chrysostom, legends of the Climentine cycle, and others) prepared the way for this subcategory.[6] Elements of it are also to be found in Apuleius' *Metamorphoses* (*The Golden Ass*). This subcategory is based on the idea of testing a holy man through suffering and temptation. The idea of testing is no longer as external and formal here as it is in the Greek romance. The hero's internal life, his *habitus* [condition], becomes an essential aspect of his image. The very nature of the test is ideologically more profound and precise, especially in passages where faith is being tested through doubt. In general this subcategory of the novel of ordeal typically combines adventures with psychology and a deep probing of problems. But here too the testing is conducted from the standpoint of a ready-made and dogmatically accepted ideal. There is no movement, no quality of emergence in the ideal itself. The tested hero is also ready-made and predetermined. The tests (suffering, temptation, doubt) do not become formative experience for him, they do not change him, and in that very immutability of the hero lies the entire point.

The next subcategory of the novel of ordeal is the medieval chivalric novel (the largest and most essential part of it), which, of course, was significantly influenced by both subcategories of the classical novel. A certain diversity of types within the chivalric novel is predicated by nuances in the ideological content of the idea of testing (a predominance of courtly, Christian, or mystical elements in the content of this idea). A brief analysis of the main types of structure in the chivalric novel-in-verse from the thirteenth, fourteenth, and subsequent centuries (up to *Amadis* [*of Gaul*] and *Palmerín*, inclusive).[7]

Finally, the most significant, historically influential, and unalloyed subcategory of the novel of ordeal is the baroque novel (d'Urfé, Scudéry, La Calprenède, Lohenstein, and others).[8] The baroque novel was able to draw from the idea of testing all the plot possibilities it held for the construction of large-scale novels. Therefore, the baroque novel best reveals the organizational possibilities of the idea of testing, and at the same time reveals the limited and narrow way in which this idea actually penetrates into reality. The baroque novel is the purest and most consistent type of *heroic novel*, a type that reveals the particular features of *novelistic heroization* as distinct from epic heroization. The baroque admits of nothing average, normal, typical, or ordinary; everything here is expanded to an immense scale. Judicial-rhetorical pathos is also expressed with great consistency and vividness here. The organization of man's image, the selection of features, their unification, and the attribution of deeds and events ("fate") to the image of the hero are determined by his defense (apology), justification, glorification, or, conversely, conviction and exposure.

The baroque novel of ordeal had two branches of development in subsequent centuries: (1) the adventure-heroic novel (Lewis, Radcliffe, Walpole, and others); (2) the pathos-filled psychological, sentimental novel (Richardson, Rousseau). The features of the novel of ordeal change significantly in these subcategories, especially where one finds a unique heroization of the weak, the heroization of the "little man."

Despite all the differences among the aforementioned historical subcategories of the novel of ordeal, they all have a certain set of essential common features that determine the significance of this type in the history of the European novel.

i. *Plot* [*sjuzhet*]. The plot of a novel of ordeal is always constructed on deviations from the normal course of the hero's life, exceptional events and situations that would not be found in the typical, normal, ordinary biography. Thus in the majority of cases the Greek romance depicts events that take place between a betrothal and the wedding or between the wedding and the wedding night, and so forth, that is, events that essentially should *not* take place, that only separate two contiguous moments of the biography from one another, that retard the course of normal life, but do not change it. In the end the lovers are always joined in wedlock and biographical life enters its normal course beyond the limits of the novel. This also determines the specific nature of novel time: it lacks any real biographical duration. Hence also the exceptional role of chance both in the Greek and, particularly, in the baroque novel. The events of a baroque novel, organized as adventures, lack any biographical or social significance or typicality: they are unexpected, unprecedented, and extraordinary. Hence also the role of crime and all kinds of anomalies in the plot of the baroque novel, its bloody and frequently perverted nature (this peculiarity is to this day inherent in that line of adventure novel that is related to the baroque novel through Lewis, Walpole, and Radcliffe—the black or Gothic novel).

The novel of ordeal always begins where a deviation from the normal social and biographical course of life begins, and it ends where life resumes its normal course. Therefore, the events of a novel of ordeal, whatever they may be, do not create a new type of life, a new human biography that is determined by the changing conditions of life. Beyond the boundaries of the novel, biography and social life remain ordinary and unchanged.

ii. *Time.* (The boundless and infinite nature of adventure time, the stringing together of adventures.) In a novel of ordeal we find first of all a further development and detailing of *adventure time* (time taken out of history and biography). One finds *fairy-tale time* (influenced by the East) here as well, particularly in the chivalric novel. This time is characterized precisely by a violation of normal temporal categories: for example, the work of several years is done in one night or, conversely, a year passes in one moment (the bewitched dream motif).

The peculiarities of the plot, which centers on deviations from the historical and biographical course, determine the overall uniqueness of time in a novel of ordeal. It lacks the means for actual measurement (historical and biographical), and it lacks historical localization, that is, significant attachment to a particular historical epoch, a link to particular historical events and conditions. The very problem of historical localization did not exist for the novel of ordeal.

To be sure, the baroque also creates a historical novel of ordeal (for example, Scudéry's *Le grand Cyrus* and Lohenstein's *Armenius und Thusnelda*), but these novels are only quasi-historical and the time in them is also quasi-historical.

The essential achievement of the novel of ordeal in the area of reworking temporal categories is *psychological time* (especially in the baroque novel). This time possesses a subjective palpability and duration (during the depiction of danger, agonizing suspense, insatiable passion, and so on). But such psychologically colored and concretized time lacks essential localization, even in the whole of the individual's life process.

iii. *Depiction of the world.* The novel of ordeal, as distinct from the travel novel, concentrates on the hero; in the majority of cases the surrounding world and the secondary characters are transformed into a mere background for the hero, into a decoration, a setting. Nonetheless, the surroundings occupy an important position in the novel (especially in the baroque novel). But the external world, attached like a background to an immobile hero, lacks independence and historicity. In addition, as distinct from the travel novel, here geographical exoticism prevails over social. Everyday life, which occupied an important place in the travel novel, is almost completely lacking here (or else it is not exotic). There is no real interaction between the hero and the world: the world is not capable of changing the hero, it only tests him; and the hero does not affect the world, he does not change its appearance; while undergoing tests and vanquishing his enemies, the hero leaves everything in the world in its place. He does not alter the social face of the world, nor does he restructure it, and he does not claim to. The problem of the interaction between subject and object, man and the world, was not raised in the novel of ordeal. This explains why the nature of heroism is so unproductive and uncreative in this type of novel (even when historical heroes are depicted).

The novel of ordeal, having reached its peak in the baroque period, lost its purity in the eighteenth and nineteenth centuries. But the type of novel that is constructed on the idea of testing a hero continues to exist, complicated, of course, by all that has been created by the biographical novel and the *Bildungsroman*. The compositional force of the idea of testing, which makes it possible to organize disparate material intrinsically and in depth around the hero, and to combine the keenly adventuristic with the profoundly problematical and complexly psychological, determines the significance of this idea in the subsequent history of the novel. Thus, the idea of testing—made much more complex and rich, of course, by the achievements of the biographical and especially the educational novel—lies at the basis of the French realistic novels. In terms of their main type of construction, the novels of Stendhal and Balzac are novels of ordeal (the baroque tradition is especially deep-seated in Balzac). Dostoevsky's novels must also be included among the significant phenomena of the nineteenth century, since, by virtue of their construction, they are also novels of ordeal.

In subsequent history the very idea of ordeal is filled with the most diverse ideological content. This type includes (in later romanticism) testing for vocation, for genius, and for membership in the elect. Another subcategory includes the testing of Napoleonic parvenus in the French novel, testing for biological health and adaptability to life (Zola), testing for artistic genius and, in parallel, the artist's fitness for life (*Künstlerroman*), and, finally, testing the liberal reformer, the Nietzschean, the immoralist, the emancipated woman, and a number of other subcategories in works produced by third-rate writers during the second half of the nineteenth century. Another special subcategory of the novel of ordeal is the Russian novel of ordeal, which tests man for his social fitness and general worthiness (the theme of the "superfluous man").

3. *The biographical novel.* During the classical period as well, the way

was being paved for the biographical novel—in classical biographies, autobiographies, and confessions of the early Christian period (ending with Augustine). But these were no more than preparation. In general the biographical novel has never actually existed in pure form. There was only the biographical (autobiographical) principle for shaping the novel's hero and certain aspects of the novel that corresponded to this configuration.

The biographical form in the novel has the following subcategories: the naive old (still classical) form of success/failure and, subsequently, works and deeds; the confessional form (biography-confession); the hagiographic form; and, finally, in the eighteenth century the most important subcategory took shape—the family-biographical novel.

All these subcategories of the biographical construction typically have a number of extremely important features, including the most primitive type, which is constructed as an enumeration of successes and failures in life.

i. The *plot* of the biographical form, as distinct from the travel novel and the novel of ordeal, is constructed not on deviations from the normal and typical course of life but precisely on the basic and typical aspects of any life course; birth, childhood, school years, marriage, the fate that life brings, works and deeds, death, and so forth, that is, exactly those moments that are located before the beginning or after the end of a novel of ordeal.

ii. Although the hero's life course is indeed depicted, his image in a purely biographical novel lacks any true process of becoming or development. The hero's life and fate change, they assume structure and evolve, but the hero himself remains essentially unchanged. Attention is concentrated either on deeds, feats, merits, and creative accomplishments, or on the structure of the hero's destiny in life, his happiness, and so on. In a biographical novel (especially autobiographical and confessional), the only essential change in the hero himself is his crisis and rebirth (the biographical hagiographies of the crisis type, Augustine's *Confessions*, and so on). The conception of life (idea of life) that underlies a biographical novel is determined either by life's objective results (works, services, deeds, feats) or by the category of happiness/unhappiness (with all of its variations).

iii. The essential feature of the biographical novel is the appearance of biographical time. As distinct from adventure and fairy-tale time, biographical time is quite realistic. All of its moments are included in the total life process, and they describe this process as limited, unrepeatable, and irreversible. Each event is localized in the whole of this life process and therefore it ceases to be adventure. The moment, the day, the night, and the immediate contiguity of short moments lose almost all of their significance in the biographical novel, which works with extended periods, organic parts of the whole of life (ages and so forth). Arranged against the background of this basic time in the biographical novel is, of course, the depiction of individual events and adventures on a larger plane, but the moments, hours, and days of this larger plane are not adventuristic and are subordinate to biographical time. They are immersed in that time, and it fills them with reality.

Biographical time as real time cannot but be included (participate) in the longer process of historical, but embryonically historical, time. Biographical life is impossible outside a larger epoch, which goes beyond the limits of a single life, whose duration is represented primarily by *generations*. There is no place for generations in the novel of travel or the novel of ordeal. Generations introduce a completely new and extremely significant aspect into the depicted world; they introduce the contiguity of lives taking place at various times (the correlation between generations and *meetings* in the adventure novel). This already provides an entry into historical duration. But the biographical novel itself does not yet know true historical time.

iv. In keeping with the features noted above, the world also assumes a special character in the biographical novel. It is no longer the background for the hero. The contiguity and the links between hero and world are no longer organized as random and unexpected meetings on the high road (and not as a means of testing the hero). Secondary characters, countries, cities, things, and so on enter into the biographical novel in significant ways and acquire a significant relationship to the whole life of the main hero. This makes it possible, in depicting the world, to surmount both the naturalistic fragmentation of the travel novel and the exoticism and abstract idealization of the novel of ordeal. Because of the link with historical time and with the epoch, it becomes possible to reflect reality in a more profoundly realistic way. (Position, occupation, and kinship were masks in the travel novel, for example, in its picaresque variant; here they acquire a life-determining essence. The links with secondary characters, institutions, countries, and so on are no longer superficially adventuristic by nature.) This is manifested especially clearly in the family-biographical novel (of the type of Fielding's *Tom Jones*).

v. The construction of the hero's image in the biographical novel.

Heroization falls away almost completely here (it remains only partially and in altered form in biographical hagiographies). The hero here is not the moving point that he was in the travel novel, devoid of inherent characteristics. Instead of abstract, sequential heroization, as in the novel of ordeal, the hero is characterized by both positive and negative features (he is not tested, but strives for actual results). But these features are fixed and ready-made, they are given from the very beginning, and throughout the entire course of the novel man remains himself (unchanged). The events shape not the man, but his destiny (though it may be a creative destiny).

Such are the basic principles for shaping the hero in the novel that took form and existed until the second half of the eighteenth century, that is, until the time of the *Bildungsroman*. All these principles for the formulation of the hero paved the way for the development of synthetic forms of the novel in the nineteenth century, and above all for the realistic novel (Stendhal, Balzac, Flaubert, Dickens, and Thackeray). In order to understand the nineteenth-century novel, one must know profoundly and evaluate all these principles for the formulation of the hero, which participate to a greater or lesser degree in the construction of that type of novel. But of special importance for the realistic novel (and to some extent for the historical novel) is the *Bildungsroman*, which appeared in Germany in the second half of the eighteenth century.

Posing the Problem of the Bildungsroman

The main theme of our essay is the time-space and the image of man in the novel. Our criterion is the assimilation of real historical time and the assimilation of historical man that takes place in that time. This problem is mainly theoretical and literary in nature, but no theoretical problem can be resolved without concrete historical material. Moreover, this problem as such is too broad, and it must be delimited somewhat in both its theoretical and historical aspects. Hence our more specific and special theme—the image of *man in the process of becoming* in the novel.

But even this particular theme must, in turn, be narrowed down and defined more precisely.

There exists a special subcategory of the novel called the "novel of education" (*Erziehungsroman* or *Bildungsroman*). Usually included (in chronological order) are the following major examples of this generic subcategory: Xenophon's *Cyropaedia* (classical), Wolfram von

Eschenbach's *Parzival* (Middle Ages), Rabelais' *Gargantua and Pantagruel*, Grimmelshausen's *Simplicissimus* (the Renaissance), Fénelon's *Télémaque* (neoclassicism), Rousseau's *Emile* (since there is a considerable novelistic element in this pedagogical treatise), Wieland's *Agathon*, Wetzel's *Tobias Knout*, Hippel's *Lebensläufe nach aufsteigender Linie*, Goethe's *Wilhelm Meister* (both novels), Jean Paul's *Titan* (and several of his other novels), Dickens' *David Copperfield*, Raabe's *Der Hungerpastor*, Gottfried Keller's *Der grüne Heinrich*, Pontoppidan's *Lucky Peter*, Tolstoy's *Childhood, Adolescence, and Youth*, Goncharov's *An Ordinary Story* and *Oblomov*, Romain Rolland's *Jean-Christophe*, Thomas Mann's *Buddenbrooks* and *Magic Mountain*, and others.[9]

Some scholars, guided by purely compositional principles (the concentration of the whole plot on the process of the hero's education), significantly limit this list (Rabelais, for example, is excluded). Others, conversely, requiring only the presence of the hero's development and emergence in the novel, considerably expand this list, including such works, for example, as Fielding's *Tom Jones* or Thackeray's *Vanity Fair*.

It is clear even at first glance that this list contains phenomena that are too diverse, from the theoretical and even from the biographical standpoint. Some of the novels are essentially biographical or autobiographical, while others are not; in some of them the organizing basis is the purely pedagogical notion of man's education, while this is not even mentioned in others; some of them are constructed on the strictly chronological plane of the main hero's educational development and have almost no plot at all, while others, conversely, have complex adventuristic plots. Even more significant are the differences in the relationship of these novels to realism, and particularly to real historical time.

All this forces us to sort out in a different way not only this list, but also the entire problem of the so-called *Bildungsroman*.

It is necessary, first of all, to single out specifically the aspect of man's essential *becoming*. The vast majority of novels (and subcategories of novels) know only the image of the *ready-made* hero. All movement in the novel, all events and escapades depicted in it, shift the hero in space, up and down the rungs of the social ladder: from beggar to rich man, from homeless tramp to nobleman. The hero sometimes attains, sometimes only approaches his goal: the bride, the victory, wealth, and so on. Events change his destiny, change his position in life and society, but he himself remains unchanged and adequate to himself.

In the majority of subcategories of the novel, the plot, composition, and entire internal structure of the novel postulate this unchanging nature, this solidity of the hero's image, this static nature of his unity. The hero is a *constant* in the novel's formula and all other quantities—the spatial environment, social position, fortune, in brief, all aspects of the hero's life and destiny—can therefore be *variables*.

The actual content of this constant (the ready-made and unchanging hero) and the actual signs of his unity, permanence, and self-identity can vary immensely, beginning with the identity provided by the empty name of the hero (in certain subcategories of the adventure novel) and ending with a complex character, whose individual aspects are disclosed only gradually, throughout the course of the entire novel. The principle for guiding the selection of essential features and combining and unifying them into the whole of the hero's image can vary. Finally, various compositional methods can be used to reveal this image.

But given all the possible differences in construction, in the image of the hero itself there is neither movement nor emergence. The hero is that immobile and fixed point around which all movement in the novel takes place. The permanence and immobility of the hero are prerequisite to novelistic movement. An analysis of typical novel plots shows that they presuppose a ready-made, unchanging hero; they presuppose the hero's static unity. Movement in the fate and life of this ready-made hero constitutes the content of the plot; but the character of the man himself, his change and emergence do not become the plot. Such is the predominant type in this category of novel.

Along with this predominant, mass type, there is another incomparably rarer type of novel that provides an image of man in the process of becoming. As opposed to a static unity, here one finds a dynamic unity in the hero's image. The hero himself, his character, becomes a variable in the formula of this type of novel. Changes in the hero himself acquire *plot* significance, and thus the entire plot of the novel is reinterpreted and reconstructed. Time is introduced into man, enters into his very image, changing in a fundamental way the significance of all aspects of his destiny and life. This type of novel can be designated in the most general sense as the novel of human *emergence*.

A human being can, however, emerge in quite diverse ways. Everything depends upon the degree of assimilation of real historical time.

In pure adventure time, of course, man's emergence is impossible (we shall return to this). But it is quite possible in cyclical time. Thus, in idyllic time one can depict man's path from childhood through youth and maturity to old age, showing all those essential internal changes in a person's nature and views that take place in him as he grows older. Such a sequence of development (emergence) of man is cyclical in nature, repeating itself in each life. Such a cyclical (purely age-oriented) novel had not been created as a pure type, but elements of it were scattered throughout the work of eighteenth-century idyllists and the work of novelists of regionalism and *Heimatskunst* in the nineteenth century. Moreover, in the *humoristic branch* of the *Bildungsroman* (in the narrow sense) represented by Hippel and Jean Paul (to some degree Sterne as well), the idyllic-cyclical ingredient is immensely significant. That ingredient is also in evidence to a greater or lesser degree in other novels of emergence (it is very strong in Tolstoy, and this links him directly to the traditions of the eighteenth century).

Another type of cyclical emergence, which retains a connection (but not such a close one) with man's age, traces a typically repeating path of man's emergence from youthful idealism and fantasies to mature sobriety and practicality. This path can be complicated in the end by varying degrees of skepticism and resignation. This kind of novel of emergence typically depicts the world and life as *experience*, as a *school*, through which every person must pass and derive one and the same result: one becomes more sober, experiencing some degree of resignation. This type is represented in its purest form in the classical novel of education in the second half of the eighteenth century, and above all in Wieland and Wetzel. To a very real extent, Keller's *Der grüne Heinrich* belongs here as well. Elements of this type are to be found in Hippel, Jean Paul, and, of course, Goethe.

The third type of novel of emergence is the biographical (and autobiographical) type. There is no longer any cyclical quality here. Emergence takes place in biographical time, and it passes through unrepeatable, individual stages. It can be typical, but this is no longer a cyclical typicality. Emergence here is the result of the entire totality of changing life circumstances and events, activity and work. Man's destiny is created and he himself, his character, is created along with it. The emergence of man's life-destiny fuses with the emergence of man himself. Fielding's *Tom Jones* and Dickens' *David Copperfield* are novels of this type.

The fourth type of novel of emergence is the didactic-pedagogical novel. It is based on a specific pedagogical ideal, understood more or less broadly, and depicts the pedagogical process of education in the strict sense of the word. Included in this pure type are such works as Xenophon's *Cyropaedia*, Fénelon's *Télémaque*, and Rousseau's *Emile*. But there are elements of this type in other subcategories of the novel of emergence as well, including works by Goethe and Rabelais.

The fifth and last type of novel of emergence is the most significant one. In it man's individual emergence is inseparably linked to historical emergence. Man's emergence is accomplished in real historical time, with all of its necessity, its fullness, its future, and its profoundly chronotopic nature. In the four preceding types, man's emergence proceeded against the immobile background of the world, ready-made and basically quite stable. If changes did take place in this world, they were peripheral, in no way affecting its foundations. Man emerged, developed, and changed within one epoch. The world, existing and stable in this existence, required that man adapt to it, that he recognize and submit to the existing laws of life. Man emerged, but the world itself did not. On the contrary, the world was an immobile orientation point for developing man. Man's emergence was his private affair, as it were, and the results of this emergence were also private and biographical in nature. And everything in the world itself remained in its place. In and of itself the conception of the world as an experience, a school, was very productive in the *Bildungsroman*: it presented a different side of the world to man, a side that had previously been foreign to the novel. It led to a radical reinterpretation of the elements of the novel's plot and opened up for the novel new and realistically productive points for viewing the world. But the world, as an experience and as a school, remained the same, fundamentally immobile and ready-made, given. It changed for the one studying in it only during the process of study (in most cases that world turned out to be more impoverished and drier than it had seemed in the beginning).

In such novels as *Gargantua and Pantagruel*, *Simplicissimus*, and *Wilhelm Meister*, however, human emergence is of a different nature. It is no longer man's own private affair. He emerges *along with the world* and he reflects the historical emergence of the world itself. He is no longer within an epoch, but on the border between two epochs, at the transition point from one to the other. This transition is accomplished in him and through him. He is forced to become a new, unprecedented type of human being. What is happening here is precisely the emergence of a new man. The organizing force held by the future is therefore extremely great here—and this is not, of course, the private biographical future, but the historical future. It is as though the very *foundations* of the world are changing, and man must change along with them. Understandably, in such a novel of emergence, problems of reality and man's potential, problems of freedom and necessity, and the problem of creative initiative rise to their full height. The image of the emerging man begins to surmount its private nature (within certain limits, of course) and enters into a completely new, *spatial* sphere of historical existence. Such is the last, realistic type of novel of emergence.

Aspects of this historical emergence of man can be found in almost all important realistic novels, and, consequently, they exist in all works that achieve a significant assimilation of real historical time.

This last type of realistic novel of emergence is the special theme of our book. The material of this type of novel serves best to reveal and clarify the overall theoretical problem of our work: the novel's assimilation of historical time in all of its essential aspects.

But, of course, the fifth type of novel cannot be understood or studied without considering its relation to the other four types of novels of emergence. This pertains particularly to the second type, the *Bildungsroman* in the narrow sense (originated by Wieland), which directly prepared the way for Goethe's novels. This novel is a most typical phenomenon of the German Enlightenment. Even in this type, problems of human potential, reality, and creative initiative were already present in rudimentary form. On the other hand, this *Bildungsroman* is directly related to the early biographical novel of emergence, namely, to Fielding's *Tom Jones* (in the very first words of his celebrated "Foreword," Wieland directly associates his *Agathon* with the type of novel—or, more precisely, hero—that was created by *Tom Jones*). Also of essential importance for understanding this problem of the assimilation of the time of human emergence is the idyllic-cyclical type of emergence as presented in Hippel and Jean Paul (linked with the more complex elements of emergence influenced by Wieland and Goethe). Finally, in order to understand the image of emerging man in Goethe, it is immensely important to consider the idea of education as it took shape during the Enlightenment, and particularly that specific subcategory that we find on German soil as the idea of the "education of the human race" in Lessing and Herder.[10]

Thus, although we shall limit our discussion to the fifth type of novel of emergence, we shall still have to touch upon all the other types of this novel. But we shall by no means attempt to make a historically exhaustive presentation of the material (after all, our main task is theoretical), or to establish all, or even the main, historical connections and correlations. Our work makes no claim whatsoever to being historically exhaustive in its consideration of this problem.

Rabelais (and, to some degree, Grimmelshausen) occupies a special place in the development of the realistic novel of emergence. His novel is the greatest attempt at constructing an image of *man growing* in *national-historical time*. Herein lies Rabelais' immense significance both for the entire problem of the assimilation of time in the novel and, particularly, for the problem of the image of emerging man. In this work we have thus devoted special attention to him, along with Goethe.

Time and Space in Goethe's Works

The ability to *see time*, to *read time*, in the spatial whole of the world and, on the other hand, to perceive the filling of space not as an immobile background, a given that is completed once and for all, but as an emerging whole, an event—this is the ability to read in everything *signs that show time in its course*, beginning with nature and ending with human customs and ideas (all the way to abstract concepts). Time reveals itself above all in nature: the movement of the sun and stars, the crowing of roosters, sensory and visual signs of the time of the year. All these are inseparably linked to corresponding moments in human life, existence, and activity (labor)—the cycles of time that are marked by degrees of intensity of labor. The growth of trees and livestock, the age of people are visible signs of longer periods. Further, there are complex visible signs of historical time in the strict sense of the word. These are visible vestiges of man's creativity, traces of his hands and his mind: cities, streets, buildings, artworks, technology, social organizations, and so on. The artist perceives in them the most complex designs of people, generations, epochs, nations, and social and class groups. The work of the seeing eye joins here with the most complex thought processes. But regardless of how profound these cognitive processes may be, how saturated with the broadest generalizations, they are never ultimately broken off from the work of the eye, from concrete sensory signs and the living figurative word. Finally, there are socioeconomic contradictions—those motive forces of development—from elementary immediate visual contrasts (the social diversity of the homeland on the high road) to their more profound and refined manifestations in human relations and ideas. These contradictions must necessarily push visible time into the future. The more profoundly they are revealed, the more essential and wide-ranging is the visible completedness of time in the novelist's images.

One of the high points of visualizing historical time in world literature was achieved by Goethe.

The Enlightenment paved the way for this vision and depiction of historical time (we have been especially unfair to the Enlightenment in this respect). Signs and categories of cyclical time are developed here: natural, everyday, and rural-labor idyllic time (of course, after a preparatory period during the Renaissance and seventeenth century, and not without the influence of the classical tradition). The themes of "times of the year," "agricultural cycles," and "the ages of man" run throughout all of the eighteenth century and can be found in a large proportion of its poetic works. It is especially important that these concepts are not confined to the thematic plane, but acquire an essentially compositional and organizational significance (in Thomson, Gessner, and other idyllists).[11] In general, the whole notion of the notorious lack of historicity during the Enlightenment should be radically revised. First, the very historicity of the first third of the nineteenth century, which so condescendingly deemed the Enlightenment to be antihistorical, was prepared for by Enlightenment thinkers. Second, the historical eighteenth century must be measured not only from the standpoint of this later historicity (we repeat, prepared for by it), but in comparison to preceding epochs. With this approach the eighteenth century emerges as an epoch of great awakening of a *sense of time*, above all a sense of time in nature and human life. Until the last third of the century, cyclical kinds of time prevailed, but they, too, despite their greatly limited nature, loosen the soil of the immobile world of preceding epochs with the plow of time. And on this soil, loosened by cyclical time, one begins to see signs of historical time. The contradictions of contemporary life, having lost their absolute, God-given, eternal nature, reveal a historical multitemporality—remnants of the past, and rudiments and tendencies of the future. Simultaneously the theme of the ages of man, evolving into the theme of generations, begins to lose its cyclical nature and begins to prepare for the phenomenon of historical perspectives. And this process of preparing for the disclosure of historical time took place more rapidly, completely, and profoundly in *literary creativity* than in the abstract philosophical and strictly historical, ideological views of Enlightenment thinkers.

In Goethe—who in this respect was the direct successor and crowning figure of the Enlightenment—artistic visualization of historical time, as we have said, reaches one of its high points (it remains unsurpassed in several respects, as we shall see).

The problem of time and historical emergence in Goethe's creativity (and especially the image of emerging man), in all of its immensity, will occupy the second half of this book. Here we shall touch on only a few of the features and peculiarities of Goethe's sense of time, so as to clarify our ideas about the chronotope and the assimilation of time in literature.

We stress, first and foremost, the exceptional significance of *visibility* for Goethe (this is generally known). All other external feelings, internal experiences, reflection, and abstract concepts are joined together around the *seeing eye* as a center, as the first and last authority. Anything essential can and should be visible; anything invisible is inessential. It is generally known that Goethe attached great significance to the *art of the eye* and that his understanding of this art was extremely broad and deep. In his understanding of the *eye* and *visibility* he was as far away from crude primitive sensualism as he was from narrow aestheticism. For him visibility was not only the first, but also the last authority, when the visible was already enriched and saturated with all the complexity of thought and cognition.

Goethe was averse to words that were not backed up by any actual *visible* experience. After visiting Venice, he exclaimed: "So, now, thank God, Venice is no longer a mere word for me, an empty name, a state of mind which had so often alarmed me who am a mortal enemy of mere words" (*Italian Journey*, p. 58).[12]

Even the most complex and crucial concepts and ideas, according to Goethe, can always be represented in *visible form*, can be *demonstrated* with a schematic or symbolic blueprint or model, or with an adequate drawing. Goethe expressed all strictly scientific ideas and constructs in the form of precise diagrams, blueprints, and drawings. And others' constructs, which he would then assimilate, he also invested with visual form. On the first evening of his friendship with Schiller, when explaining his "Metamorphosis of Plants" to him, with several typical strokes of the pen Goethe made a symbolic flower appear before the eyes of his listener (*Annals*, p. 391).[13] During their subsequent joint reflections "about nature, art, and morality," Goethe and Schiller felt a vital need to turn to tables and symbolic blueprints ("die Notwendigkeit von tabellarischer und symbolischer Behandlung"). They compiled a "rose of temperaments" and a table of the useful and harmful effects of dilettantism; and they drew diagrams of Goethe's table of colors—"Farbenlehre" (*Annals*, p. 64).

Even the very basis of a philosophical world view can be revealed in a simple and clear visual image. When traveling from Naples to Sicily, Goethe found himself on the open sea for the first time, encircled by the line of the horizon. He said, "No-one who has never seen himself surrounded on all sides by nothing but the sea can have a true conception of the world and his own relation to it" (*IJ*, p. 220).

For Goethe the *word* coincided with the clearest visibility. In his *Autobiography*, he tells about a "singular expedient" to which he frequently resorted. With a few strokes he would sketch on paper a subject or locality that interested him, and he would fill in the details with *words*, which he inscribed directly on the drawing. These remarkable artistic hybrids enabled him to fix precisely in his memory any locality (*Localität*) he might need for a poem or a story (*Goethe's Autobiography*, vol. 2, p. 394).[14]

Thus, Goethe wished and was able to perceive everything with his eyes. The invisible did not exist for him. But at the same time his eyes did not want to (and could not) see that which was *ready-made* and *immobile*. His eyes did not recognize simple spatial contiguities or the simple coexistence of things and phenomena. Behind each static multiformity he saw multitemporality: for him diversity was distributed in various stages (epochs) of development, that is, it acquired a temporal significance. In the short note "More about My Relations with Schiller," Goethe defines this peculiarity of his as follows: "I used an evolutionary method which disclosed development [*die entwickelnde entfaltende Methode*], but it was by no means a method that ordered things through juxtaposition; I did not know what to do with phenomena that were situated next to one another or, rather, I could not deal with their affiliation" (*Annals*, p. 393).

The simple spatial contiguity (*nebeneinander*) of phenomena was profoundly alien to Goethe, so he saturated and imbued it with *time*, revealed emergence and development in it, and he distributed that which was contiguous in *space* in various *temporal* stages, epochs of becoming.[15] For him contemporaneity—both in nature and in human life—is revealed as an essential multitemporality: as remnants or relics of various stages and formations of the past and as rudiments of stages in the more or less distant future.

Goethe's heroic struggle to introduce the ideas of emergence and development into natural sciences is generally known. This is not the place to discuss his scientific works in depth. Let us simply note that in them as well concrete visibility loses its static quality and fuses with time. Everywhere here the *seeing eye* seeks and finds *time*—development, emergence, and history. Behind the ready-made it perceives what is emerging and being prepared. And he sees all this with exceptional clarity. In crossing the Alps, he observes the movement of the clouds and the atmosphere around the mountains, and he creates his own theory of the emergence of weather. Plainsmen have good or bad weather in *ready-made form*, but in the mountains people are present during its *emergence*.

Here is a brief illustration of this "vision of emergence" from *Italian Journey*.

> When we look at mountains, whether from far or near, and see their summits, now glittering in the sunshine, now shrouded in mists or wreathed in storm-tossed clouds, now lashed by rain or covered with snow, we attribute all these phenomena to the atmosphere, because all of its changes and movements are visible to the eye. To the eye, on the other hand, shapes of the mountains always remain immobile; and because they seem rigid, inactive and at rest, we believe them to be dead. But for a long time I have felt convinced that most manifest atmospheric changes are really due to their imperceptible and secret influence. (*IJ*, p. 13)

Goethe goes on to develop his hypothesis that the attractive force of the earth's mass, and particularly of its extrusive parts (mountain chains), is not something constant and unchanging, but is, on the contrary, under the influence of various factors. It sometimes increases, sometimes decreases, and it constantly *pulsates*. This pulsation of the very mass of the mountains exerts an essential influence on changes in the atmosphere. Weather, too, which is experienced in ready-made form by plainsmen, is created as a result of this internal activity of the mountains themselves.

The scientific groundlessness of this hypothesis is quite unimportant to us here. What is important are the characteristic features of Goethe's way of seeing. After all, for the ordinary observer, mountains are the epitome of stasis, the embodiment of immobility and immutability. But in fact mountains are not at all inanimate.[16] They have congealed, but they are certainly not inactive. They seem so because they are at peace and at rest (*sie ruhen*). And the gravitational forces of the mass are not a constant quantity that is always equal to itself. It changes, pulsates, and oscillates. Therefore, the mountains, too, in which this force seems to congeal, change internally, become active, and create weather.

As a result, the picture with which Goethe began changes sharply and *in principle.* Initially there were abrupt changes in the atmosphere (the bright sunshine, fog, thunderclouds, pouring rains, and snow) against the immobile background of the eternally unchanging mountains. But in the end this did not prove to be an immobile and immutable background at all. It has entered into a more essential and profound movement than the clear, but peripheral, movement of the atmosphere. It has become active, and, moreover, the real movement and activity have shifted to it—to this background.

This particular feature of Goethe's way of seeing, revealed in our small example, is manifested everywhere in one form or another (depending on the material) and with varying degrees of visibility. Everywhere, whatever served as and appeared to be a stable and immutable background for all movements and changes became for Goethe a part of emergence, saturated through and through with time, and emergence took on a more essential and creative mobility than ever. We shall see below, when analyzing *Wilhelm Meister,* how everything that usually serves in the novel as a stable background, an unchanging quantity, an immobile prerequisite for plot movement, becomes for Goethe an essential vehicle of movement, its initiator, an organizational center for plot movement through which the novel's plot itself changes in a fundamental way. For the "great genius" Goethe, essential movement was revealed against that immobile background of the world's buttresses (socioeconomic, political, and moral) that the "narrow philistine" Goethe himself frequently proclaimed to be unchanging and eternal. In *Wilhelm Meister* this background of the world's buttresses begins to pulsate like the mountain masses in the example above, and this pulsation determines the more superficial movement and alteration of human destinies and human outlooks. But this will be discussed later.

Thus, we arrive at Goethe's startling ability to see time in space. One is impressed by the exceptional freshness and clarity of this way of visualizing time (as, incidentally, is generally true of writers of the eighteenth century, to whom it seemed that time was being revealed for the first time). To be sure, this is partially due to the relative simplicity and elementary nature of this time, and therefore to its more perceptible graphic quality. Goethe had a keen eye for all visible markers and signs of time in nature. He could, for example, quickly determine the ages of trees by sight, he knew the growth rates of their various species, and he could see epochs and ages. He had an exceptionally keen insight into all visible signs of time in human life—from everyday time that is measured by the sun and the ordinary sequence of man's day, to the time of the whole of human life—ages and epochs of man's emergence. The significance of this latter *biographical time* for Goethe and his profound visualization of this time are demonstrated in his own autobiographical and biographical works, which comprise an immense proportion of his creative work—and that constant interest in autobiographical and biographical literature that he shared with his epoch (Goethe's biographical methods are included in our treatment of this subject).[17]

As for everyday time in Goethe, we recall with what love and tender concern he analyzes and depicts the everyday time of the Italians in his *Italian Journey*.

> In a country where everyone enjoys the day but the evening even more, sunset is an important moment. All work stops; those who were strolling about return to their homes; the father wants to see his daughter back in the house—the day has ended. We Cimmerians hardly know the real meaning of day. With our perpetual fogs and cloudy skies we do not care if it is day or night, since we are so little given to take walks and enjoy ourselves out of doors. But here, when night falls, the day consisting of evening and morning is definitely over, twenty-four hours have been spent, and time begins afresh. The bells ring, the rosary is said, the maid enters the room with a lighted lamp and says: "*Felicissima notte!*" This period of time varies in length according to the season, and people who live here are so full of vitality that this does not confuse them, because the pleasures of their existence are related not to the precise hour, but to the time of day. If one were to force a German clock hand on them, they would be at a loss, for their own method of time measurement is closely bound up with their nature. And an hour or an hour and a half before sunset, the nobility set out in their carriages. . . . (*IJ*, p. 42)

Goethe goes on to develop in detail the method he has chosen for translating organic Italian time into German, that is, ordinary time, and he appends a sketch in which he uses concentric circles to give a visually graphic image of the relationship between the two kinds of time (*IJ*, p. 44).

This organic Italian time (the calculation of time proceeds from the *actual* setting of the sun, which, of course, takes place at different hours during different times of the year) is inseparably interwoven with all of Italian life, and Goethe repeatedly turns his attention to the latter. All his descriptions of Italian everyday life are pervaded with a sense of everyday time, measured by the pleasures and labor of the vital human life. This feeling for time profoundly permeates his celebrated description of the Roman carnival (*IJ*, pp. 445–69).

Against the background of these times of nature, daily existence, and life, which are still cyclical to one degree or another, Goethe also sees interwoven with them signs of historical time—essential traces of human hands and minds that change nature, and the way human reality and all man has created are reflected back on his customs and views. Goethe searches for and finds primarily the visible movement of *historical time*, which is inseparable from the natural setting (*Localität*) and the entire totality of objects created by man, which are essentially connected to this natural setting. And here Goethe displays exceptional keenness and concreteness of vision.

Here is one example in which Goethe takes advantage of the historical sharp-sightedness of his eye. While driving along the road to Pyrmont through the town of Einbeck, Goethe immediately saw with his *eye* that about thirty years ago this town had an excellent Bürgermeister (*Annals*, p. 76).

What, specifically, did he see? He saw a great deal of greenery, many trees, and he saw that they had not been planted at random. And he saw in them a *vestige of a single human will acting in a planned way*. From the age of the trees, which he determined approximately by sight, he saw the time when this will, acting in a planned way, was manifested.

Regardless of how random the above-cited case of historical vision may be in itself, how microscopic its scale, and how elementary it is, it reveals very clearly and precisely the very structure of this vision. Let us discuss it.

Here, first of all, we have an *essential* and *living* vestige of the past in the present. We emphasize essential and living because this is no inanimate, even if picturesque, ruin that has no essential connection with the living present surrounding it and has no influence on it. Goethe did not like "ruinlike," antiquated, museumlike external coverings of the naked past. He called them ghosts (*Gespenster*) and drove them away.[18] They burst into the present like foreign bodies. They were extraneous and could not be comprehended in it. To mix the past and present mechanically, without making any real temporal connection, was profoundly offensive to Goethe. Therefore, he disliked those idle historical reminiscences of historical places that one usually hears from tourists who have visited them. He hated the stories that guides tell about historical events that had occurred there at one time. All these were ghosts that lacked any *necessary* and visible connection with the surrounding living reality.

One time in Sicily, near Palermo, in a luxuriant, extravagantly fertile valley, a guide described in detail to Goethe the terrible battles and extraordinary feats Hannibal had once performed there. "I strictly forbade him," said Goethe, "this fatal summoning of ghosts that had disappeared (*das fatale Hervorrufen solcher abgeschiedenen Gespenster*)." Indeed, what necessary and creative (historically productive) link can there be between these cultivated fields with their extravagant fertility and the recollection of Hannibal's horses and elephants trampling them down?

The guide was surprised at Goethe's indifference to these recollections of the classical period. "And I could not make him understand my objections to that *mixing-up of past and present.*"

The guide was even more surprised when Goethe, "indifferent to classical recollections," began carefully to gather certain little stones on the bank of the river. "Again, I could not explain to him that the quickest way to get an idea of any mountainous region is to examine the types of rock fragments washed down by its streams, or that there was any point in studying the rubble to get the idea of these eternal classical heights of the prehistoric earth" (*IJ*, p. 222).

The excerpt cited here is highly characteristic. It is not important to us here that there is a certain element of Rousseauism in it (the juxtaposition of natural time and creativity: "the eternally classical peaks of the ancient period of the earth's existence" and the fertile valley, human history with its wars and devastation). The importance lies elsewhere. First, this is a manifestation of Goethe's characteristic dislike for the *estranged* past, for the past in and of itself, that past of which the romantics were so fond. He wanted to see *necessary connections* between this past and the living present, to understand the *necessary place* of this past in the *unbroken line of historical development*. And the isolated, estranged chunk of the past was for him a "ghost," profoundly loathsome and even frightening. Thus, he also contrasts to these "disappeared ghosts" fragments of rocks on the bank of a stream, because from these fragments one can create a unified idea of the nature of the entire mountainous territory and of the earth's inevitable past. He sees clearly the entire lengthy process that necessarily resulted in the appearance of these fragments today, here and now, on the bank of the stream. He sees clearly what kind they are, their geological age, and he sees clearly their position in the earth's continuous development. This is no longer a random, mechanical mixing of the past and present. Everything has its *stable* and *necessary* place in *time.*

Second—and this is a very important feature of the Goethean vision of historical time—the past itself must be *creative.* It must have its *effect* in the present (even if this effect is negative or one Goethe considers undesirable). Such a creatively effective past, determining the present, produces in conjunction with the present a particular direction for the future, and, to a certain degree, predetermines the future. Thus, one achieves a *fullness of time,* and it is a graphic, visible completeness. This is the past he had seen on a microscopic scale near the town of Einbeck. This past—planned plantings—continues to live effectively in the present (in this case in the literal sense, since the planted trees are still living and continue to grow, they determine the present by creating a certain physiognomy for the town of Einbeck and, of course, they influence its future to a certain microscopic degree).

We must also emphasize another aspect of our small example. Goethe's historical vision always relied on a deep, painstaking, and concrete perception of the locality (*Localität*). The creative past must be revealed as necessary and productive under the conditions of a given locality, as a creative humanization of this locality, which transforms a portion of terrestrial space into a place of historical life for people, into a corner of the historical world.

A locality or a landscape in which there is no place for man and his creative activity, which cannot be populated and built up, which cannot become the arena for human history, was alien and unpleasant for Goethe.

As we know, it was typical of this epoch to bring wild nature, virgin and inaccessible to man, primordial landscape, into both literature and painting. Goethe was deeply opposed to this practice. And in a later epoch Goethe also took a negative attitude toward similar tendencies that developed on the soil of realism.

In 1820, Friedrich Gmelin sent his copper engravings to Weimar.[19] They were intended for an elegant edition of Vergil's *Aeneid* produced by Hannibal Caro.[20] The artist depicted the desolate marshy localities of the Roman Campagna in a realistic manner. While giving the artist's talent its due, Goethe disapproved of his direction. "What can be more pathetic," he said, "than attempts to help the poet (Vergil) by depicting *desolate localities* which even the most lively imagination could not *build up and populate* again" (*Annals*, p. 340).

Before all else, Goethe's creative imagination built up and populated any locality. It was only from the viewpoint, as it were, of building up and populating that Goethe could even consider any locality. When separated from man, from his needs and activities, a locality lost all apparent sense or significance for Goethe, because all criteria for evaluation, all measures, and the entire living human scale of the locality can be understood only from the standpoint of *man the builder*, from the standpoint of its transformation into a small part of historical life. We shall see this artistic viewpoint applied frequently and consistently when we analyze *Wilhelm Meister*.

Such are the structural peculiarities of the Goethean vision as revealed in the elementary example above.

More complex material will demonstrate this point more concretely and in more depth.

In his *Autobiography*, Goethe makes an admission that is very important in this connection:

> One feeling, which prevailed greatly with me, and could never find an expression odd enough for itself, was a sense of the past and present together in one—a phenomenon which brought something spectral into the present. It is expressed in many of my smaller and larger works, and always has a beneficial influence in a poem, though, whenever it began to mix itself up with actual life, it must have appeared to every one strange, inexplicable, perhaps gloomy.
>
> Cologne was a place where antiquity had such an incalculable effect upon me. The ruins of the cathedral (for an unfinished work is like one destroyed) called up the emotions to which I had been accustomed in Strasbourg. (*GA*, vol. 2, p. 258)

This remarkable admission adds a certain corrective to what we said above about Goethe's revulsion for the romantic sense of the past, for "ghosts of the past" that cloud the present. It turns out that this feeling could affect him as well.

This feeling of the past and present merging into one, which Goethe discusses in his comments above, was a *complex* feeling. It included also a romantic (as we shall arbitrarily call it), "ghostly" component. In certain early stages of Goethe's creative work (primarily in the Strasbourg period), this component was stronger and almost set the tone for all feeling. This also created a certain amount of romanticism in

Goethe's corresponding (mainly small-scale, and exclusively poetic) works.

But alongside this conventionally romantic component in the feeling of a merged past and present, there also existed from the very beginning a *realistic* component (as we shall call it, also arbitrarily). It is precisely because the realistic component existed *from the very beginning* that we do not find a purely romantic sense of time anywhere in Goethe. In Goethe's subsequent development, the realistic component became increasingly strong, crowded out the romantic component, and, as early as the beginning of the Weimar period, gained an almost total victory. Here Goethe already displays a profound *revulsion* for the romantic component, which becomes especially acute during the period of the Italian journey. The evolution of the sense of time in Goethe, which can be reduced to a consistent surmounting of the romantic component and the total victory of the realistic, could be traced in those works that served as a transition from the early period to the late one, primarily in *Faust* and partially in *Egmont*.

In the process of developing a sense of time, Goethe overcomes the ghostly (*Gespenstermässiges*), the terrifying (*Unerfreuliches*), and the unaccountable (*Unzuberechnendes*), which were strong in his initial feeling of a merged past and present. But the very sense of the merging of times remained in complete and undiminished force and freshness until the end of his life, blossoming into an authentic fullness of time. The ghostly, terrifying, and unaccountable in it were surmounted by the structural aspects, already disclosed by us above, which are inherent in this way of visualizing time: the aspect of an *essential link* between the past and present, the aspect of the *necessity* of the past and the necessity of its place in a line of continuous development, the aspect of the *creative effectiveness* of the past, and, finally, the aspect of the past and present being linked to a *necessary future*.

The fresh wind of the future blows ever stronger through Goethe's sense of time, purging it of all that is dark, ghostly, and unaccountable. And perhaps we feel the draft of this wind most strongly in *Wilhelm Meisters Wanderjahre* (and in the last scenes of part 2 of *Faust*). Thus, in Goethe, from a murky sense of the past and present that frightened even him, there arose a realistic sense of time that was exceptional in world literature in its force and, at the same time, its distinct clarity.

Let us look more closely at the chronotopic visualizing of locality and landscape in Goethe. His seeing eye saturates landscape with time—creative, historically productive time. As we have noted above, the point of view of man-the-builder determines Goethe's contemplation and understanding of landscape. His creative imagination is also restricted and subordinated to the *necessity* of a given locality, the ironclad logic of its historical and geographical existence.

Goethe strove above all to penetrate this geological and historical logic of the existence of a locality, and this logic had to be *visible*, interpretive and graphic, from beginning to end. For this he had his own primary means of orientation.

In his *Autobiography*, regarding his journey through Alsace, Goethe says:

> Already, in my limited wanderings through the world, I had remarked how important it is in travelling to ascertain the course of the waters, and even to ask with respect to the smallest brook, whither in reality it runs. One thus acquires a general survey of every stream-region in which one happens to be, a conception of the heights and depths which bear relation to each other, and by these leading lines, which assist the contemplation as well as the memory, extricates one's self in the surest manner from the geological and political labyrinth. (*GA*, vol. 2, pp. 26–27)

And in the very beginning of *Italian Journey*:

> The land rises steadily all the way to Tischenreuth, and the streams flow towards the Eger and the Elbe. After Tischenreuth, the land falls to the south and the streams run down toward the Danube. I find I can quickly get a topographical idea of a region by looking at even the smallest stream and noting in which direction it flows and which drainage basin it belongs to. Even in a region which one cannot survey as a whole, one can obtain in this way a mental picture of the relation between the mountains and valleys. (*IJ*, p. 5)

Goethe discusses this same method of his for contemplating regions in the *Annals* as well (see, for example, p. 161).

The living, dynamic marker provided by flowing rivers and streams also gives a graphic idea of the country's water basins, its topography, its natural boundaries and natural connections, its land and water routes and transshipment points, its fertile and arid areas, and so on. This is not an abstract geological and geographical landscape. For Goethe it reveals potential for historical life. This is an arena of historical events, a firmly delineated boundary of that spatial riverbed along which the current of historical time flows. Historically active man is placed in this living, graphic, visual system of waterways, mountains, valleys, boundaries, and routes. He builds, drains marshes, lays routes across mountains and rivers, develops the minerals, cultivates the irrigated valleys, and so on. One sees the *essential* and *necessary* character of man's historical activity. And if he wages wars, one can understand *how* he will wage them (that is, there will be necessity here, too).

In the *Annals*, Goethe relates: "For whatever small amount of clarity I possess in the area of geology and geography I am obliged to the mountain map of Europe compiled by Sorrio.[21] Thus, it became immediately clear to me how treacherous the area in Spain was for a military leader (with a regular army) and how favorable it was for guerrillas. On my map of Spain I drew in its main *watershed* and immediately gained a clear and comprehensible picture of each land route, each military campaign, each undertaking of a regular or irregular nature" (*Annals*, p. 303).

Goethe cannot and will not see or conceive of any locality, any natural landscape, as an abstract thing, for the sake of its self-sufficient naturalness, as it were. It must be illuminated by human activity and historical events. A piece of the earth's space must be incorporated into the history of humanity. Outside this history it is lifeless and incomprehensible, and nothing can be done with it. But, conversely, nothing can be done with the historical event, with the abstract historical recollection, if it is not localized in terrestrial space, if one does not understand (does not see) the *necessity* of its occurrence at a particular time and in a particular place.

Goethe wants to reveal this *visible* concrete *necessity* of human creativity and of the historical event. Any fantasy, fabrication, dreamlike recollection, or abstract judgment must be restrained, suppressed, and let go. It must give way to the work of the eye that contemplates the need for performance and creativity in a *particular place* and at a *particular time.* "I try to keep my eyes open all the time, remember as much as I can and not judge more than I can help" (*IJ*, p. 112). And somewhat later, having noted how difficult it is to create for oneself an understanding of classical antiquity from surviving ruins, he adds:

> The so-called classic soil is another matter. If we do not approach it fancifully but consider this soil in its reality as it presents itself to our senses, it still appears as the stage upon which the greatest events were enacted and decided. I have always looked at landscape with the eye of a geologist and a topographer, and suppressed my imagination and emotions in order to preserve my faculty for clear and unbiased observation. If one does this first, then history follows naturally and

pace and time are bound together into one inseparable knot.
rial space and human history are inseparable from one another
he's integrated concrete vision. This is what makes historical
his creative work so dense and materialized, and space so hu-
nterpreted and intensive.

is the major way in which necessity manifests itself in artistic
ty. In regard to Winckelmann's Italian letters, Goethe says:[22]
from the objects of Nature, who in all her realms is true and
nt, nothing speaks so loudly as the impression left by a good
elligent man, or by authentic works of art which are just as un-
s Nature. One feels this particularly strongly in Rome, where
y caprices have been given free rein and so many absurdities
uated by wealth and power" (*IJ*, p. 137).

in Rome that Goethe experiences especially keenly this im-
e condensation of historical time, its fusion with terrestrial

history, above all, that one reads quite differently here from
re else in the world. Everywhere else one starts from the out-
d works inward; here it seems to be the other way around. All
is encamped about us and all history sets forth again from us.
oes not apply only to Roman history, but to the history of the
world. From here I can accompany the conquerors to the Weser
e Euphrates. . . ." (*IJ*, p. 142). Or another instance: "My expe-
with natural history is repeating itself here, for the entire his-
the world is linked up with this city, and I reckon my second
very rebirth, from the day when I entered Rome" (*IJ*, p. 136).
in another place, when justifying his intention to visit Sicily, he
To me Sicily implies Asia and Africa, and it will mean more than
to me to stand at that miraculous centre upon which so many
f world history converge" (*IJ*, p. 212).

as though the essence of historical time in that small section of
rth in Rome, the *visible* coexistence of various epochs in it,
the person who contemplates it to participate in the great coun-
world destinies. Rome is a great chronotope of human history:

> is an entity which has suffered so many drastic changes in the
> se of two thousand years, yet is still the same soil, the same hill,
> n even the same column or the same wall, and in its people one
> finds traces of their ancient character. Contemplating this, the
> rver becomes, as it were, a contemporary of the great decrees of
> iny, and this makes it difficult for him to follow the evolution of

logically in all its astonishing wonder. Or
want to do is to read Tacitus in Rome. (*I.*

Thus, in a correctly understood, objec
terated by fantasy and feeling) one discov
sity of history (that is, of a particular hist
Goethe saw the same internal necessit
cient peoples.

> I walked up to Spoleto and stood on the a
> as a bridge from one hill to the other. Th
> span the valley have been quietly standin
> turies, and the water still gushes in all qu
> third work of antiquity which I have seen,
> noble spirit. A sense of the civic good, wh
> architecture, was *second nature* to the ancie
> theatre, the temple, the aqueduct. For the
> I always detested *arbitrary* constructions,
> Weissenstein, for example, which is a *poin*
> piece of confectionery—and I have felt th
> other buildings. Such things are still-born,
> have a true *raison d'être* is lifeless and cann
> so. (*IJ*, pp. 111–12)

Human creativity has its own internal la
civilly expedient), but it must also be *neces*
like nature. Any arbitrariness, fabrication,
pulsive to Goethe.

Not abstract moral truth (abstract justice,
the *necessity* of any creative work or historic
thing for Goethe. And this leads to the sha
and Schiller, between him and the majo
the Enlightenment with their abstractly m
criteria.

As we have already pointed out, necessit
center for Goethe's sense of time. He want
unite the present, past, and future with th
Goethean necessity was very far both from
from mechanical natural necessity (in natu
visible, concrete, and material, but it was a m
cal necessity.

An authentic vestige is a sign of history that

In it, s
Terres
in Goe
time ir
manly
This
creativ
"Aside
consist
and in
erring
so mai
perpet
It is
pressiv
space.
"It
anywh
side a
history
This d
whole
and th
rience
tory o
life, a
And
says, "
a littl
radii c
It is
the e
allows
cil of

> He
> cou
> ofte
> still
> obs
> des

> the city, to grasp not only how Modern Rome follows Ancient, but also how, within both, one epoch follows another. (*IJ*, p. 120)

Synchronism, the coexistence of times at one point in space, the space of Rome, revealed for Goethe the "fullness of time," as he experienced it in his classical period (the Italian journey was its culmination point):

> On me, the ultimate effect of this tour was to strengthen my sense of really standing on classic soil and convince my senses and my spirit that here greatness was, is and ever will be. It lies in the nature of time and the mutual interaction of physical and moral forces that greatness and splendour must perish, but my ultimate feeling was less of sadness at all that had been destroyed than of joy at so much which had been preserved and even reconstructed more splendidly and impressively than it had been before.
>
> The Church of St. Peter, for example, is a bolder and grander conception than any antique temple. Even the fluctuations in taste, now a striving for simple grandeur, now a return to a love for the multiple and small, are signs of vitality, and in Rome the history of art and the history of mankind confront us simultaneously.
>
> The observation that all greatness is transitory should not make us despair; on the contrary, the realization that the past was great should stimulate us to create something of consequence ourselves, which, even when, in its turn, it has fallen in ruins, may continue to inspire our descendants to a noble activity such as our ancestors never lacked. (*IJ*, pp. 433–34)

We have quoted this long passage so that it can serve as a summary conclusion to the series of passages we have cited above. Unfortunately, in this summary of his impressions of Rome, Goethe did not repeat the motif of necessity, which for him was the actual connecting link of times. Therefore, the final paragraph of the quotation, which introduces a new motif of historical generations (we find a more profound interpretation of it in *Wilhelm Meister*), somewhat simplifies and degrades—in the sense of Herder's "Idea"—Goethe's historical vision.[23]

Let us sum up our preliminary analysis of Goethe's mode of visualizing time. The main features of this visualization are the merging of time (past with present), the fullness and clarity of the visibility of the time in space, the inseparability of the time of an event from the specific place of its occurrence (*Localität und Geschichte*), the visible *essential* connection of time (present and past), the creative and active nature of time (of the past in the present and of the present itself), the necessity that penetrates time and links time with space and different times with one another, and, finally, on the basis of the necessity that pervades localized time, the inclusion of the future, crowning the fullness of time in Goethe's images.

One must especially single out and emphasize the aspects of *necessity and fullness of time.* Goethe is intimately and fundamentally linked to a *feeling for time* that awakened in the eighteenth century and reached its culmination on German soil in Lessing, Winckelmann, and Herder. In these two areas he escapes the limitations of the Enlightenment, its abstract morality, rationality, and utopianism. On the other hand, an understanding of necessity as humanly creative, historical necessity ("second nature"—the aqueduct that serves as a bridge between two mountains; see *IJ*, p. 111) separates him from the mechanical materialism of Holbach and others (see his opinion of "The System of Nature" in the eleventh book of *Dichtung und Wahrheit* [*GA*, vol. 2, pp. 108–9]). These same two aspects clearly separate Goethe from subsequent romantic historicity as well.

All we have said reveals the exceedingly chronotopic nature of Goethe's mode of visualization and thought in all areas and spheres of his multifaceted activity. He saw everything not *sub specie aeternitatis* (from the point of view of eternity), as his teacher, Spinoza, did, but in time and in the *power of time.* But the power of this time is a productive and creative power. Everything—from an abstract idea to a piece of rock on the bank of a stream—bears the stamp of time, is saturated with time, and assumes its form and meaning in time. Therefore, everything is intensive in Goethe's world; it contains no inanimate, immobile, petrified places, no immutable background that does not participate in action and emergence (in events), no decorations or sets. On the other hand, this time, in all its essential aspects, is localized in concrete space, imprinted on it. In Goethe's world there are no events, plots, or temporal motifs that are not related in an essential way to the particular spatial place of their occurrence, that could occur anywhere or nowhere ("eternal" plots and motifs). Everything in this world is a *time-space,* a true *chronotope.*

Hence the unrepeatably concrete and visible world of human space and human history to which all images of Goethe's creative imagination belong, serving as a mobile background and an inexhaustible source of his artistic visualization and depiction. Everything is visible, everything is concrete, everything is corporeal, and everything is material in this world, and at the same time everything is intensive, interpreted, and creatively necessary.

The large epic form (the large epic), including the novel as well, should provide an integrated picture of the world and life, it should reflect the *entire* world and *all* of life. In the novel, the entire world and all of life are given in the cross section of the *integrity of the epoch*. The events depicted in the novel should somehow *substitute for* the total life of the epoch. In their capacity to represent the real-life whole lies their artistic essentiality. Novels differ enormously in their degrees of this essentiality and, consequently, in their artistic significance. These novels depend above all on their realistic penetration into this real-life integrity of the world, from which the formalized essentiality shaped in the novelistic whole is extracted. "The entire world" and its history, like the reality that confronted the romantic artist, had by Goethe's time changed profoundly and in a fundamental way. As little as three centuries ago, the "entire world" was a unique symbol that could not be adequately represented by any model, by any map or globe. In this symbol the "entire world," visible and cognized, embodied and real, was a small and detached patch of terrestrial space and an equally small and severed segment of real time. Everything else vanished in the fog, became mixed up and interwoven with other worlds—separate, ideal, fantastic, and utopian worlds. But the otherworldly and fantastic not only filled in the gaps of that impoverished reality, and conjoined and rounded out that patch of reality into a mythological whole; the otherworldly also disorganized and bled this present reality. The otherworldly admixture absorbed and broke down the real compactness of the world and prevented the real world and real history from gathering themselves together and rounding themselves out into a unified, compact, and complete whole. The otherworldly future, severed from the horizontal of terrestrial space and time, rose as an otherworldly vertical to the real flow of time, bleeding the real future and terrestrial space as an arena for this real future, ascribing symbolic significance to everything, and devaluing and discarding everything that did not yield to symbolic interpretation.

During the Renaissance the "entire world" began to condense into a real and compact whole. The earth became firmly rounded out, and it occupied a particular position in the real space of the universe. And the earth itself began to acquire a geographical definition (still far from complete) and a historical interpretation (even less complete). In Rabelais and Cervantes we see a fundamental condensation of reality that is no longer bled by otherworldly rounding out; but this reality rises up against the still very unstable and nebulous background of the entire world and human history.

The process by which the real world was rounded out, filled in, and integrated first reached its culmination in the eighteenth century, precisely by Goethe's time. The earth's position in the solar system and its relation to other worlds of this system were determined; it became subject to interpretation and, in a real-life sense, historical. It is not just a matter of the quantity of great discoveries, new journeys, and acquired knowledge, but rather of that new *quality* in the comprehension of the real world that resulted from all this: from being a fact of abstract consciousness, theoretical constructs, and *rare books*, the new, *real* unity and integrity of the world became a fact of concrete (ordinary) consciousness and practical orientation, a fact of ordinary books and everyday thoughts. These facts were linked to permanent visual images and became a graphically visual unity. Visual equivalents could be found for things that could not be directly perceived with vision. The immensely growing real material contact (economic and then cultural) with almost all of the geographical world and technical contact with complex forces of nature (the visible effect of the application of these forces) played an extremely large role in this concretization and visual clarification. Such a thing as Newton's law of gravity, in addition to its direct significance in natural and philosophical sciences, made an exceptional contribution to the visual clarification of the world. It made the new unity of the real world and its new natural law almost graphically visible and perceptible.

The eighteenth century, the most abstract and antihistorical century, was in fact a time of concretization and visual clarification of the new real world and its history. From a world of the sage and the scholar, it became the world of the everyday working consciousness of the vanguard.

The philosophical and publicistic struggle of Enlightenment thinkers against everything that was otherworldly and authoritarian, that nourished outlooks, art, daily life, the social order, and so on, played an immense role in this process of purification and condensation of reality. As a result of Enlightenment criticism, the world, as it were, became qualitatively poorer in the most immediate way; there turned out to be much less that was actually real in it than was previously thought; it was as if the absolute mass of reality, of actual existence, had been compressed and reduced; the world had been made poorer and drier.[24]

But this abstract negative criticism of Enlightenment thinkers, by dispersing the residue of otherworldly cohesion and mythical unity, helped reality to gather itself together and condense into the visible whole of the new world. New aspects and infinite prospects were revealed in this condensing reality. And this positive productivity of the Enlightenment reaches one of its high points in the work of Goethe.

This process of finally rounding out and complementing the real world can be traced in the biography of Goethe as an artist. This is not the place to discuss it in any detail. To find a good map of the mountains of Europe was still an event for him. There was a very large proportion of travel accounts, other geography books (their proportion was great even in Goethe's father's library), archeology books, and books on history (especially the history of art) in Goethe's *working* library.

We repeat that this process of concretization, graphic clarification, and completion was just coming to an end. That is the reason why all this is so fresh and prominent in Goethe. The "historical radii" from Rome and Sicily were new, and this very feeling of the fullness of *world* history (Herder) was new and fresh.

In Goethe's novels (*Lehrjahre* and *Wanderjahre*), the integrity of the world and life in the cross section of the epoch are relegated for the first time to this new, concretized, graphically clarified, and complemented real world. Behind the whole of the novel stands the large, real wholeness of the world in history. Any important novel in any epoch of this genre's development was encyclopedic. *Gargantua and Pantagruel* was encyclopedic, *Don Quixote* was encyclopedic, and the important baroque novels were encyclopedic (it goes without saying that *Amadis* and *Palmerín* were). But in Renaissance novels, late chivalric tales (*Amadis*), and baroque novels it was an abstract and bookish encyclopedicity, which was not backed by any *model* of the world whole.

Therefore, even to select what was essential and round it out into a novelistic whole was a different project before the middle of the eighteenth century (before Fielding, Sterne, and Goethe) from what it later became.

Of course, this essential condensation of the whole of life, which the novel (and the large epic in general) should be, is by no means a concise exposition of this entire whole, a summation of all its parts. That is out of the question. And, of course, no such summation can be found in Goethe's novels. There, action takes place on a limited section of terrestrial space and embraces an extremely brief segment of historical time. But, nonetheless, this new, complemented world always stands behind the world of the novel. Each part of it transmits to the novel its representatives and deputies, who reflect its new and real fullness and concreteness (geographic and historical in the broadest sense of these words). Far from everything is mentioned in the novel itself, but the compact wholeness of the real world is sensed in each of its images; it is precisely in this world that each image lives and acquires its form. The real fullness of the world also determines the very type of essentiality in it. The novel, to be sure, also includes utopian and symbolic elements, but both their character and their functions are completely transformed. The entire nature of novelistic images is determined by that new relationship through which they enter into the new, already real wholeness of the world.

We shall touch briefly here on that new attitude toward the new world, using the material of Goethe's creative plans (an analysis of the novels comes next).

In his autobiographical essays—*Autobiography, Italian Journey,* and *Annals*—Goethe discusses in detail a number of his artistic plans that either were not realized at all "on paper" or were realized only fragmentarily. Such are "Mohamet," "The Eternal Jew," "Nausicaa," "Tell," and "Pyrmont" (as we shall arbitrarily call it), and, finally, the children's tale "The New Paris" and a multilingual epistolary novel also for children. We shall discuss certain of them that are most characteristic of Goethe's chronotopic artistic imagination.

One feature of the children's fairy tale "The New Paris" is typical (see *GA*, book 2): the precise designation of that actual place where the fantastic event portrayed in the tale took place, part of Frankfurt's city wall that bears the name "bad wall." There actually was a niche with a fountain there and an inscribed stone tablet set into the wall, and old hazelnut trees rose up behind the wall. The fairy tale added a mysterious gate to the actual markers of the place, and brought the niche with the fountain, the hazelnut trees, and the tablet closer together. Subsequently it was as though these three objects were intermixed, sometimes coming closer together and sometimes moving apart from one another. This mixing of real spatial markers with fantastic ones created the unique charm of the fairy tale. The fairy tale plot was interwoven into visible reality, as if it arose directly from this ancient "bad wall" that was surrounded by certain legends, with its fountain in the deep niche, the old hazelnut trees, and the inset stone tablet. And this feature of the fairy tale had a special effect on Goethe's young audience: each of them made a pilgrimage to the "bad wall" and saw the actual markers—the niche, the fountain, and the hazelnut trees. With this fairy tale it was as though Goethe had created a "local legend," on the basis of which a small "local cult" arose (pilgrimage to the "bad wall").

Goethe wrote this fairy tale in 1757–58. During these same years the same kind of "local cult," but on a larger scale, was created on the shores of Lake Geneva, where the events of Rousseau's *La nouvelle Héloïse* took place. A similar "local cult" was created earlier by Richardson's *Clarissa Harlowe,* and later the "local cult" of Werther would come into being. We had a similar cult associated with Karamzin's *Poor Liza.*[25]

These unique "local cults" engendered by literary works are a typical feature of the second half of the eighteenth century, and gave evidence of a certain reorientation of the artistic image with respect to actual reality. It was as though the artistic image felt an organic striving for attachment to a particular time and, more importantly, to a particular concrete and graphically visible position in space. Here it is not a matter of how artistically realistic the image may be in and of itself (which, of course, in no way requires a precise geographical determination, a "nonfictitious" place of action). In this epoch the image typically conveys a direct *geographical reality,* and it strives not so much for internal verisimilitude as for an idea of it as an event that actually occurred, that is, *in real time* (and hence an attitude toward the artistic image of man as a living person, which is especially typical of sentimentalism, and the artistically deliberate "naive realism" of the image and of its perception by the public). The relationship of the artistic image to the new, geographically and historically concrete, graphically presented world is manifest here in an elementary, but still clear and graphic, form. These "local cults" attest above all to a completely *new sense of space and time* in the artistic work.

The striving for concrete geographical localization is also manifested in the multilingual children's novel on which Goethe worked somewhat later (see *GA,* book 4). "To obtain matter for filling up this singular form, I studied the geography of the countries in which my creations resided, and by inventing for those dry localities all sorts of human incidents which had some affinity with the characters and employments of my heroes" (*GA,* vol. 1, pp. 127–28). And here we see the same characteristic humanization of concrete geographical localities.

In *Italian Journey*, Goethe discusses the origin and the nature of the plan for the drama "Nausicaa." This plan took shape in Sicily, where the country's marine and insular landscape immediately evoked images of the *Odyssey* for Goethe. "A wealth of secondary motives was to have added interest to this simple fable, and there was to have been a sea-island quality about the imagery and atmosphere to give a pervading tone to the whole play" (*IJ*, p. 283). And somewhat later: "Now that my mind is stored with images of all these coasts and promontories, gulfs and bays, islands and headlands, rocky cliffs, fields, flower gardens, tended trees, festooned vines, mountains wreathed in clouds, eternally serene plains, and the all-encircling sea with its ever-changing colours and moods, for the first time the *Odyssey* has become a living truth to me" (*IJ*, p. 305).

Even more typical in this regard is the plan for *William Tell*. Its images arose directly from live contemplation of the corresponding historical localities of Switzerland. In the *Annals*, Goethe says: "When on the way there and back (during a journey through Switzerland in 1797) I again saw with a free and open eye Vierwaldstaetter See, Schwyz, Fluelen and Altdorf. They forced my imagination to populate these localities with characters that represent this immense (*ungeheure*) landscape. And what images could appear to my imagination more quickly than the image of Tell and his bold contemporaries?" (*Annals*, pp. 141–42). Tell himself appeared to Goethe as an embodiment of the people (*eine Art von Demos*) in the image of the colossal force of one who lifts weights, who all his life carried heavy animal hides and other goods across his native mountains.

Finally, we shall discuss the creative plan that appeared to Goethe when he was in Pyrmont.

The Pyrmont locality is steeped in historical time. It is mentioned in the works of Roman writers. The Roman outpost reached this far; here passed one of those radii of world history that Goethe contemplated from Rome. The ancient ramparts still remain; hills and valleys tell of the battles that took place here; remnants of antiquity can be found in the etymology of the names of various places and mountains and in the customs of the population; everywhere there are markers of the historical past penetrating space. "Here you feel as though you are enclosed in a magic circle," says Goethe. "You equate the past with the present, you contemplate general spatiality through the prism of the given immediate spatial surroundings, and, finally, you feel good, since for a moment it begins to seem that the most elusive thing has become an object of unmediated contemplation" (*Annals*, p. 81).

Here, under these specific conditions, a plan also emerges for a work that was to be written in the style of the late sixteenth century. The entire outline of the plot, which Goethe sketched quite precisely, is interwoven with motifs of the locality and, as it were, its historical transformation. It depicts the people's spontaneous migration toward Pyrmont's miraculous spring. At the head of the movement is a knight, who organizes it and leads the people to Pyrmont. We see the social and characterological diversity of the masses of people. An essential aspect is the depiction of the construction of a new settlement and the parallel social differentiation and separation of the aristocracy ("nobles"). The main theme is the work of the creatively organizing human will on the raw material of a spontaneous mass migration. The result is the appearance of a new city on the ancient historical site of Pyrmont. In conclusion the motif of the future greatness of Pyrmont is introduced in the form of a prophecy of three strange newcomers—a youth, an adult, and an elder (a symbol of historical generations). This entire plan is nothing other than an attempt to transform historically creative will into a plot, both the spontaneous mass will of the people and the organizing will of the leader, of which Pyrmont is a direct visible vestige—or, in other words, to grasp the "most elusive" course of pure historical time and fix it through "unmediated contemplation."

Such are Goethe's unrealized creative projects. All of them are profoundly chronotopic. Time and space merge here into an inseparable unity, both in the plot itself and in its individual images. In the majority of cases, a definite and absolutely concrete locality serves as the starting point for the creative imagination. But this is not an abstract landscape, imbued with the mood of the contemplator—no, this is a piece of human history, historical time condensed in space. Therefore, the plot (the sum of depicted events) and the characters do not enter it from outside, are not invented to fit the landscape, but are unfolded in it as though they were present from the very beginning. They are like those creative forces that formulated and humanized this landscape, made it a speaking vestige of the movement of history (historical time), and, to a certain degree, predetermined its subsequent course as well, or like those creative forces a given locality needs in order to organize and continue the historical process embodied in it.

Such an approach to locality and to history, their inseparable unity and interpenetrability, became possible only because the locality ceased to be a part of abstract nature, a part of an indefinite, interrupted, and only symbolically rounded out (supplemented) world, and the event ceased to be a segment of the same indefinite time that was always equal to itself, reversible, and symbolically embodied. The locality became an irreplaceable part of the geographically and historically determined world, of *that* completely real and essentially visible world of human history, and the event became an essential and nontransferable moment in the time of this particular human history that occurred in this, and only in this, geographically determined human world. The world and history did not become poorer or smaller as a result of this process of mutual concretization and interpenetration. On the contrary, they were condensed, compacted, and filled with the creative possibilities of subsequent *real* emergence and development. Goethe's world is a *germinative seed*, utterly real, visibly available, and at the same time filled with an equally real future that is growing out of it.

And it is this new sense of space and time that has led to an essential change in the orientation of the artistic image: that image felt an irresistible attraction to a particular place and to a particular time in this world that had become definite and real. And this orientation is manifest both in the elementary (but well-outlined) form of naive realistic "local cults" for literary heroes and in the more profound and complex form of such works as *Wilhelm Meister*, which lie on the border between the novel and the new large epic.

Let us discuss briefly a somewhat earlier stage in the eighteenth century's development of the sense of time, as represented in Rousseau.

Rousseau's artistic imagination was also chronotopic. He opened up for literature (and particularly for the novel) a special and very important chronotope—"nature" (to be sure, this discovery, like all real discoveries, was prepared for by centuries of preceding development).[26] He had a profound sense of time in nature. The time of nature and the time of human life entered into the closest interaction and interpenetration in his work. But the real historicity of time was still very weak. For him the only time that was separated from the background of natural time was idyllic time (also still cyclical) and biographical time, which had already surmounted its cyclical nature, but had not yet completely merged with real historical time. Therefore, creative historical necessity was almost completely foreign to Rousseau.

When contemplating landscape, Rousseau, like Goethe, populates it with images of people; he humanizes it. However, these people are neither creators nor builders, but people of idyllic and individual biological life. Hence the quality of his plots is also poor (in most cases they involve love, with its suffering and joy, and idyllic labor) and his future is utopian in the manner of a "Golden Age" (historical inversion) and lacking any creative necessity.[27]

During his journey to Turin on foot, Rousseau admires the rural landscape and populates it with images of his imagination. "I imagined," he says in his *Confessions*,

> that every house was filled with joyous frivolity, the meadows resounded with sports and revelry, the rivers offered refreshing baths, delicious fish wantoned in these streams, and how delightful it was to ramble along the flowery banks! The trees were loaded with the choicest fruit while their shade afforded the most charming and voluptuous retreats to happy lovers; the mountains abounded with milk and cream, peace and leisure, simplicity and joy, mingled with the charm of going I knew not whither, and everything I saw carried to my heart some new cause for rapture.[28]

The utopian aspect of Rousseau's artistic imagination emerges even more clearly in a letter to Malesherbes (of 26 January 1762):

> I soon populated it [i.e., beautiful nature—M. B.] with beings that pleased me . . . and transported into that sanctuary of nature people who were worthy of inhabiting it. I formed a charming society for myself . . . my fantasy resurrected the Golden Age and, filling these beautiful days with all the scenes of my life that left a sweet memory with me and also those which my heart could still desire, I was moved to tears, thinking about mankind's satisfactions, so charming and so pure, which are now very distant from people.[29]

These confessions of Rousseau's are very revealing even in themselves, but their significance becomes especially clear when they are compared to the corresponding confessions of Goethe cited above. Instead of man the creator and builder, here appears the idyllic man of pleasure, play, and love. Nature, as if bypassing history with its past and present, directly gives way to the "Golden Age," that is, the utopian past that is transferred into the utopian future. Pure and blissful nature gives way to pure and blissful people. Here the desired and the ideal are torn away from real time and necessity: they are not necessary, they are only desired. Therefore, the time of all these games, country meals, passionate meetings, and so forth also lacks real duration and irreversibility. If within the idyllic day there is a change from morning to evening to night, all idyllic days are alike and repeat one another. It is also quite understandable that such contemplation in no way impedes the penetration of subjective desires, emotions, personal remembrances, and fantasy into the contemplated thing, that is, this contemplation does not involve the factors that restricted and suppressed Goethe's contemplation as he was striving to see the necessity of occurrences, independent of his desires and feelings.

Of course, what we have related far from exhausts the peculiar features of Rousseau's sense of time, even of natural time. His novels and his autobiographical essays reveal other, more profound and essential, aspects of his sense of time. He also knew idyllic labor time, biographical time, and family-biographical time, and he introduced new and essential elements into the understanding of the ages of man, and so forth. We shall have to deal further with all these below.

The second half of the eighteenth century in England and Germany is characterized, as we know, by an increased interest in folklore. One can even speak with a certain amount of justification about the *discovery of folklore* for literature, which occurred in this epoch. This was primarily a matter of national and local (within the boundaries of the national) folklore. The folksong, the folktale, the heroic and historical legend, and the saga were above all a new and powerful means of humanizing and intensifying one's native space. With folklore there burst into literature a new, powerful, and extremely productive wave of *national-historical time* that exerted an immense influence on the development of the historical outlook in general and on the development of the historical novel in particular.

Folklore is in general saturated with time; all of its images are profoundly chronotopic. Time in folklore, the fullness of time in it, the folkloric future, the folkloric human yardsticks of time—all these are very important and fundamental problems. We cannot, of course, discuss them here, even though folkloric time exerted an immense and productive influence on literature.

We are interested here in another aspect of the matter—in the utilization of local folklore, particularly heroic and historical legends and sagas, in order to intensify the native soil and thus prepare for the historical novel. Local folklore interprets and saturates space with time, and draws it into history.

Pindar's utilization of local myths on classical soil is very typical in this respect. Through a complex and skillful interweaving of local myths with general Hellenic ones, he incorporated each corner of Greece, retaining all of its local wealth, into the *unity* of the Greek world. Each spring, hillock, grove, and bend in the coastline had its own legend, its own memories, its own events, and its own heroes. Using skillful associations, metaphoric correspondences, and genealogical links, Pindar interspersed these local myths with general Hellenic myths and created a unified and closely woven fabric that embraced the entire Greek land and produced a kind of national poetic substitute for an inadequate political unity.[30]

Sir Walter Scott utilizes local folklore in the same way, although under different historical conditions and for different purposes.

Typical for Walter Scott is a striving after precisely local folklore. He covered every inch of his native Scotland on foot, especially the areas bordering England, and he knew every bend of the Tweed, all the ruins of castles, and for him all this was consecrated by legend, song, and ballad. For him each clump of land was saturated with certain events from local legends, was profoundly intensified with legend time, but, on the other hand, each event was strictly localized, condensed in spatial markers. His eye could see time in space.

But in Walter Scott during that early period, when he created *Minstrelsy of the Scottish Border* and his poems ("Lay of the Last Minstrel," "St. John's Eve," "Lady of the Lake," and others), this time still had the nature of a *closed past*. Herein lies the essential difference between him and Goethe. This past, read by Walter Scott in the ruins and in various details of the Scottish landscape, was not creatively operative in the present. It was self-sufficient, and it was a closed world of a specific past. And the visible in the present only evoked a *remembrance* of this past. It was a storehouse not of the past itself in its living and operative form, but a storehouse precisely of remembrances of it. Therefore, the *fullness of time* was minimal even in Walter Scott's best folkloric poems.

In Scott's subsequent "novelistic" period, he overcomes this limitation (to be sure, still not completely). The profound chronotopic nature of his artistic thinking and his ability to read time in space remain from the preceding period, as do elements of the folkloric coloring of time (national-historical time). And all these aspects become extremely productive for the historical novel. At the same time he assimilates novelistic subcategories from the preceding development of the genre, particularly the Gothic and family-biographical novel, and, finally, he assimilates historical drama. Here he also overcomes the closed nature of the past and achieves the fullness of time necessary for the historical novel. We have briefly sketched one of the most important stages on the path to the assimilation of real historical time in literature, a stage that was represented above all by the figure of Goethe. We believe we have also demonstrated the exceptional importance of the very problem of the assimilation of time in literature, and particularly in the novel.

Notes

1. Gaius Petronius (d. A.D. 66) is probably the author of the *Satyricon*, the fragmentary manuscript in prose and verse that is generally (and specifically by Bakhtin) considered to be one of the major landmarks in the history of the novel.

Lucius Apuleius (fl. c. A.D. 155), author of the prose romance *Metamorphoses*, or *The Golden Ass*, the only Latin novel to survive in its entirety.

Encolpius is the narrator of Petronius' *Satyricon*. At times he plays a direct part in the action (as at his famous feast), while at other times he is quite removed from the plot.

Lucius, the first-person narrator of Apuleius' *Metamorphoses*, intends to swallow the potion that will turn him into an owl, but he takes instead a potion that transforms him into an ass. In this form he travels through Greece, passing through the hands of various masters, seeing life from a variety of social perspectives, and collecting stories that are interspersed throughout his narrative.

La vida de Lazarillo de Tormes (1554) is a picaresque novel by an anonymous author sometimes identified with Diego Hurtado de Mendoza.

La vida del Pícaro Guzmán de Alfarache (part 1, 1599; part 2, 1604) is a picaresque novel by Mateo Alemán.

Vraie histoire comique de Francion (1623–33) is a novel by Charles Sorel (1597–1674) that is important in Bakhtin's history of the novel not only because it is picaresque, but because it is a protest against the "fine style" of such idealized romances as *L'Astrée*.

Histoire de Gil Blas de Santillane (1714, 1724, 1735) is a picaresque novel by Lesage (1668–1747).

2. *The Life, Adventures and Piracies of the Famous Captain Singleton* (1720) is a first-person narrative of piracy and buccaneer raids on the African coast written by Daniel Defoe (1660–1731).

Moll Flanders (1722), the full title of which is almost a volume in itself, is perhaps Defoe's greatest picaresque and one of the earliest social novels in English.

Roderick Random (1748) is a picaresque loosely based on *Gil Blas* by Tobias Smollett (1721–71).

Peregrine Pickle (1751) is another picaresque by Smollett.

Humphry Clinker (1771) is a travel novel in epistolary form by Smollett.

3. *Aethiopica* (*an Ethiopian Tale*) is the longest of the still extant Greek novels. The presumed author, Heliodorus (fl. A.D. 220–50) is variously associated with several figures: the novel was influential even in modern times: Scaliger, Calderón, and Cervantes all admired and imitated it.

Leucippe and Clitophon by Achilles Tatius (fl. second century A.D.) was much admired by Byzantine critics for its pure Attic diction, but its licentiousness was considered scandalous.

4. The Russian here is *stanovlenie*, a word Bakhtin uses early and late in his career. It is closer to the German *das Werden* (becoming): the process of development that is never complete in the life course of an individual. It is Bakhtin's way of insisting that identity is never complete but always in process. Where possible it has been rendered in English as "becoming," but where this is too barbarous the word "emergence" has been used.

5. The so-called Second Sophistic is a movement that began in the second century with the aim of reviving the literary glories of the great classical period of antiquity.

6. John Chrysostom (c. 345–407) became the patriarch of Constantinople in A.D. 398. His attempts at reform alienated other members of the clergy, and he was condemned on false charges in 403.

The Climentine cycle was made up of works of early Christian hagiographic literature from the third century. In literary form it was similar to the ancient novel, and it was one of the sources of *Das Faustbuch* in the sixteenth century.

7. *Amadis de Gaula* (1508) is a Spanish chivalric romance. The first extant version was compiled by Garcia Ordóñez or Rodríguez Montalvo, who stated that he was merely revising the original text. The origin of the story is still obscure, though it was known in both Spain and Portugal at least as early as the fourteenth century.

Palmerín is the hero of several sixteenth-century Spanish romances. According to tradition, the first work in the series, *Palmerín de Oliva* (1511) is of disputed authorship, but was enormously popular; the last of the series, *Palmerín de Inglaterra* (1547–48) is generally regarded as the best.

8. Honoré d'Urfé (1568–1625) is best known as the author of *L'Astrée* (1607–27), a vast pastoral romance in prose that enjoyed great popularity and helped revive a taste for the pastoral as a genre.

Madeleine de Scudéry (1607–1701), under the name of Sappho, wrote *Artamène, ou le grand Cyrus* (10 vols., 1649–53).

Gautier de la Calprenède is best known for his enormous historical romances, all of which run to ten or twelve large volumes.

Daniel Caspar von Lohenstein (1635–83) was a German dramatist, poet, and novelist of the late baroque. His historical novel *Arminius* (1689) is closely tied to the political realities of his day.

9. *Cyropaedia* is a biography of Cyrus, the Persian emperor, by the Athenian Xenophon (c. 430–c. 355 B.C.), modified to suit the author's didactic purposes. It is an example of the "mirror for princes" (*Fürstenspiegel*) genre, with much attention devoted to the prince's education.

Parzival is a verse epic of the early thirteenth century by Wolfram von Eschenbach.

Der abenteurliche Simplicissimus (1668), a picaresque by Jakob von Grimmelshausen (1625–76), sometimes thought of as the first biographical novel.

Télémaque (1699), a didactic romance by Fénelon (1651–1715) written for his pupil, the duc de Bourgogne. Translations of this work played an important role in eighteenth-century Russian literature.

Geschichte des Agathons (1766, final version 1798) is a psychological novel by Wieland (1733–1813) about the development of a youth in classical Greece, generally considered to be an important forerunner of the *Bildungsroman*.

Tobias Knout (1773) by Johann Wetzel (1747–1819), one of Bakhtin's favorite books due to the playfulness and complexity of the authorial point of view. It was reprinted in 1971 (Stuttgart: Metzler).

Lebensläufe nach aufsteigender Linie is a novel in four volumes (1778–81) by von Hippel (1741–96) that owes its combination of sentimental effusions and Enlightenment rationalism to Sterne.

Titan is a novel (1800–1803) by the humorist and aesthetician Jean Paul Richter (1763–1825).

Der Hungerpastor is an 1864 novel by the German realistic novelist Wilhelm Raabe (1831–1910).

Der grüne Heinrich is an 1854 novel of education (second version 1879–80) by the Swiss poet and novelist Gottfried Keller (1819–90).

Lykke-Per (8 volumes, 1898–1904), a series of works by the Danish novelist Henrik Pontoppidan (1857–1943). Pontoppidan shared the Nobel Prize for literature in 1917.

Jean-Christophe is a long novel series begun in 1889 by Romain Rolland (1866–1944).

10. Gotthold Lessing (1729–81), German dramatist, aesthetician, and critic. Among his many works, those most important for Bakhtin are *Laocoön, or On the Limits of Painting and Poetry* (1766), because of its concern with the representation of time in art; *How the Ancients Represented Death* (1780), because it is one of the first important exercises in philosophical anthropology; and a work of particular importance in Bakhtin's conception of the *Bildungsroman, The Education of the Human Race* (1770).

Johann Gottfried Herder (1744–1803), philosopher and historian whose ideas about the importance of intuition in both creative work and criticism were taken up by Goethe, with whom he was closely associated. The basic works that have a bearing on Bakhtin's discussion here are *On German Character and Art* (1733), *Yet Another Philosophy of History for the Furthering of Humanity* (1774), and *Letters for the Furthering of Humanity* (1793–97).

11. James Thomson (1700–1748), Scottish-born English poet, a forerunner of romanticism in an era when neoclassicism held sway. Such well-known poems as "The Castle of Indolence" (1748) and, especially, "The Seasons" (completed in 1730) were enormously popular throughout Europe due to their love of nature, fantasy, and sensuous imagery.

Salomon Gessner (1730–88), Swiss writer, landscape painter, and engraver who wrote and illustrated prose idylls.

12. *Italienische Reise* passages are taken from the translation by W. H. Auden and Elizabeth Mayer, *The Italian Journey* (London: Collins, 1962), with page numbers in the text referring to this edition (hereafter cited as *IJ*).

13. *The Annals* are cited from the Jubiläum edition: *Goethes sämtliche Werke* (Stuttgart-Berlin, 1902–7), vol. 30.

14. Page references to *Goethe's Autobiography* are from the translation of *Dichtung*

und Wahrheit by John Oxenford (Chicago-London: University of Chicago Press, 1974), with page numbers in the text referring to this edition (hereafter cited as *GA*).

15. Compare this description of Goethe's creative vision with Dostoevsky's vision in *Problems of Dostoevsky's Poetics*, ed. and tr. Caryl Emerson (Minneapolis: University of Minnesota Press, 1984, p. 28):

> An artist such as Goethe, for example, gravitates organically toward an evolving sequence. He strives to perceive all existing contradictions as various stages of some unified development; in every manifestation of the present he strives to glimpse a trace of the past, a peak of the present-day or a tendency of the future; and as a consequence, nothing for him is arranged along a single extensive plane. Such in any case was the basic tendency of his mode for viewing and understanding the world.
>
> In contrast to Goethe, Dostoevsky attempted to perceive the very stages themselves in their *simultaneity*, to *juxtapose* and *counterpose* them dramatically, and not to stretch them into an evolving sequence. For him, to get one's bearings in the world meant to conceive all its content as simultaneous, and *to guess at their interrelationships in the cross section of a single moment.*

16. Bakhtin was an admirer of the great geochemist, V. I. Vernadsky (1863–1945), whose concept of the biosphere (*La biosphère,* Paris, 1929) is based on the idea that all matter in the cosmos is alive. (Cf. note 6 in "From Notes Made in 1970–71.")

17. The prospectus for Bakhtin's book on the novel of education contains remarks about Goethe's autobiographical methods in *Dichtung und Wahrheit*:

> . . . in depicting the epoch, the literary figures of the time and, finally, the participants in the life of the time, Goethe combines the viewpoint of his current creative work on his own autobiography. Goethe's task is to present not only the world of his past (and participants in his past life) in light of his present and enriched with the perspective of time, but also his past awareness and understanding of this world (of childhood, youth, and young adulthood). This past consciousness is the same sort of object of depiction as the objective world of the past. These two consciousnesses, separated by decades and looking at one and the same world, are not crudely divided and are not separated from the object of depiction "out there": they enliven this object, introduce a unique dynamic into it, a temporal movement, and adorn the world with living, emerging humanness: childhood, youth, and maturity—without any detriment to the objectivity of the depicted world. On the contrary, the presence of the two aspects makes the objectivity of the depicted reality stand out in even bolder relief. This subjectivity that pervades the depicted world is not the bloodless subjectivity of a romantic such as Novalis, but a concrete, red-blooded subjectivity, one that is growing, maturing, and aging. (*Estetika*, pp. 397–398)

18. Goethe shares the antiquarian-archeological enthusiasm of his epoch. We need only remember the enormous international success of the "archeological"

novel *Anarchisis* (1788), which describes the travels of its hero around fourth-century B.C. Greece, by the French archeologist Jean Berthélémy (1716–95), who created the genre of the archeological novel.

19. Wilhelm Friedrich Gmelin (1745–1821), engraver whose best works are after Claude Lorrain and Nicolas Poussin.

20. *The Aeneid* was translated into Italian by the sixteenth-century poet Hannibal Caro.

21. Refers to *A General Mountain and Water Map of Europe* compiled by A. Sorrio in 1816.

22. Johann Joachim Winckelmann (1717–86), German classical scholar especially interested in painting and sculpture. He conceived of ancient Greece as characterized by noble simplicity and silent greatness, an idea that influenced Weimar classicism.

23. Reference here is to Herder's (cf. note 10 above, this section) *Outlines of the Philosophy of Man* (*Ideen zur Philosophie der Menschheit,* 1784–91), a work that Bakhtin among many others considered a simplified version of Goethe's theory of history.

24. As Bocharov observes in his footnote to the Russian edition at this point, Bakhtin's prospectus for the book on the *Bildungsroman* placed special emphasis on the outcome of Enlightenment philosophy, which "impoverished" the world and created a "narrowed conception of the real" in Enlightenment realism. Bakhtin makes a distinction between Enlightenment realism and Goethe's realism:

> Finally, in the novel of education up to Goethe this leads not to an enrichment, but to a certain impoverishment of the world and man. Much in the world turns out to be unreal, illusory, and it is cast out as prejudice, fantasy, or fabrication; the world turns out to be more impoverished than it had seemed to others in past ages or to the hero himself in his youth. Many of the hero's illusions about himself are dispelled, and he becomes more serious, drier, and more impoverished. Such unification of the world and man is typical of the critical and abstract realism of the Age of the Enlightenment. (*Estetika,* p. 398)

Compare also the entry in the preparatory materials: "The narrowed concept of actuality (daily life, reality) of the eighteenth century, *Et voilà tout!* as a typical tendency of thought, diminishing and impoverishing reality, leaving it with much less than it had before." These lines are taken from Bakhtin's materials on the *Bildungsroman* in his archive.

25. Nikolay Karamzin (1766–1826), historian and author whose work created a vogue for sentimentalism. The jilted heroine of his tale *Poor Liza* (1702) commits suicide by drowning in a pool outside Moscow, which soon became a place of pilgrimage.

26. The materials for the book mention the special role of Petrarch, his "discovery of man and nature" (including the "discovery of the lonely stroll").

27. Concerning "historical inversion," see "Forms of Time and the Chronotope in the Novel" in Mikhail Bakhtin, *The Dialogic Imagination* (Austin: University of Texas Press, 1981), p. 147.

28. *Confessions,* tr. E. Hedouin (Paris, 1881), part 1, book 2, p. 52.

29. From M. N. Rozanov, *Zh. Zh. Russo i literaturnoe dvizhenie kontsa XVIII i nachala XIX v.* (Moscow, 1910), p. 50.

30. In Pindar's epicurean odes it is the hero-victor in the games—his name, his lineage, his city—who himself served as the center point, the pivot from which lines of association and connection spread out in all directions.

The Problem of Speech Genres

I. Statement of the Problem and Definition of Speech Genres

All the diverse areas of human activity involve the use of language. Quite understandably, the nature and forms of this use are just as diverse as are the areas of human activity. This, of course, in no way disaffirms the national unity of language.[1] Language is realized in the form of individual concrete utterances (oral and written) by participants in the various areas of human activity. These utterances reflect the specific conditions and goals of each such area not only through their content (thematic) and linguistic style, that is, the selection of the lexical, phraseological, and grammatical resources of the language, but above all through their compositional structure. All three of these aspects—thematic content, style, and compositional structure—are inseparably linked to the *whole* of the utterance and are equally determined by the specific nature of the particular sphere of communication. Each separate utterance is individual, of course, but each sphere in which language is used develops its own *relatively stable types* of these utterances. These we may call *speech genres.*

The wealth and diversity of speech genres are boundless because the various possibilities of human activity are inexhaustible, and because each sphere of activity contains an entire repertoire of speech genres that differentiate and grow as the particular sphere develops and becomes more complex. Special emphasis should be placed on the extreme *heterogeneity* of speech genres (oral and written). In fact, the category of speech genres should include short rejoinders of daily dialogue (and these are extremely varied depending on the subject matter, situation, and participants), everyday narration, writing (in all its various forms), the brief standard military command, the elaborate and detailed order, the fairly variegated repertoire of business documents (for the most part standard), and the diverse world of commentary (in the broad sense of the word: social, political). And we must also include here the diverse forms of scientific statements and all literary genres (from the proverb to the multivolume novel). It might seem that speech genres are so heterogeneous that they do not have and cannot have a single common level at which they can be studied. For here, on one level of inquiry, appear such heterogeneous phenomena as the single-word everyday rejoinder and the multivolume novel, the military command that is standardized even in its intonation and the profoundly individual lyrical work, and so on. One might think that such functional heterogeneity makes the common features of speech genres excessively abstract and empty. This probably explains why the general problem of speech genres has never really been raised. Literary genres have been studied more than anything else. But from antiquity to the present, they have been studied in terms of their specific literary and artistic features, in terms of the differences that distinguish one from the other (within the realm of literature), and not as specific types of utterances distinct from other types, but sharing with them a common *verbal* (language) nature. The general linguistic problem of the utterance and its types has hardly been considered at all. Rhetorical genres have been studied since antiquity (and not much has been added in subsequent epochs to classical theory). At that time, more attention was already being devoted to the verbal nature of these genres as utterances: for example, to such aspects as the relation to the listener and his influence on the utterance, the specific verbal finalization of the utterance (as distinct from its completeness of thought), and so forth. But here, too, the specific features of rhetorical genres (judicial, political) still overshadowed their general linguistic nature. Finally, everyday speech genres have been studied (mainly rejoinders in everyday dialogue), and from a general linguistic standpoint (in the school of Saussure and among his later followers—the Structuralists, the American behaviorists, and, on a completely different linguistic basis, the Vosslerians).[2] But this line of inquiry could not lead to a correct determination of the general linguistic nature of the utterance either, since it was limited to the specific features of everyday oral speech, sometimes being directly and deliberately oriented toward primitive utterances (American behaviorists).

The extreme heterogeneity of speech genres and the attendant difficulty of determining the general nature of the utterance should in no way be underestimated. It is especially important here to draw attention to the very significant difference between primary (simple) and secondary (complex) speech genres (understood not as a functional difference). Secondary (complex) speech genres—novels, dramas, all kinds of scientific research, major genres of commentary, and so forth—arise in more complex and comparatively highly developed and organized cultural communication (primarily written) that is artistic, scientific, sociopolitical, and so on. During the process of their formation, they absorb and digest various primary (simple) genres that have taken form in unmediated speech communion. These primary genres are altered and assume a special character when they enter into complex ones. They lose their immediate relation to actual reality and to the real utterances of others. For example, rejoinders of everyday dialogue or letters found in a novel retain their form and their everyday significance only on the plane of the novel's content. They enter into actual reality only via the novel as a whole, that is, as a literary-artistic event and not as everyday life. The novel as a whole is an utterance just as rejoinders in everyday dialogue or private letters are (they do have a common nature), but unlike these, the novel is a secondary (complex) utterance.

The difference between primary and secondary (ideological) genres is very great and fundamental,[3] but this is precisely why the nature of the utterance should be revealed and defined through analysis of both types. Only then can the definition be adequate to the complex and profound nature of the utterance (and encompass its most important facets). A one-sided orientation toward primary genres inevitably leads to a vulgarization of the entire problem (behaviorist linguistics is an extreme example). The very interrelations between primary and secondary genres and the process of the historical formation of the latter shed light on the nature of the utterance (and above all on the complex problem of the interrelations among language, ideology, and world view).

A study of the nature of the utterance and of the diversity of generic forms of utterances in various spheres of human activity is immensely important to almost all areas of linguistics and philology. This is because any research whose material is concrete language—the history of a language, normative grammar, the compilation of any kind of dictionary, the stylistics of language, and so forth—inevitably deals with concrete utterances (written and oral) belonging to various spheres of human activity and communication: chronicles, contracts, texts of laws, clerical and other documents, various literary, scientific, and commentarial genres, official and personal letters, rejoinders in everyday dialogue (in all of their diverse subcategories), and so on. And it is here that scholars find the language data they need. A clear idea of the nature of the utterance in general and of the peculiarities of the various types of utterances (primary and secondary), that is, of various speech genres, is necessary, we think, for research in any special area. To ignore the nature of the utterance or to fail to consider the peculiarities of generic subcategories of speech in any area of linguistic study leads to perfunctoriness and excessive abstractness, distorts the historicity of the research, and weakens the link between language and life. After all, language enters life through concrete utterances (which manifest language) and life enters language through concrete utterances as well. The utterance is an exceptionally important node of problems. We shall approach certain areas and problems of the science of language in this context.

First of all, stylistics. Any style is inseparably related to the utterance and to typical forms of utterances, that is, speech genres. Any utterance—oral or written, primary or secondary, and in any sphere of communication—is individual and therefore can reflect the individuality of the speaker (or writer); that is, it possesses individual style. But not all genres are equally conducive to reflecting the individuality of the speaker in the language of the utterance, that is, to an individual style. The most conducive genres are those of artistic literature: here the individual style enters directly into the very task of the utterance, and this is one of its main goals (but even within artistic literature various genres offer different possibilities for expressing individuality in language and various aspects of individuality). The least favorable conditions for reflecting individuality in language obtain in speech genres that require a standard form, for example, many kinds of business documents, military commands, verbal signals in industry, and so on. Here one can reflect only the most superficial, almost biological aspects of individuality (mainly in the oral manifestation of these standard types of utterances). In the vast majority of speech genres (except for literary-artistic ones), the individual style does not enter into the intent of the utterance, does not serve as its only goal, but is, as it were, an epiphenomenon of the utterance, one of its by-products. Various genres can reveal various layers and facets of the individual personality, and individual style can be found in various interrelations with the national language. The very problem of the national and the individual in language is basically the problem of the utterance (after all, only here, in the utterance, is the national language embodied in individual form). The very determination of style in general, and individual style in particular, requires deeper study of both the nature of the utterance and the diversity of speech genres.

The organic, inseparable link between style and genre is clearly revealed also in the problem of language styles, or functional styles. In essence, language, or functional, styles are nothing other than generic styles for certain spheres of human activity and communication. Each sphere has and applies its own genres that correspond to its own specific conditions. There are also particular styles that correspond to these genres. A particular function (scientific, technical, commentarial, business, everyday) and the particular conditions of speech communication specific for each sphere give rise to particular genres, that is, certain relatively stable thematic, compositional, and stylistic types of utterances. Style is inseparably linked to particular thematic unities and—what is especially important—to particular compositional unities: to particular types of construction of the whole, types of its completion, and types of relations between the speaker and other participants in speech communication (listeners or readers, partners, the other's speech, and so forth). Style enters as one element into the generic unity of the utterance. Of course, this does not mean that language style cannot be the subject of its own independent study. Such a study, that is, of language stylistics as an independent discipline, is both feasible and necessary. But this study will be correct and productive only if based on a constant awareness of the generic nature of language styles, and on a preliminary study of the subcategories of speech genres. Up to this point the stylistics of language has not had such a basis. Hence its weakness. There is no generally recognized classification of language styles. Those who attempt to create them frequently fail to meet the fundamental logical requirement of classification: a unified basis.[4] Existing taxonomies are extremely poor and undifferentiated.[a] For example, a recently published academy grammar of the Russian language gives the following stylistic subcategories of language: bookish speech, popular speech, abstract-scientific, scientific-technical, journalistic-commentarial, official-business, and familiar everyday speech, as well as vulgar common parlance. In addi-

---

[a]The same kinds of classifications of language styles, impoverished and lacking clarity, with a fabricated foundation, are given by A. N. Gvozdev in his book *Ocherki po stilistike russkogo jazyka* (Essays on the stylistics of the Russian language) (Moscow, 1952, pp. 13–15). All of these classifications are based on an uncritical assimilation of traditional ideas about language styles.

tion to these linguistic styles, there are the stylistic subcategories of dialectical words, archaic words, and occupational expressions. Such a classification of styles is completely random, and at its base lies a variety of principles (or bases) for division into styles. Moreover, this classification is both inexhaustive and inadequately differentiated. All this is a direct result of an inadequate understanding of the generic nature of linguistic styles, and the absence of a well-thought-out classification of speech genres in terms of spheres of human activity (and also ignorance of the distinction between primary and secondary genres, which is very important for stylistics).

It is especially harmful to separate style from genre when elaborating historical problems. Historical changes in language styles are inseparably linked to changes in speech genres. Literary language is a complex, dynamic system of linguistic styles. The proportions and interrelations of these styles in the system of literary language are constantly changing. Literary language, which also includes nonliterary styles, is an even more complex system, and it is organized on different bases. In order to puzzle out the complex historical dynamics of these systems and move from a simple (and, in the majority of cases, superficial) description of styles, which are always in evidence and alternating with one another, to a historical explanation of these changes, one must develop a special history of speech genres (and not only secondary, but also primary ones) that reflects more directly, clearly, and flexibly all the changes taking place in social life. Utterances and their types, that is, speech genres, are the drive belts from the history of society to the history of language. There is not a single new phenomenon (phonetic, lexical, or grammatical) that can enter the system of language without having traversed the long and complicated path of generic-stylistic testing and modification.[b]

In each epoch certain speech genres set the tone for the development of literary language. And these speech genres are not only secondary (literary, commentarial, and scientific), but also primary (certain types of oral dialogue—of the salon, of one's own circle, and other types as well, such as familiar, family-everyday, sociopolitical, philosophical, and so on). Any expansion of the literary language that results from drawing on various extraliterary strata of the national lan-

---

[b]This thesis of ours has nothing in common with the Vosslerian idea of the primacy of the stylistic over the grammatical. Our subsequent exposition will make this completely clear.

guage inevitably entails some degree of penetration into all genres of written language (literary, scientific, commentarial, conversational, and so forth) to a greater or lesser degree, and entails new generic devices for the construction of the speech whole, its finalization, the accommodation of the listener or partner, and so forth. This leads to a more or less fundamental restructuring and renewal of speech genres. When dealing with the corresponding extraliterary strata of the national language, one inevitably also deals with the speech genres through which these strata are manifested. In the majority of cases, these are various types of conversational-dialogical genres. Hence the more or less distinct dialogization of secondary genres, the weakening of their monological composition, the new sense of the listener as a partner-interlocutor, new forms of finalization of the whole, and so forth. Where there is style there is genre. The transfer of style from one genre to another not only alters the way a style sounds, under conditions of a genre unnatural to it, but also violates or renews the given genre.

Thus, both individual and general language styles govern speech genres. A deeper and broader study of the latter is absolutely imperative for a productive study of any stylistic problem.

However, both the fundamental and the general methodological question of the interrelations between lexicon and grammar (on the one hand) and stylistics (on the other) rests on the same problem of the utterance and of speech genres.

Grammar (and lexicon) is essentially different from stylistics (some even oppose it to stylistics), but at the same time there is not a single grammatical study that can do without stylistic observation and excursus. In a large number of cases the distinction between grammar and stylistics appears to be completely erased. There are phenomena that some scholars include in the area of grammar while others include them in the area of stylistics. The syntagma is an example.

One might say that grammar and stylistics converge and diverge in any concrete language phenomenon. If considered only in the language system, it is a grammatical phenomenon, but if considered in the whole of the individual utterance or in a speech genre, it is a stylistic phenomenon. And this is because the speaker's very selection of a particular grammatical form is a stylistic act. But these two viewpoints of one and the same specific linguistic phenomenon should not be impervious to one another and should not simply replace one another mechanically. They should be organically combined (with, however, the most clear-cut methodological distinction between them) on the basis of the real unity of the language phenomenon. Only a profound understanding of the nature of the utterance and the particular features of speech genres can provide a correct solution to this complex methodological problem.

It seems to us that a study of the nature of the utterance and of speech genres is of fundamental importance for overcoming those simplistic notions about speech life, about the so-called speech flow, about communication and so forth—ideas which are still current in our language studies. Moreover, a study of the utterance as a *real unit of speech communion* will also make it possible to understand more correctly the *nature of language units* (as a system): words and sentences.

We shall now turn to this more general problem.

II. The Utterance as a Unit of Speech Communion: The Difference between This Unit and Units of Language (Words and Sentences)

Nineteenth-century linguistics, beginning with Wilhelm von Humboldt, while not denying the communicative function of language, tried to place it in the background as something secondary.[5] What it foregrounded was the function of thought emerging *independently of communication*. The famous Humboldtian formula goes like this: "Apart from the communication between one human and another, speech is a necessary condition for reflection *even in solitude*." Others, Vosslerians for example, emphasize the so-called expressive function. With all the various ways individual theoreticians understand this function, it essentially amounts to the expression of the speaker's individual discourse. Language arises from man's need to express himself, to objectify himself. The essence of any form of language is somehow reduced to the spiritual creativity of the individuum. Several other versions of the function of language have been and are now being suggested, but it is still typical to underestimate, if not altogether ignore, the communicative function of language. Language is regarded from the speaker's standpoint as if there were only *one* speaker who does not have any *necessary* relation to *other* participants in speech communication. If the role of the other is taken into account at all, it is the role of a listener, who understands the speaker only passively. The utterance is adequate to its object (i.e., the content of the uttered thought) and to the person who is pronouncing the utterance. Language essentially needs only a speaker—one speaker—and an object for his speech. And if language also serves as a means of communication, this is a secondary function that has nothing to do with its essence. Of course, the language collective, the plurality of speakers, cannot be ignored when speaking of language, but when defining the essence of language this aspect is not a necessary one that determines the nature of language. Sometimes the language collective is regarded as a kind of collective personality, "the spirit of the people," and so forth, and immense significance is attached to it (by representatives of the "psychology of nations"),[6] but even in this case the plurality of speakers, and others with respect to each given speaker, is denied any real essential significance.

Still current in linguistics are such *fictions* as the "listener" and "understander" (partners of the "speaker"), the "unified speech flow," and so on. These fictions produce a completely distorted idea of the complex and multifaceted process of active speech communication. Courses in general linguistics (even serious ones like Saussure's) frequently present graphic-schematic depictions of the two partners in speech communication—the speaker and the listener (who perceives the speech)—and provide diagrams of the active speech processes of the speaker and the corresponding passive processes of the listener's perception and understanding of the speech. One cannot say that these diagrams are false or that they do not correspond to certain aspects of reality. But when they are put forth as the actual whole of speech communication, they become a scientific fiction. The fact is that when the listener perceives and understands the meaning (the language meaning) of speech, he simultaneously takes an active, responsive attitude toward it. He either agrees or disagrees with it (completely or partially), augments it, applies it, prepares for its execution, and so on. And the listener adopts this responsive attitude for the entire duration of the process of listening and understanding, from the very beginning—sometimes literally from the speaker's first word. Any understanding of live speech, a live utterance, is inherently responsive, although the degree of this activity varies extremely. Any understanding is imbued with response and necessarily elicits it in one form or another: the listener becomes the speaker. A passive understanding of the meaning of perceived speech is only an abstract aspect of the actual whole of actively responsive understanding, which is then actualized in a subsequent response that is actually articulated. Of course, an utterance is not always followed immediately by an articulated response. An actively responsive understanding of what is heard (a command, for example) can be directly realized in action (the execution of an order or command that has been understood and accepted for execution), or it can remain, for the time being, a silent responsive understanding (certain speech genres are intended exclusively for this kind of responsive understanding, for example, lyrical genres), but this is, so to speak, responsive understanding with a delayed reaction. Sooner or later what is heard and actively understood will find its response in the subsequent speech or behavior of the listener. In most cases, genres of complex cultural communication are intended precisely for this kind of actively responsive understanding with delayed action. Everything we have said here also pertains to written and read speech, with the appropriate adjustments and additions.

Thus, all real and integral understanding is actively responsive, and constitutes nothing other than the initial preparatory stage of a response (in whatever form it may be actualized). And the speaker himself is oriented precisely toward such an actively responsive understanding. He does not expect passive understanding that, so to speak, only duplicates his own idea in someone else's mind. Rather, he expects response, agreement, sympathy, objection, execution, and so forth (various speech genres presuppose various integral orientations and speech plans on the part of the speakers or writers). The desire to make one's speech understood is only an abstract aspect of the speaker's concrete and total speech plan. Moreover, any speaker is himself a respondent to a greater or lesser degree. He is not, after all, the first speaker, the one who disturbs the eternal silence of the universe. And he presupposes not only the existence of the language system he is using, but also the existence of preceding utterances—his own and others'—with which his given utterance enters into one kind of relation or another (builds on them, polemicizes with them, or simply presumes that they are already known to the listener). Any utterance is a link in a very complexly organized chain of other utterances.

Thus, the listener who understands passively, who is depicted as the speaker's partner in the schematic diagrams of general linguistics, does not correspond to the real participant in speech communication. What is represented by the diagram is only an abstract aspect of the real total act of actively responsive understanding, the sort of understanding that evokes a response, and one that the speaker anticipates. Such scientific abstraction is quite justified in itself, but under one condition: that it is clearly recognized as merely an abstraction and is not represented as the real concrete whole of the phenomenon. Otherwise it becomes a fiction. This is precisely the case in linguistics, since such abstract schemata, while perhaps not claiming to reflect real speech communication, are not accompanied by any indication of the great complexity of the actual phenomenon. As a result, the schema distorts the actual picture of speech communication, removing precisely its most essential aspects. The active role of the *other* in the process of speech communication is thus reduced to a minimum.

This disregard for the active role of the other in the process of speech communication, and the desire generally to bypass this process, are manifested in the imprecise and ambiguous use of such terms as "speech" or "speech flow." These deliberately indefinite terms are usually intended to designate something that can be divided into language units, which are then interpreted as segments of language: phonetic (phoneme, syllable, speech rhythm [*takt*]) and lexical (sentence and word). "The speech flow can be broken down . . ."; "Our speech is divided . . ." This is the way those sections of grammars devoted to the study of such language units are usually introduced into general courses in linguistics and grammar, and also into special research on phonetics and lexicology. Unfortunately, even our recently published academy grammar uses the same indefinite and ambiguous term "our speech." Here is how the section on phonetics is introduced: "*Our speech* is basically divided into sentences, which in turn can be broken down into phrases and words. The word is clearly divided into small sound units—*syllables* . . . syllables are divided into individual speech sounds or phonemes. . . ."[7]

But what sort of thing is this "speech flow" and what is meant by "our speech"? What is the nature of their duration? Do they have a beginning and an end? If their length is indefinite, which of their segments do we use when we break them down into units? These questions have not been raised or defined at all. Linguists have not yet transformed the imprecise *word* "speech"—which can designate language, the speech process (i.e., speaking), the individual utterance, an entire long indefinite series of such utterances, or a particular speech genre ("he gave a speech")—into a definite (defined) *term* with clear-cut semantic boundaries (similar situations also exist in other languages). This can be explained by the almost complete lack of research into the problem of the utterance and speech genres (and, consequently, of speech communion as well). What we almost always find is a confused play with all these meanings (except for the last). Most frequently the expression "our speech" simply means any utterance of any person. But this meaning is never consistently sustained throughout.[c]

And if it is indefinite and unclear just what it is that is divided and broken down into units of language, this lack of definition and confusion also spread to these units themselves.

The terminological imprecision and confusion in this methodologically central point of linguistic thinking result from ignoring the *real unit* of speech communication: the utterance. For speech can exist in reality only in the form of concrete utterances of individual speaking people, speech subjects. Speech is always cast in the form of an utterance belonging to a particular speaking subject, and outside this form it cannot exist. Regardless of how varied utterances may be in terms of their length, their content, and their compositional structure, they have common structural features as units of speech communication and, above all, quite clear-cut boundaries. Since these boundaries are so essential and fundamental they must be discussed in detail.

The boundaries of each concrete utterance as a unit of speech communication are determined by a *change of speaking subjects*, that is, a change of speakers. Any utterance—from a short (single-word) rejoinder in everyday dialogue to the large novel or scientific treatise—has, so to speak, an absolute beginning and an absolute end: its beginning is preceded by the utterances of others, and its end is followed by the responsive utterances of others (or, although it may be silent, others' active responsive understanding, or, finally, a responsive action based on this understanding). The speaker ends his utterance in order to relinquish the floor to the other or to make room for the other's active responsive understanding. The utterance is not a conventional unit, but a real unit, clearly delimited by the change of speaking sub-

---

[c] And it cannot be sustained. For example, such an utterance as "Ah!" (a rejoinder in dialogue) cannot be broken down into sentences, phrases, or syllables. Consequently, not just *any* utterance will do. Further, they divide up the utterance (speech) and obtain units of language. Frequently the sentence is then defined as the simplest utterance and, consequently, it cannot be a *unit* of the utterance. It is tacitly assumed that there is only one speaker, and dialogical overtones are thus ignored.

As compared to the boundaries of the utterance, all other boundaries (between sentences, phrases, syntagmic units, and words) are relative and arbitrary.

jects, which ends by relinquishing the floor to the other, as if with a silent *dixi*, perceived by the listeners (as a sign) that the speaker has finished.

This change of speaking subjects, which creates clear-cut boundaries of the utterance, varies in nature and acquires different forms in the heterogeneous spheres of human activity and life, depending on the functions of language and on the conditions and situations of communication. One observes this change of speaking subjects most simply and clearly in actual dialogue where the utterances of the interlocutors or partners in dialogue (which we shall call rejoinders) alternate. Because of its simplicity and clarity, dialogue is a classic form of speech communication. Each rejoinder, regardless of how brief and abrupt, has a specific quality of completion that expresses a particular position of the speaker, to which one may respond or may assume, with respect to it, a responsive position. We shall discuss further this specific quality of completion of the utterance, one of its main markers. But at the same time rejoinders are all linked to one another. And the sort of relations that exist among rejoinders of dialogue—relations between question and answer, assertion and objection, assertion and agreement, suggestion and acceptance, order and execution, and so forth—are impossible among units of language (words and sentences), either in the system of language (in the vertical cross section) or within the utterance (on the horizontal plane). These specific relations among rejoinders in a dialogue are only subcategories of specific relations among whole utterances in the process of speech communication. These relations are possible only among utterances of different speech subjects; they presuppose *other* (with respect to the speaker) participants in speech communication. The relations among whole utterances cannot be treated grammatically since, we repeat, such relations are impossible among units of language, and not only in the system of language, but within the utterance as well.

In secondary speech genres, especially rhetorical ones, we encounter phenomena that apparently contradict this tenet. Quite frequently within the boundaries of his own utterance the speaker (or writer) raises questions, answers them himself, raises objections to his own ideas, responds to his own objections, and so on. But these phenomena are nothing other than a conventional playing out of speech communication and primary speech genres.[d] This kind of playing out is

[d]The seam of boundaries in secondary genres.

typical of rhetorical genres (in the broad sense, which would include certain kinds of scientific popularization), but other secondary genres (artistic and scholarly) also use various forms such as this to introduce primary speech genres and relations among them into the construction of the utterance (and here they are altered to a greater or lesser degree, for the speaking subject does not really change). Such is the nature of secondary genres. But the relations among the reproduced primary genres cannot be treated grammatically in any of these phenomena, even though they appear within a single utterance. Within the utterance they retain their own specific nature, which is essentially different from the nature of relations among words and sentences (and other language units, i.e., phrases and so forth).

Here, drawing on material from dialogue and the rejoinders that comprise it, we must provisionally pose the problem of the *sentence* as a *unit of language*, as distinct from the *utterance* as a unit of speech communication.

(The question of the nature of the sentence is one of the most complicated and difficult in linguistics. The clash of opinions regarding this question continues in our scholarship to this day. Of course, the task we set for ourselves here does not include an investigation of this problem in all its complexity; we intend to mention only one of its aspects. But it seems to us that this aspect is essential to the entire problem. It is important for us to define precisely the relationship between the sentence and the utterance. This will give us a clearer picture of both the utterance and the sentence.)

But this will come later. Here we shall simply note that the boundaries of the sentence as a unit of language are never determined by a change of speaking subjects. Such a change, framing the sentence on both sides, transforms the sentence into an entire utterance. Such a sentence assumes new qualities and is perceived quite differently from the way it would be if it were framed by other sentences within the single utterance of one and the same speaker. The sentence is a relatively complete thought, directly correlated with the other thoughts of a single speaker within his utterance as a whole. The speaker pauses at the end of a sentence in order then to move on to his own next thought, continuing, supplementing, and substantiating the preceding one. The context of the sentence is the speech of one speaking subject (speaker). The sentence itself is not correlated directly or personally with the extraverbal context of reality (situation, setting, prehistory) or with the utterances of other speakers; this takes place only indirectly, through its entire surrounding context, that is, through the utterance as a whole. And if the sentence is not surrounded by a context of the speech of the same speaker, that is, if it constitutes an entire completed utterance (a rejoinder in dialogue), then it (itself) directly confronts reality (the extraverbal context of the speech) and the different utterances of *others*. It is not followed by a pause that the speaker himself designates and interprets. (Any pause that is grammatical, calculated, or interpreted is possible only within the speech of a single speaker, i.e., within a single utterance. Pauses between utterances are, of course, not grammatical but real. Such real pauses—psychological, or prompted by some external circumstance—can also interrupt a single utterance. In secondary artistic genres such pauses are calculated by the artist, director, or actor. But these pauses differ essentially from both grammatical and stylistic pauses—for example, among syntagmas—within the utterance.) One expects them to be followed by a response or a responsive understanding on the part of another speaker. Such a sentence, having become an entire utterance, acquires a special semantic fullness of value. One can assume a responsive position with respect to it; one can agree or disagree with it, execute it, evaluate it, and so on. But a sentence in context cannot elicit a response. It acquires this capability (or, rather, assimilates to it) only in the entirety of the whole utterance.

All these completely new qualities and peculiarities belong not to the sentence that has become a whole utterance, but precisely to the utterance itself. They reflect the nature of the utterance, not the nature of the sentence. They attach themselves to the sentence, augmenting it until it is a complete utterance. The sentence as a language unit lacks all of these properties; it is not demarcated on either side by a change of speaking subjects; it has neither direct contact with reality (with an extraverbal situation) nor a direct relation to others' utterances; it does not have semantic fullness of value; and it has no capacity to determine directly the responsive position of the *other* speaker, that is, it cannot evoke a response. The sentence as a language unit is grammatical in nature. It has grammatical boundaries and grammatical completedness and unity. (Regarded in the whole of the utterance and from the standpoint of this whole, it acquires stylistic properties.) When the sentence figures as a whole utterance, it is as though it has been placed in a frame made of quite a different material. When one forgets this in analyzing a sentence, one distorts the nature of the sentence (and simultaneously the nature of the utterance as well, by treating it grammatically). A great many linguists and linguistic schools (in the area of syntax) are held captive by this confusion, and what they study as a sentence is in essence a kind of *hybrid* of the sentence (unit of language) and the utterance (unit of speech communication). One does not exchange sentences any more than one exchanges words (in the strict linguistic sense) or phrases. One exchanges utterances that are constructed from language units: words, phrases, and sentences. And an utterance can be constructed both from one sentence and from one word, so to speak, from one speech unit (mainly a rejoinder in dialogue), but this does not transform a language unit into a unit of speech communication.

The lack of a well-developed theory of the utterance as a unit of speech communication leads to an imprecise distinction between the sentence and the utterance, and frequently to a complete confusion of the two.

Let us return to real-life dialogue. As we have said, this is the simplest and the most classic form of speech communication. The change of speaking subjects (speakers) that determines the boundaries of the utterance is especially clear here. But in other spheres of speech communication as well, including areas of complexly organized cultural communication (scientific and artistic), the nature of the boundaries of the utterance remains the same.

Complexly structured and specialized works of various scientific and artistic genres, in spite of all the ways in which they differ from rejoinders in dialogue, are by nature the same kind of units of speech communication. They, too, are clearly demarcated by a change of speaking subjects, and these boundaries, while retaining their *external* clarity, acquire here a special internal aspect because the speaking subject—in this case, the *author* of the work—manifests his own individuality in his style, his world view, and in all aspects of the design of his work. This imprint of individuality marking the work also creates special internal boundaries that distinguish this work from other works connected with it in the overall processes of speech communication in that particular cultural sphere: from the works of predecessors on whom the author relies, from other works of the same school, from the works of opposing schools with which the author is contending, and so on.

The work, like the rejoinder in dialogue, is oriented toward the response of the other (others), toward his active responsive understanding, which can assume various forms: educational influence on the readers, persuasion of them, critical responses, influence on followers and successors, and so on. It can determine others' responsive positions under the complex conditions of speech communication in a particular cultural sphere. The work is a link in the chain of speech communion. Like the rejoinder in a dialogue, it is related to other work-utterances: both those to which it responds and those that respond to it. At the same time, like the rejoinder in a dialogue, it is separated from them by the absolute boundaries created by a change of speaking subjects.

Thus, the change of speaking subjects, by framing the utterance and creating for it a stable mass that is sharply delimited from other related utterances, is the first constitutive feature of the utterance as a unit of speech communication, a feature distinguishing it from units of language. Let us turn to this second feature, which is inseparably linked to the first. This second feature is the specific *finalization* of the utterance.

The finalization of the utterance is, if you will, the inner side of the change of speech subjects. This change can only take place because the speaker has said (or written) *everything* he wishes to say at a particular moment or under particular circumstances. When hearing or reading, we clearly sense the end of the utterance, as if we hear the speaker's concluding *dixi*. This finalization is specific and is determined by special criteria. The first and foremost criterion for the finalization of the utterance is *the possibility of responding to it* or, more precisely and broadly, of assuming a responsive attitude toward it (for example, executing an order). This criterion is met by a short everyday question, for example, "What time is it?" (one may respond to it), an everyday request that one may or may not fulfill, a scientific statement with which one may agree or disagree (partially or completely), or a novel, which can be evaluated as a whole. Some kind of finalization is necessary to be able to react to an utterance. It is not enough for the utterance to be understood in terms of *language*. An absolutely understood and completed sentence, if it is a sentence and not an utterance comprised of one sentence, cannot evoke a responsive reaction: it is comprehensible, but it is still not *all*. This *all*—the indicator of the *wholeness* of the utterance—is subject neither to grammatical nor to abstract semantic definition.

This finalized wholeness of the utterance, guaranteeing the possibility of a response (or of responsive understanding), is determined by three aspects (or factors) that are inseparably linked in the organic whole of the utterance: 1. semantic exhaustiveness of the theme; 2.

the speaker's plan or speech will; 3. typical compositional and generic forms of finalization.

The first aspect—the referential and semantic exhaustiveness of the theme of the utterance—differs profoundly in various spheres of communication. This exhaustiveness can be almost complete in certain spheres of everyday life (questions that are purely factual and similarly factual responses to them, requests, orders, and so forth), in certain business circles, in the sphere of military and industrial commands and orders, that is, in those spheres where speech genres are maximally standard by nature and where the creative aspect is almost completely lacking. Conversely, in creative spheres (especially, of course, in scientific ones), the semantic exhaustiveness of the theme may be only relative. Here one can speak only of a certain minimum of finalization making it possible to occupy a responsive position. We do not objectively exhaust the subject, but, by becoming the *theme* of the utterance (i.e., of a scientific work) the subject achieves a relative finalization under certain conditions, when the problem is posed in a particular way, on the basis of particular material, with particular aims set by the author, that is, already within the boundaries of a *specific authorial intent*. Thus, we inevitably come to the second aspect, which is inseparably linked to the first.

In each utterance—from the single-word, everyday rejoinder to large, complex works of science or literature—we embrace, understand, and sense the speaker's *speech plan* or *speech will*, which determines the entire utterance, its length and boundaries. We imagine to ourselves what the speaker *wishes* to say. And we also use this speech plan, this speech will (as we understand it), to measure the finalization of the utterance. This plan determines both the choice of the subject itself (under certain conditions of speech communication, in necessary connection with preceding utterances), as well as its boundaries and its semantic exhaustiveness. It also determines, of course, the choice of a generic form in which the utterance will be constructed (this is already the third aspect, to which we shall turn next). This plan—the subjective aspect of the utterance—combines in an inseparable unity with the objective referentially semantic aspect, limiting the latter by relating it to a concrete (individual) situation of speech communication with all its individual circumstances, its personal participants, and the statement-utterances that preceded it. Therefore, the immediate participants in communication, orienting themselves with respect to the situation and the preceding utterances, easily and quickly grasp the speaker's speech plan, his speech will. And from the very beginning of his words they sense the developing whole of the utterance.

Let us turn to the third and, for us, most important aspect: the stable *generic* forms of the utterance. The speaker's speech will is manifested primarily in the *choice of a particular speech genre.* This choice is determined by the specific nature of the given sphere of speech communication, semantic (thematic) considerations, the concrete situation of the speech communication, the personal composition of its participants, and so on. And when the speaker's speech plan with all its individuality and subjectivity is applied and adapted to a chosen genre, it is shaped and developed within a certain generic form. Such genres exist above all in the great and multifarious sphere of everyday oral communication, including the most familiar and the most intimate.

We speak only in definite speech genres, that is, all our utterances have definite and relatively stable typical *forms of construction of the whole.* Our repertoire of oral (and written) speech genres is rich. We use them confidently and skillfully *in practice,* and it is quite possible for us not even to suspect their existence *in theory.* Like Molière's Monsieur Jourdain who, when speaking in prose, had no idea that was what he was doing, we speak in diverse genres without suspecting that they exist. Even in the most free, the most unconstrained conversation, we cast our speech in definite generic forms, sometimes rigid and trite ones, sometimes more flexible, plastic, and creative ones (everyday communication also has creative genres at its disposal). We are given these speech genres in almost the same way that we are given our native language, which we master fluently long before we begin to study grammar. We know our native language—its lexical composition and grammatical structure—not from dictionaries and grammars but from concrete utterances that we hear and that we ourselves reproduce in live speech communication with people around us. We assimilate forms of language only in forms of utterances and in conjunction with these forms. The forms of language and the typical forms of utterances, that is, speech genres, enter our experience and our consciousness together, and in close connection with one another. To learn to speak means to learn to construct utterances (because we speak in utterances and not in individual sentences, and, of course, not in individual words). Speech genres organize our speech in almost the same way as grammatical (syntactical) forms do. We learn to cast our speech in generic forms and, when hearing others' speech, we guess its genre from the very first words; we predict a certain length (that is, the approximate length of the speech whole) and a certain compositional structure; we foresee the end; that is, from the very beginning we have a sense of the speech whole, which is only later differentiated during the speech process. If speech genres did not exist and we had not mastered them, if we had to originate them during the speech process and construct each utterance at will for the first time, speech communication would be almost impossible.

The generic forms in which we cast our speech, of course, differ essentially from language forms. The latter are stable and compulsory (normative) for the speaker, while generic forms are much more flexible, plastic, and free. Speech genres are very diverse in this respect. A large number of genres that are widespread in everyday life are so standard that the speaker's individual speech will is manifested only in its choice of a particular genre, and, perhaps, in its expressive intonation. Such, for example, are the various everyday genres of greetings, farewells, congratulations, all kinds of wishes, information about health, business, and so forth. These genres are so diverse because they differ depending on the situation, social position, and personal interrelations of the participants in the communication. These genres have high, strictly official, respectful forms as well as familiar ones.[e] And there are forms with varying degrees of familiarity, as well as intimate forms (which differ from familiar ones). These genres also require a certain tone; their structure includes a certain expressive intonation. These genres, particularly the high and official ones, are compulsory and extremely stable. The speech will is usually limited here to a choice of a particular genre. And only slight nuances of expressive intonation (one can take a drier or more respectful tone, a colder or warmer one; one can introduce the intonation of joy, and so forth) can express the speaker's individuality (his emotional speech intent). But even here it is generally possible to re-accentuate genres. This is typical of speech communication: thus, for example, the generic form of greeting can

[e]These and other phenomena have interested linguists (mainly language historians) in the purely stylistic level as a reflection in language of historically changed forms of etiquette, courtesy, and hospitality. See, for example, F. Brunot, *Histoire de la langue française des origines à 1900*, 10 vols. (Paris: A. Colin, 1905).

move from the official sphere into the sphere of familiar communication, that is, it can be used with parodic-ironic re-accentuation. To a similar end, one can deliberately mix genres from various spheres.

In addition to these standard genres, of course, freer and more creative genres of oral speech communication have existed and still exist: genres of salon conversations about everyday, social, aesthetic, and other subjects, genres of table conversation, intimate conversations among friends, intimate conversations within the family, and so on. (No list of oral speech genres yet exists, or even a principle on which such a list might be based.) The majority of these genres are subject to free creative reformulation (like artistic genres, and some, perhaps, to a greater degree). But to use a genre freely and creatively is not the same as to create a genre from the beginning; genres must be fully mastered in order to be manipulated freely.

Many people who have an excellent command of a language often feel quite helpless in certain spheres of communication precisely because they do not have a practical command of the generic forms used in the given spheres. Frequently a person who has an excellent command of speech in some areas of cultural communication, who is able to read a scholarly paper or engage in a scholarly discussion, who speaks very well on social questions, is silent or very awkward in social conversation. Here it is not a matter of an impoverished vocabulary or of style, taken abstractly: this is entirely a matter of the inability to command a repertoire of genres of social conversation, the lack of a sufficient supply of those ideas about the whole of the utterance that help to cast one's speech quickly and naturally in certain compositional and stylistic forms, the inability to grasp a word promptly, to begin and end correctly (composition is very uncomplicated in these genres).

The better our command of genres, the more freely we employ them, the more fully and clearly we reveal our own individuality in them (where this is possible and necessary), the more flexibly and precisely we reflect the unrepeatable situation of communication—in a word, the more perfectly we implement our free speech plan.

Thus, a speaker is given not only mandatory forms of the national language (lexical composition and grammatical structure), but also forms of utterances that are mandatory, that is, speech genres. The latter are just as necessary for mutual understanding as are forms of language. Speech genres are much more changeable, flexible, and plastic than language forms are, but they have a normative significance for the speaking individuum, and they are not created by him but are given to him. Therefore, the single utterance, with all its individuality and creativity, can in no way be regarded as a *completely free combination* of forms of language, as is supposed, for example, by Saussure (and by many other linguists after him), who juxtaposed the utterance (*la parole*), as a purely individual act, to the system of language as a phenomenon that is purely social and mandatory for the individuum.[f] The vast majority of linguists hold the same position, in theory if not in practice. They see in the utterance only an individual combination of purely linguistic (lexical and grammatical) forms and they neither uncover nor study any of the other normative forms the utterance acquires in practice.

Ignoring speech genres as relatively stable and normative forms of the utterance inevitably led to the confusion we have already pointed out between the utterance and the sentence, and it had to lead them to the position (which, to be sure, was never consistently defended) that our speech is cast solely in stable sentence forms that are given to us; and the number of these interrelated sentences we speak in a row and when we stop (end)—this is completely subject to the individual speech will of the speaker or to the caprice of the mythical "speech flow."

When we select a particular type of sentence, we do so not for the sentence itself; but out of consideration for what we wish to express with this one given sentence. We select the type of sentence from the standpoint of the *whole* utterance, which is transmitted in advance to our speech imagination and which determines our choice. The idea of the form of the whole utterance, that is, of a particular speech genre, guides us in the process of our speaking. The plan of the utterance as a whole may require only one sentence for its implementation, but it may also require a large number of them. The chosen genre predetermines for us their type and their compositional links.

One reason why forms of utterances are ignored in linguistics is that these forms are extremely diverse in compositional structure, particularly in size (speech length)—from the single-word rejoinder to a large

---

[f]Saussure defines the utterance (*la parole*) as an "individual act. It is willful and intellectual. Within the act, we should distinguish between (1) the combinations by which the speaker uses the language code for expressing his own thought; and (2) the psychological mechanism that allows him to exteriorize those combinations" (*Course in General Linguistics* [New York: McGraw-Hill, 1966], p. 14). Thus, Saussure ignores the fact that in addition to forms of language there are also *forms of combinations* of these forms, that is, he ignores speech genres.

novel. There is also a great range of sizes in oral speech genres. Thus, speech genres appear incommensurable and unacceptable as units of speech.

This is why many linguists (mainly those investigating syntax) try to find special forms that lie somewhere between the sentence and the utterance, forms with the completeness of the utterance and at the same time the commensurability of the sentence. Such are the "phrase" (i.e., in Kartsevsky) and "communication" (in Shakhmatov and others).[8] There is no common understanding of these units among researchers who use them because no definite and clearly delimited reality corresponds to them in the life of language. All these artificial and conventional units neglect the change of speech subjects that takes place in any real live speech communication, and therefore the most essential boundaries are erased in all spheres of language activity: boundaries between utterances. Hence (in consequence of this) one also forfeits the main criterion for the finalization of the utterance as a true unit of speech communication: the capability of determining the active responsive position of the other participants in the communication.

We shall conclude this section with a few more remarks about the sentence (and return to discuss this issue in detail in the summary of our essay).

The sentence as a unit of language lacks the capability of determining the directly active responsive position of the speaker. Only after becoming a complete utterance does the individual sentence acquire this capability. Any sentence can act as a complete utterance, but then, as we know, it is augmented by a number of very essential nongrammatical aspects that change it radically. And this circumstance also causes a special syntactic aberration. When the individual sentence is analyzed separately from its context, it is interpreted to the point of becoming a whole utterance. As a result, it acquires that degree of finalization that makes a response possible.

The sentence, like the word, is a signifying unit of language. Therefore, each individual sentence, for example, "The sun has risen," is completely comprehensible, that is, we understand its language *meaning*, its *possible* role in an utterance. But in no way can we assume a responsive position with respect to this individual sentence unless we know that with this sentence the speaker has said *everything* he wishes to say, that this sentence is neither preceded nor followed by other sentences of the same speaker. But then this is no longer a sentence, but a full-fledged utterance consisting of one sentence. It is framed and delimited by a change of speech subjects and it directly reflects an extraverbal reality (situation). It is possible to respond to such an utterance.

But if this sentence were surrounded by context, then it would acquire a fullness of its own *sense* only in this context, that is, only in the whole of the utterance, and one could respond only to this entire utterance whose signifying element is the given sentence. The utterance, for example, can be thus: "The sun has risen. It's time to get up." The responsive understanding (or articulated response): "Yes, it really is time." But it can also be thus: "The sun has risen. But it's still very early. Let's get some more sleep." Here the *sense* of the utterance and the responsive reaction to it will be different. Such a sentence can also enter into the composition of an artistic work as an element of landscape. Here the responsive reaction—the artistic-ideological impression and evaluation—can pertain only to the entire landscape. In the context of another work this sentence can acquire symbolic significance. In all such cases the sentence is a signifying element of the whole utterance, which acquires its final meaning only in this whole.

If our sentence figures as a completed utterance, then it acquires its own integral sense under the particular concrete circumstances of speech communication. Thus, it can be a response to another's question: "Has the sun risen?" (of course, under the particular circumstances that justify this question). Here this utterance is an assertion of a particular fact, an assertion that can be true or false, with which one can agree or disagree. A sentence that is assertive in its *form* becomes a *real* assertion in the context of a particular utterance.

When this individual sentence is analyzed, it is usually perceived as a completed utterance in some extremely simplified situation: the sun really has risen and the speaker states: "The sun has risen." The speaker sees that the grass is green and announces: "The grass is green." Such senseless "communications" are often directly regarded as classic examples of the sentence. But in reality any communication like that, addressed to someone or evoking something, has a particular purpose, that is, it is a real link in the chain of speech communion in a particular sphere of human activity or everyday life.

The sentence, like the word, has a finality of meaning and a finality of *grammatical* form, but this finality of meaning is abstract by nature and this is precisely why it is so clear-cut: this is the finality of an element, but not of the whole. The sentence as a unit of language, like the word, has no author. Like the word, it belongs to *nobody*, and only by functioning as a whole utterance does it become an expression of the position of someone speaking individually in a concrete situation of speech communication. This leads us to a new, third feature of the utterance—the relation of the utterance to the *speaker himself* (the author of the utterance) and to the *other* participants in speech communication.

Any utterance is a link in the chain of speech communion. It is the active position of the speaker in one referentially semantic sphere or another. Therefore, each utterance is characterized primarily by a particular referentially semantic content. The choice of linguistic means and speech genre is determined primarily by the referentially semantic assignments (plan) of the speech subject (or author). This is the first aspect of the utterance that determines its compositional and stylistic features.

The second aspect of the utterance that determines its composition and style is the *expressive* aspect, that is, the speaker's subjective emotional evaluation of the referentially semantic content of his utterance. The expressive aspect has varying significance and varying degrees of force in various spheres of speech communication, but it exists everywhere. There can be no such thing as an absolutely neutral utterance. The speaker's evaluative attitude toward the subject of his speech (regardless of what his subject may be) also determines the choice of lexical, grammatical, and compositional means of the utterance. The individual style of the utterance is determined primarily by its expressive aspect. This is generally recognized in the area of stylistics. Certain investigators even reduce style directly to the emotionally evaluative aspect of speech.

Can the expressive aspect of speech be regarded as a phenomenon of *language* as a system? Can one speak of the expressive aspect of language units, that is, words and sentences? The answer to these questions must be a categorical "no." Language as a system has, of course, a rich arsenal of language tools—lexical, morphological, and syntactic—for expressing the speaker's emotionally evaluative position, but all these tools as language tools are absolutely neutral with respect to any particular real evaluation. The word "darling"—which is affectionate in both the meaning of its root and its suffix—is in itself, as a language unit, just as neutral as the word "distance."[9] It is only a language tool for the possible expression of an emotionally evaluative attitude toward reality, but it is not applied to any particular reality, and this application, that is, the actual evaluation, can be accomplished only by the speaker in his concrete utterance. Words belong to nobody, and in themselves they evaluate nothing. But they can serve any speaker and be used for the most varied and directly contradictory evaluations on the part of the speakers.

The sentence as a unit of language is also neutral and in itself has no expressive aspect. It acquires this expressive aspect (more precisely, joins itself to it) only in a concrete utterance. The same aberration is possible here. A sentence like "He died" obviously embodies a certain expressiveness, and a sentence like "What joy!" does so to an even greater degree. But in fact we perceive sentences of this kind as entire utterances, and in a typical situation, that is, as kinds of speech genres that embody typical expression. As sentences they lack this expressiveness and are neutral. Depending on the context of the utterance, the sentence "He died" can also reflect a positive, joyful, even a rejoicing expression. And the sentence "What joy!" in the context of the particular utterance can assume an ironic or bitterly sarcastic tone.

One of the means of expressing the speaker's emotionally evaluative attitude toward the subject of his speech is expressive intonation, which resounds clearly in oral speech.[g] Expressive intonation is a constitutive marker of the utterance. It does not exist in the system of language as such, that is, outside the utterance. Both the word and the sentence as *language units* are devoid of expressive intonation. If an individual word is pronounced with expressive intonation it is no longer a word, but a completed utterance expressed by one word (there is no need to develop it into a sentence). Fairly standard types of evaluative utterances are very widespread in speech communication, that is, evaluative speech genres that express praise, approval, rapture, reproof, or abuse: "Excellent!" "Good for you!" "Charming!" "Shame!" "Revolting!" "Blockhead!" and so forth. Words that acquire special weight under particular conditions of sociopolitical life become expressive exclamatory utterances: "Peace!" "Freedom!" and so forth. (These constitute a special sociopolitical speech genre.) In a particular situation a word can acquire a profoundly expressive meaning in the form of an exclamatory utterance: "Thalassa, Thalassa!" [The sea! The sea!] (exclaimed 10,000 Greeks in Xenophon).

In each of these cases we are dealing not with the individual word as

[g] Of course, intonation is recognized by us and exists as a stylistic factor even with silent reading of written speech.

a unit of language and not with the *meaning* of this word but with a complete utterance and with a *specific sense*—the content of a given utterance.[10] Here the meaning of the word pertains to a particular actual reality and particular real conditions of speech communication. Therefore here we do not understand the meaning of a given word simply as a word of a language; rather, we assume an active responsive position with respect to it (sympathy, agreement or disagreement, stimulus to action). Thus, expressive intonation belongs to the utterance and not to the word. But still it is very difficult to abandon the notion that each word of a language itself has or can have an "emotional tone," "emotional coloring," an "evaluative aspect," a "stylistic aura," and so forth, and, consequently, also an expressive intonation that is inherent in the word as such. After all, one might think that when selecting a word for an utterance we are guided by an emotional tone inherent in the individual word: we select those that in their tone correspond to the expression of our utterance and we reject others. Poets themselves describe their work on the word in precisely this way, and this is precisely the way this process is interpreted in stylistics (see Peshkovsky's "stylistic experiment").[11]

But still this is not what really happens. It is that same, already familiar aberration. When selecting words we proceed from the planned whole of our utterance,[h] and this whole that we have planned and created is always expressive. The utterance is what radiates its expression (rather, our expression) to the word we have selected, which is to say, invests the word with the expression of the whole. And we select the word because of its meaning, which is not in itself expressive but which can accommodate or not accommodate our expressive goals in combination with other words, that is, in combination with the whole of our utterance. The neutral meaning of the word applied to a particular actual reality under particular real conditions of speech communication creates a spark of expression. And, after all, this is precisely what takes place in the process of creating an utterance. We

---

[h] When we construct our speech, we are always aware of the whole of our utterance: both in the form of a particular generic plan and in the form of an individual speech plan. We do not string words together smoothly and we do not proceed from word to word; rather, it is as though we fill in the whole with the necessary words. Words are strung together only in the first stage of the study of a foreign language, and then only when the methodological guidance is poor.

repeat, only the contact between the language meaning and the concrete reality that takes place in the utterance can create the spark of expression. It exists neither in the system of language nor in the objective reality surrounding us.

Thus, emotion, evaluation, and expression are foreign to the word of language and are born only in the process of its live usage in a concrete utterance. The meaning of a word in itself (unrelated to actual reality) is, as we have already said, out of the range of emotion. There are words that specifically designate emotions and evaluations: "joy," "sorrow," "wonderful," "cheerful," "sad," and so forth. But these meanings are just as neutral as are all the others. They acquire their expressive coloring only in the utterance, and this coloring is independent of their meaning taken individually and abstractly. For example: "Any joy is now only bitterness to me." Here the word "joy" is given an expressive intonation that resists its own meaning, as it were.

But the above far from exhausts the question. The matter is considerably more complicated. When we select words in the process of constructing an utterance, we by no means always take them from the system of language in their neutral, *dictionary* form. We usually take them from *other utterances*, and mainly from utterances that are kindred to ours in genre, that is, in theme, composition, or style. Consequently, we choose words according to their generic specifications. A speech genre is not a form of language, but a typical form of utterance; as such the genre also includes a certain typical kind of expression that inheres in it. In the genre the word acquires a particular typical expression. Genres correspond to typical situations of speech communication, typical themes, and, consequently, also to particular contacts between the *meanings* of words and actual concrete reality under certain typical circumstances. Hence also the possibility of typical expressions that seem to adhere to words. This typical expression (and the typical intonation that corresponds to it) does not have that force of compulsoriness that language forms have. The generic normative quality is freer. In our example, "Any joy is now bitterness to me," the expressive tone of the word "joy" as determined by the context is, of course, not typical of this word. Speech genres in general submit fairly easily to re-accentuation, the sad can be made jocular and gay, but as a result something new is achieved (for example, the genre of comical epitaphs).

This typical (generic) expression can be regarded as the word's "stylistic aura," but this aura belongs not to the word of language as such but to that genre in which the given word usually functions. It is an echo of the generic whole that resounds in the word.

The word's generic expression—and its generic expressive intonation—are impersonal, as speech genres themselves are impersonal (for they are typical forms of individual utterances, but not the utterances themselves). But words can enter our speech from others' individual utterances, thereby retaining to a greater or lesser degree the tones and echoes of individual utterances.

The words of a language belong to nobody, but still we hear those words only in particular individual utterances, we read them in particular individual works, and in such cases the words already have not only a typical, but also (depending on the genre) a more or less clearly reflected individual expression, which is determined by the unrepeatable individual context of the utterance.

Neutral dictionary meanings of the words of a language ensure their common features and guarantee that all speakers of a given language will understand one another, but the use of words in live speech communication is always individual and contextual in nature. Therefore, one can say that any word exists for the speaker in three aspects: as a neutral word of a language, belonging to nobody; as an *other's* word, which belongs to another person and is filled with echoes of the other's utterance; and, finally, as *my* word, for, since I am dealing with it in a particular situation, with a particular speech plan, it is already imbued with my expression. In both of the latter aspects, the word is expressive, but, we repeat, this expression does not inhere in the word itself. It originates at the point of contact between the word and actual reality, under the conditions of that real situation articulated by the individual utterance. In this case the word appears as an expression of some evaluative position of an individual person (authority, writer, scientist, father, mother, friend, teacher, and so forth), as an abbreviation of the utterance.

In each epoch, in each social circle, in each small world of family, friends, acquaintances, and comrades in which a human being grows and lives, there are always authoritative utterances that set the tone—artistic, scientific, and journalistic works on which one relies, to which one refers, which are cited, imitated, and followed. In each epoch, in all areas of life and activity, there are particular traditions that are expressed and retained in verbal vestments: in written works, in utterances, in sayings, and so forth. There are always some verbally expressed leading ideas of the "masters of thought" of a given epoch, some basic tasks, slogans, and so forth. I am not even speaking about those examples from school readers with which children study their native language and which, of course, are always expressive.

This is why the unique speech experience of each individual is shaped and developed in continuous and constant interaction with others' individual utterances. This experience can be characterized to some degree as the process of *assimilation*—more or less creative—of others' words (and not the words of a language). Our speech, that is, all our utterances (including creative works), is filled with others' words, varying degrees of otherness or varying degrees of "our-own-ness," varying degrees of awareness and detachment. These words of others carry with them their own expression, their own evaluative tone, which we assimilate, rework, and re-accentuate.

Thus, the expressiveness of individual words is not inherent in the words themselves as units of language, nor does it issue directly from the meaning of these words: it is either typical generic expression or it is an echo of another's individual expression, which makes the word, as it were, representative of another's whole utterance from a particular evaluative position.

The same thing must be said about the sentence as a unit of language: it, too, is devoid of expressiveness. We discussed this at the beginning of this section. We need only supplement what we have already said. The fact is that there are types of sentences that usually function as whole utterances belonging to particular generic types. Such are interrogatory, exclamatory, and imperative sentences. There are a great many everyday and special genres (i.e., military and industrial commands and orders) in which expression, as a rule, is effected by one sentence of the appropriate type. However, one encounters this type of sentence quite rarely in the cohesive context of developed utterances. And when sentences of this type do enter into a developed, cohesive context, they are clearly somewhat separated from its composition and, moreover, usually strive to be either the first or the last sentence of the utterance[i] (or a relatively independent part of it).

[i]The first and last sentences of an utterance are unique and have a certain additional quality. For they are, so to speak, sentences of the "front line" that stand right at the boundary of the change of speech subjects.

These types of sentences become especially interesting in the broad context of our problem, and we shall return to them below. But for the moment we need only note that this type of sentence knits together very stably with its generic expression, and also that it absorbs individual expression especially easily. Such sentences have contributed much to reinforcing the illusion that the sentence is by nature expressive.

One more remark. The sentence as a unit of language has a special grammatical intonation, but no expressive intonation at all. Special grammatical intonations include: the intonation of finalization; explanatory, distributive, enumerative intonations, and so forth. Storytelling, interrogatory, explanatory, and imperative intonations occupy a special position. It is as though grammatical intonation crosses with generic intonation here (but not with expressive intonation in the precise sense of this word). The sentence acquires expressive intonation only in the whole utterance. When giving an example of a sentence for analysis, we usually supply it with a particular typical intonation, thereby transforming it into a completed utterance (if we take the sentence from a particular text, of course, we intone it according to the expression of the given text).

So the expressive aspect is a constitutive feature of the utterance. The system of the language has necessary forms (i.e., language means) for reflecting expression, but the language itself and its semantic units—words and sentences—are by their very nature devoid of expression and neutral. Therefore, they can serve equally well for any evaluations, even the most varied and contradictory ones, and for any evaluative positions as well.

Thus, the utterance, its style, and its composition are determined by its referentially semantic element (the theme) and its expressive aspect, that is, the speaker's evaluative attitude toward the referentially semantic element in the utterance. Stylistics knows no third aspect. Stylistics accounts only for the following factors, which determine the style of the utterance: the language system, the theme of the speech, and the speaker himself with his evaluative attitude toward the object. The selection of language means, according to ordinary stylistic conceptions, is determined solely by referentially semantic and expressive considerations. These also determine language styles, both general and individual. The speaker with his world view, with his evaluations and emotions, on the one hand, and the object of his speech and the language system (language means), on the other—

these alone determine the utterance, its style, and its composition. Such is the prevailing idea.

But in reality the situation is considerably more complicated. Any concrete utterance is a link in the chain of speech communication of a particular sphere. The very boundaries of the utterance are determined by a change of speech subjects. Utterances are not indifferent to one another, and are not self-sufficient; they are aware of and mutually reflect one another. These mutual reflections determine their character. Each utterance is filled with echoes and reverberations of other utterances to which it is related by the communality of the sphere of speech communication. Every utterance must be regarded primarily as a *response* to preceding utterances of the given sphere (we understand the word "response" here in the broadest sense). Each utterance refutes, affirms, supplements, and relies on the others, presupposes them to be known, and somehow takes them into account. After all, as regards a given question, in a given matter, and so forth, the utterance occupies a particular *definite* position in a given sphere of communication. It is impossible to determine its position without correlating it with other positions. Therefore, each utterance is filled with various kinds of responsive reactions to other utterances of the given sphere of speech communication. These reactions take various forms: others' utterances can be introduced directly into the context of the utterance, or one may introduce only individual words or sentences, which then act as representatives of the whole utterance. Both whole utterances and individual words can retain their alien expression, but they can also be re-accentuated (ironically, indignantly, reverently, and so forth). Others' utterances can be repeated with varying degrees of reinterpretation. They can be referred to as though the interlocutor were already well aware of them; they can be silently presupposed; or one's responsive reaction to them can be reflected only in the expression of one's own speech—in the selection of language means and intonations that are determined not by the topic of one's own speech but by the others' utterances concerning the same topic. Here is an important and typical case: very frequently the expression of our utterance is determined not only—and sometimes not so much—by the referentially semantic content of this utterance, but also by others' utterances on the same topic to which we are responding or with which we are polemicizing. They also determine our emphasis on certain elements, repetition, our selection of harsher (or, conversely, milder) expressions, a contentious (or, conversely, conciliatory) tone, and so forth. The expression of an utterance can never be fully understood or explained if its thematic content is all that is taken into account. The expression of an utterance always *responds* to a greater or lesser degree, that is, it expresses the speaker's attitude toward others' utterances and not just his attitude toward the object of his utterance.[j] The forms of responsive reactions that supplement the utterance are extremely varied and have not yet undergone any special study at all. These forms are sharply differentiated, of course, depending on the differences among those spheres of human activity and everyday life in which speech communication takes place. However monological the utterance may be (for example, a scientific or philosophical treatise), however much it may concentrate on its own object, it cannot but be, in some measure, a response to what has already been said about the given topic, on the given issue, even though this responsiveness may not have assumed a clear-cut external expression. It will be manifested in the overtones of the style, in the finest nuances of the composition. The utterance is filled with *dialogic overtones,* and they must be taken into account in order to understand fully the style of the utterance. After all, our thought itself—philosophical, scientific, and artistic—is born and shaped in the process of interaction and struggle with others' thought, and this cannot but be reflected in the forms that verbally express our thought as well.

Others' utterances and others' individual words—recognized and singled out as such and inserted into the utterance—introduce an element that is, so to speak, irrational from the standpoint of language as system, particularly from the standpoint of syntax. The interrelations between inserted other's speech and the rest of the speech (one's own) are analogous neither to any syntactical relations within a simple or complex syntactic whole nor to the referentially semantic relations among grammatically unrelated individual syntactic wholes found within a single utterance. These relations, however, are analogous (but, of course, not identical) to relations among rejoinders in dialogue. Intonation that isolates others' speech (in written speech, designated by quotation marks) is a special phenomenon: it is as though the *change of speech subjects* has been internalized. The *boundaries* created by this change are weakened here and of a special sort: the speaker's expression penetrates through these boundaries and spreads to the other's speech, which is transmitted in ironic, indignant, sympathetic,

---

[j] Intonation is especially sensitive and always points beyond the context.

or reverential tones (this expression is transmitted by means of expressive intonation—in written speech we guess and sense it precisely because of the context that frames the other's speech, or by means of the extraverbal situation that suggests the appropriate expression). The other's speech thus has a dual expression: its own, that is, the other's, and the expression of the utterance that encloses the speech. All this takes place primarily when the other's speech (even if it is only one word, which here acquires the force of an entire utterance) is openly introduced and clearly demarcated (in quotation marks). Echoes of the change of speech subjects and their dialogical interrelations can be heard clearly here. But any utterance, when it is studied in greater depth under the concrete conditions of speech communication, reveals to us many half-concealed or completely concealed words of others with varying degrees of foreignness. Therefore, the utterance appears to be furrowed with distant and barely audible echoes of changes of speech subjects and dialogic overtones, greatly weakened utterance boundaries that are completely permeable to the author's expression. The utterance proves to be a very complex and multiplanar phenomenon if considered not in isolation and with respect to its author (the speaker) only, but as a link in the chain of speech communication and with respect to other, related utterances (these relations are usually disclosed not on the verbal—compositional and stylistic—plane, but only on the referentially semantic plane).

Each individual utterance is a link in the chain of speech communion. It has clear-cut boundaries that are determined by the change of speech subjects (speakers), but within these boundaries the utterance, like Leibniz's monad,[12] reflects the speech process, others' utterances, and, above all, preceding links in the chain (sometimes close and sometimes—in areas of cultural communication—very distant).

The topic of the speaker's speech, regardless of what this topic may be, does not become the object of speech for the first time in any given utterance; a given speaker is not the first to speak about it. The object, as it were, has already been articulated, disputed, elucidated, and evaluated in various ways. Various viewpoints, world views, and trends cross, converge, and diverge in it. The speaker is not the biblical Adam, dealing only with virgin and still unnamed objects, giving them names for the first time. Simplistic ideas about communication as a logical-psychological basis for the sentence recall this mythical Adam. Two ideas combine in the soul of the speaker (or, conversely, one complex idea is divided into two simple ones), and he utters a sentence like the following: "The sun is shining," "The grass is green," "I am sitting," and so forth. Such sentences, of course, are quite possible, but either they are justified and interpreted by the context of the whole utterance that attaches them to speech communication (as a rejoinder in a dialogue, a popular scientific article, a teacher's discussion in class, and so forth) or they are completed utterances and are somehow justified by a speaking situation that includes them in the chain of speech communication. In reality, and we repeat this, any utterance, in addition to its own theme, always responds (in the broad sense of the word) in one form or another to others' utterances that precede it. The speaker is not Adam, and therefore the subject of his speech itself inevitably becomes the arena where his opinions meet those of his partners (in a conversation or dispute about some everyday event) or other viewpoints, world views, trends, theories, and so forth (in the sphere of cultural communication). World views, trends, viewpoints, and opinions always have verbal expression. All this is others' speech (in personal or impersonal form), and it cannot but be reflected in the utterance. The utterance is addressed not only to its own object, but also to others' speech about it. But still, even the slightest allusion to another's utterance gives the speech a dialogical turn that cannot be produced by any purely referential theme with its own object. The attitude toward another's word is in principle distinct from the attitude toward a referential object, but the former always accompanies the latter. We repeat, an utterance is a link in the chain of speech communication, and it cannot be broken off from the preceding links that determine it both from within and from without, giving rise within it to unmediated responsive reactions and dialogic reverberations.

But the utterance is related not only to preceding, but also to subsequent links in the chain of speech communion. When a speaker is creating an utterance, of course, these links do not exist. But from the very beginning, the utterance is constructed while taking into account possible responsive reactions, for whose sake, in essence, it is actually created. As we know, the role of the *others* for whom the utterance is constructed is extremely great. We have already said that the role of these others, for whom my thought becomes actual thought for the first time (and thus also for my own self as well) is not that of passive listeners, but of active participants in speech communication. From the very beginning, the speaker expects a response from them, an active responsive understanding. The entire utterance is constructed, as it were, in anticipation of encountering this response.

An essential (constitutive) marker of the utterance is its quality of being directed to someone, its *addressivity*. As distinct from the signifying units of a language—words and sentences—that are impersonal, belonging to nobody and addressed to nobody, the utterance has both an author (and, consequently, expression, which we have already discussed) and an addressee. This addressee can be an immediate participant-interlocutor in an everyday dialogue, a differentiated collective of specialists in some particular area of cultural communication, a more or less differentiated public, ethnic group, contemporaries, like-minded people, opponents and enemies, a subordinate, a superior, someone who is lower, higher, familiar, foreign, and so forth. And it can also be an indefinite, unconcretized *other* (with various kinds of monological utterances of an emotional type). All these varieties and conceptions of the addressee are determined by that area of human activity and everyday life to which the given utterance is related. Both the composition and, particularly, the style of the utterance depend on those to whom the utterance is addressed, how the speaker (or writer) senses and imagines his addressees, and the force of their effect on the utterance. Each speech genre in each area of speech communication has its own typical conception of the addressee, and this defines it as a genre.

The addressee of the utterance can, so to speak, coincide *personally* with the one (or ones) to whom the utterance responds. This personal coincidence is typical in everyday dialogue or in an exchange of letters. The person to whom I respond is my addressee, from whom I, in turn, expect a response (or in any case an active responsive understanding). But in such cases of personal coincidence one individual plays two different roles, and the difference between the roles is precisely what matters here. After all, the utterance of the person to whom I am responding (I agree, I object, I execute, I take under advisement, and so forth) is already at hand, but his response (or responsive understanding) is still forthcoming. When constructing my utterance, I try actively to determine this response. Moreover, I try to act in accordance with the response I anticipate, so this anticipated response, in turn, exerts an active influence on my utterance (I parry objections that I foresee, I make all kinds of provisos, and so forth). When speaking I always take into account the apperceptive background of the addressee's perception of my speech: the extent to which he is familiar with the situation, whether he has special knowledge of the given cultural area of communication, his views and convictions, his prejudices (from my viewpoint), his sympathies and antipathies—because all this will determine his active responsive understanding of my utterance. These considerations also determine my choice of a genre for my utterance, my choice of compositional devices, and, finally, my choice of language vehicles, that is, the *style* of my utterance. For example, genres of popular scientific literature are addressed to a particular group of readers with a particular apperceptive background of responsive understanding; special educational literature is addressed to another kind of reader, and special research work is addressed to an entirely different sort. In these cases, accounting for the addressee (and his apperceptive background) and for the addressee's influence on the construction of the utterance is very simple: it all comes down to the scope of his specialized knowledge.

In other cases, the matter can be much more complicated. Accounting for the addressee and anticipating his responsive reaction are frequently multifaceted processes that introduce unique internal dramatism into the utterance (in certain kinds of everyday dialogue, in letters, and in autobiographical and confessional genres). These phenomena are crucial, but more external, in rhetorical genres. The addressee's social position, rank, and importance are reflected in a special way in utterances of everyday and business speech communication. Under the conditions of a class structure and especially an aristocratic class structure, one observes an extreme differentiation of speech genres and styles, depending on the title, class, rank, wealth, social importance, and age of the addressee and the relative position of the speaker (or writer). Despite the wealth of differentiation, both of basic forms and of nuances, these phenomena are standard and external by nature: they cannot introduce any profound internal dramatism into the utterance. They are interesting only as instances of very crude, but still very graphic expressions of the addressee's influence on the construction and style of the utterance.[k]

Finer nuances of style are determined by the nature and degree of *personal* proximity of the addressee to the speaker in various familiar

---

[k] I am reminded of an apposite observation of Gogol's: "One cannot enumerate all the nuances and fine points of our communication . . . we have slick talkers who will speak quite differently with a landowner who has 200 souls than with one who has 300, and again he will not speak the same way with one who has 300 as he will with one who has 500, and he will not speak the same way with one who has 500 as he will with one who has 800; in a word, you can go up to a million and you will still find different nuances" (*Dead Souls*, chapter 3).

speech genres, on the one hand, and in intimate ones, on the other. With all the immense differences among familiar and intimate genres (and, consequently, styles), they perceive their addressees in exactly the same way: more or less outside the framework of the social hierarchy and social conventions, "without rank," as it were. This gives rise to a certain *candor* of speech (which in familiar styles sometimes approaches cynicism). In intimate styles this is expressed in an apparent desire for the speaker and addressee to merge completely. In familiar speech, since speech constraints and conventions have fallen away, one can take a special unofficial, volitional approach to reality.[1] This is why during the Renaissance familiar genres and styles could play such a large and positive role in destroying the official medieval picture of the world. In other periods as well, when the task was to destroy traditional official styles and world views that had faded and become conventional, familiar styles became very significant in literature. Moreover, familiarization of styles opened literature up to layers of language that had previously been under speech constraint. The significance of familiar genres and styles in literary history has not yet been adequately evaluated. Intimate genres and styles are based on a maximum internal proximity of the speaker and addressee (in extreme instances, as if they had merged). Intimate speech is imbued with a deep confidence in the addressee, in his sympathy, in the sensitivity and goodwill of his responsive understanding. In this atmosphere of profound trust, the speaker reveals his internal depths. This determines the special expressiveness and internal candor of these styles (as distinct from the loud street-language candor of familiar speech). Familiar and intimate genres and styles (as yet very little studied) reveal extremely clearly the dependence of style on a certain sense and understanding of the addressee (the addressee of the utterance) on the part of the speaker, and on the addressee's actively responsive understanding that is anticipated by the speaker. These styles reveal especially clearly the narrowness and incorrectness of traditional stylistics, which tries to understand and define style solely from the standpoint of the semantic and thematic content of speech and the speaker's expressive attitude toward this content. Unless one accounts for the speaker's attitude toward the *other* and his utterances (existing or anticipated), one can understand neither the genre nor the style of

---

[1]The loud candor of the streets, calling things by their real names, is typical of this style.

speech. But even the so-called neutral or objective styles of exposition that concentrate maximally on their subject matter and, it would seem, are free of any consideration of the other still involve a certain conception of their addressee. Such objectively neutral styles select language vehicles not only from the standpoint of their adequacy to the subject matter of speech, but also from the standpoint of the presumed apperceptive background of the addressee. But this background is taken into account in as generalized a way as possible, and is abstracted from the expressive aspect (the expression of the speaker himself is also minimal in the objective style). Objectively neutral styles presuppose something like an identity of the addressee and the speaker, a unity of their viewpoints, but this identity and unity are purchased at the price of almost complete forfeiture of expression. It must be noted that the nature of objectively neutral styles (and, consequently, the concept of the addressee on which they are based) is fairly diverse, depending on the differences between the areas of speech communication.

This question of the concept of the speech addressee (how the speaker or writer senses and imagines him) is of immense significance in literary history. Each epoch, each literary trend and literary-artistic style, each literary genre within an epoch or trend, is typified by its own special concepts of the addressee of the literary work, a special sense and understanding of its reader, listener, public, or people. A historical study of changes in these concepts would be an interesting and important task. But in order to develop it productively, the statement of the problem itself would have to be theoretically clear.

It should be noted that, in addition to those real meanings and ideas of one's addressee that actually determine the style of the utterances (works), the history of literature also includes conventional or semiconventional forms of address to readers, listeners, posterity, and so forth, just as, in addition to the actual author, there are also conventional and semiconventional images of substitute authors, editors, and various kinds of narrators. The vast majority of literary genres are secondary, complex genres composed of various transformed primary genres (the rejoinder in dialogue, everyday stories, letters, diaries, minutes, and so forth). As a rule, these secondary genres of complex cultural communication *play out* various forms of primary speech communication. Here also is the source of all literary/conventional characters of authors, narrators, and addressees. But the most complex and ultra-composite work of a secondary genre as a whole (viewed as a whole) is a single integrated real utterance that has a real author and real addressees whom this author perceives and imagines.

Thus, addressivity, the quality of turning to someone, is a constitutive feature of the utterance; without it the utterance does not and cannot exist. The various typical forms this addressivity assumes and the various concepts of the addressee are constitutive, definitive features of various speech genres.

As distinct from utterances (and speech genres), the signifying units of a language—the word and the sentence—lack this quality of being directed or addressed to someone: these units belong to nobody and are addressed to nobody. Moreover, they in themselves are devoid of any kind of relation to the other's utterance, the other's word. If an individual word or sentence is directed at someone, addressed to someone, then we have a completed utterance that consists of one word or one sentence, and addressivity is inherent not in the unit of language, but in the utterance. A sentence that is surrounded by context acquires the addressivity only through the entire utterance, as a constituent part (element) of it.[m]

Language as a system has an immense supply of purely linguistic means for expressing formal address: lexical, morphological (the corresponding cases, pronouns, personal forms of verbs), and syntactical (various standard phrases and modifications of sentences). But they acquire addressivity only in the whole of a concrete utterance. And the expression of this actual addressivity is never exhausted, of course, by these special language (grammatical) means. They can even be completely lacking, and the utterance can still reflect very clearly the influence of the addressee and his anticipated responsive reaction. The choice of *all* language means is made by the speaker under varying degrees of influence from the addressee and his anticipated response.

When one analyzes an individual sentence apart from its context, the traces of addressivity and the influence of the anticipated response, dialogical echoes from others' preceding utterances, faint traces of changes of speech subjects that have furrowed the utterance from within—all these are lost, erased, because they are all foreign to the sentence as a unit of language. All these phenomena are connected with the whole of the utterance, and when this whole escapes the field

[m] We note that interrogatory and imperative types of sentences, as a rule, act as completed utterances (in the appropriate speech genres).

of vision of the analyst they cease to exist for him. Herein lies one of the reasons for that narrowness of traditional stylistics we commented upon above. A stylistic analysis that embraces all aspects of style is possible only as an analysis of the *whole* utterance, and only in that chain of speech communion of which the utterance is an inseparable *link*.

Notes

1. "National unity of language" is a shorthand way of referring to the assemblage of linguistic and translinguistic practices common to a given region. It is, then, a good example of what Bakhtin means by an open unity. See also Otto Jesperson, *Mankind, Nation, and Individual* (Bloomington: Indiana University Press, 1964).

2. Saussure's teaching is based on a distinction between language (*la langue*)—a system of interconnected signs and forms that normatively determine each individual speech act and are the special object of linguistics—and speech (*la parole*)—individual instances of language use. Bakhtin discusses Saussure's teachings in *Marxism and the Philosophy of Language* as one of the two main trends in linguistic thought (the trend of "abstract objectivism") that he uses to shape his own theory of the utterance. See V. N. Voloshinov, *Marxism and the Philosophy of Language*, tr. Ladislav Matejka and I. R. Titunik (New York: Seminar Press, 1973), esp. pp. 58–61.

"Behaviorists" here refers to the school of psychology introduced by the Harvard physiologist J. B. Watson in 1913. It seeks to explain animal and human behavior entirely in terms of observable and measurable responses to external stimuli. Watson, in his insistence that behavior is a physiological reaction to environmental stimuli, denied the value of introspection and of the concept of consciousness. He saw mental processes as bodily movements, even when unperceived, so that thinking in his view is subvocal speech. There is a strong connection as well between the behaviorist school of psychology and the school of American descriptive linguistics, which is what Bakhtin is referring to here. The so-called descriptivist school was founded by the eminent anthropologist Franz Boas (1858–1942). Its closeness to behaviorism consists in its insistence on careful observation unconditioned by presuppositions or categories taken from traditional language structure. Leonard Bloomfield (1887–1949) was the chief spokesman for the school and was explicit about his commitment to a "mechanist approach" (his term for the behaviorist school of psychology): "Mechanists demand that the facts be presented without any assumption of such auxiliary factors [as a version of the mind]. I have tried to meet this demand. . . ." (*Language* [New York: Holt, Rinehart, and Winston, 1933], p. vii). Two prominent linguists sometimes associated with the descriptivists, Edward Sapir (1884–1939) and his pupil Benjamin Lee Whorf (1897–1941), differ from Bloomfield insofar as behaviorism plays a relatively minor role in their work.

"Vosslerians" refers to the movement named after the German philologist Karl Vossler (1872–1949), whose adherents included Leo Spitzer (1887–1960). For

Vosslerians, the reality of language is the continuously creative, constructive activity that is prosecuted through speech acts; the creativity of language is likened to artistic creativity, and stylistics becomes the leading discipline. Style takes precedence over grammar, and the standpoint of the speaker takes precedence over that of the listener. In a number of aspects, Bakhtin is close to the Vosslerians, but differs in his understanding of the utterance as the concrete reality of language life. Bakhtin does not, like the Vosslerians, conceive the utterance to be an individual speech act; rather, he emphasizes the "inner sociality" in speech communication—an aspect that is objectively reinforced in speech genres. The concept of speech genres is central to Bakhtin, then, in that it separates his translinguistics from both Saussureans and Vosslerians in the philosophy of language.

3. "Ideology" should not be confused with the politically oriented English word. Ideology as it is used here is essentially any system of ideas. But ideology is semiotic in the sense that it involves the concrete exchange of signs in society and history. Every word/discourse betrays the ideology of its speaker; every speaker is thus an ideologue and every utterance an ideologeme.

4. A unified basis for classifying the enormous diversity of utterances is an obsession of Bakhtin's, one that relates him directly to Wilhelm von Humboldt (1767–1835), the first in the modern period to argue systematically that language is the vehicle of thought. He calls language the "labor of the mind" (*Arbeit des Geistes*) in his famous formulation "[language] itself is not [mere] work (*ergon*), but an activity (*energeia*) . . . it is in fact the labor of the mind that otherwise would eternally repeat itself to make articulated sound capable of the expression of thought" (*Über die Verschiedenheit des menschlichen Sprachbaues*, in *Werke*, vol. 7 [Berlin: De Gruyter, 1968], p. 46). What is important here is that for Bakhtin, as for von Humboldt, the diversity of languages *is itself of philosophical significance*, for if thought and speech are one, does not each language embody a unique way of thinking? It is here that Bakhtin also comes very close to the work of Sapir and, especially, of Whorf. See Benjamin Lee Whorf, *Language, Thought, and Reality*, ed. John B. Carroll (Cambridge, Mass.: MIT Press, 1956), esp. pp. 212–19 and 239–45.

5. See Wilhelm von Humboldt, *Linguistic Variability and Intellectual Development* (Coral Gables: University of Miami Press, 1971).

6. The phrase "psychology of nations" refers to a school organized around the nineteenth-century journal *Zeitschrift für Volkerpsychologie und Sprachwissenschaft*, whose leading spokesman, Kermann Steinthal, was among the first to introduce psychology (especially that of the Kantian biologist Herbart) into language (and vice versa). Steinthal was attracted to von Humboldt's idea of "innere Sprachform" and was important in Potebnya's attempts to wrestle with inner speech.

7. *Grammatika russkogo jazyka* (Grammar of the Russian language) (Moscow, 1952), vol. 1, p. 51.

8. S. D. Kartsevsky, Russian linguist of the Geneva School who also participated in the Prague Linguistic Circle. He argued that the "phrase" should be used as a different kind of language unit from that of the sentence. Unlike the sentence, the phrase "does not have its own grammatical structure. But it has its own phonetic structure, which consists in its intonation. It is intonation that forms the phrase" (S. Karcewski, "Sur la phonologie de la phrase," in *Travaux du Cercle lin-*

guistique de Prague 4 [1931], 190). "The sentence, in order to be realized, must be given the intonation of the phrase. . . . The phrase is a function of dialogue. It is a unit of exchange among conversing parties. . . ." (S. Karcewski, "Sur la parataxe et la syntaxe en russe," in *Cahiers Ferdinand de Saussure*, no. 7 [1948], 34).

Aleksey Shakhmatov (1864–1920), linguist and academician whose most important works were devoted to the history of the Russian language, modern Russian, and comparative studies of the grammars of different Slavic languages. "Communication" has a rather distinctive meaning for Shakhmatov: it refers to the act of thinking, this being the psychological basis of the sentence, the mediating link "between the psyche of the speaker and its manifestation in the discourse toward which it strives" (A. Shakhmatov, *Sintaksis russkogo jazyka* [Syntax of the Russian language] [Leningrad, 1941], pp. 19–20).

9. The Russian word Bakhtin uses here (*milenkij*) is a diminutive of *milyj*, itself a term of endearment meaning "nice" or "sweet."

10. In *Marxism and the Philosophy of Language*, the specific sense of an utterance is defined as its *theme* (*tema*): "The theme of an utterance is essentially individual and unrepeatable, like the utterance itself. . . . The theme of the utterance is essentially indivisible. The significance of the utterance, on the contrary, breaks down into a number of significances that are included in its linguistic elements" (pp. 101–2).

11. Aleksandr Peshkovsky (1878–1933), Soviet linguist specializing in grammar and stylistics in the schools. His "stylistic experiment" consisted in artificially devising stylistic variants of the text, a device he used for analyzing artistic speech. See A. M. Peshkovsky, *Voprosy metodiki rodnogo jazyka, lingvistiki i stilistiki* (Problems in the methodology of folk language, linguistics, and stylistics) (Moscow-Leningrad, 1930), p. 133.

12. Leibniz identified monads with the metaphysical individuals or souls, conceived as unextended, active, indivisible, naturally indestructible, and teleological substances ideally related in a system of preestablished harmony.

The Problem of the Text in Linguistics, Philology, and the Human Sciences: An Experiment in Philosophical Analysis

Our analysis must be called philosophical mainly because of what it is not: it is not a linguistic, philological, literary, or any other special kind of analysis (study). The advantages are these: our study will move in the liminal spheres, that is, on the borders of all the aforementioned disciplines, at their junctures and points of intersection.

The text (written and oral) is the primary given of all these disciplines and of all thought in the human sciences and philosophy in general (including theological and philosophical thought at their sources). The text is the unmediated reality (reality of thought and experience), the only one from which these disciplines and this thought can emerge. Where there is no text, there is no object of study, and no object of thought either.

The "implied" text: if the word "text" is understood in the broad sense—as any coherent complex of signs—then even the study of art (the study of music, the theory and history of fine arts) deals with texts (works of art). Thoughts about thoughts, experiences of experiences, words about words, and texts about texts. Herein lies the basic distinction between our disciplines (human sciences) and the natural ones (about nature), although there are no absolute, impenetrable boundaries here either. Thought about the human sciences originates as thought about others' thoughts, wills, manifestations, expressions, and signs, behind which stand manifest gods (revelations) or people (the laws of rulers, the precepts of ancestors, anonymous sayings, riddles, and so forth). A scientifically precise, as it were, authentication of the texts and criticism of texts come later (in thought in the human sciences, they represent a complete about-face, the origin of *skepticism*). Initially, *belief* required only understanding—*interpretation*. This belief was brought to bear on profane texts (the study of languages and so forth). We do not intend to delve into the history of the human sciences, and certainly not into philology or linguistics. We are interested rather in the specific nature of thought in the human sciences that is directed toward other thoughts, ideas, meanings, and so forth, which are realized and made available to the researcher only in the form of a *text*. Regardless of the goals of the research, the only possible point of departure is the text.

We shall be interested only in the problem of *verbal* texts, which are the initial givens of the corresponding human sciences—primarily linguistics, philology, literary scholarship, and so forth.

Every text has a subject or author (speaker or writer). Various types, subcategories, and forms of authorship are possible. Within certain limits, linguistic analysis can disregard authorship altogether. The text can be interpreted as an *example* (model judgments, syllogisms in logic, sentences in grammar, "commutations" in linguistics, and so forth).[1] There are imagined texts (exemplary and other kinds) and constructed texts (for purposes of linguistic or stylistic experiment). Special kinds of authors appear everywhere in this area: those who think up examples and experimenters with their special authorial responsibility (there is even a second subject here: the person who could speak this way).

The problem of the limits of the text. The text as *utterance*. The problem of the functions of the text and textual genres.

Two aspects that define the text as an utterance: its plan (intention) and the realization of this plan. The dynamic interrelations of these aspects, their struggle, which determine the nature of the text. Their divergence can reveal a great deal. "Pelestradal" (Leo Tolstoy).[2] Freudian slips of the tongue and slips of the pen (expression of the unconscious). Change of the plan in the process of its realization. Failure to fulfill the phonetic intention.

The problem of the second subject who is reproducing (for one purpose or another, including for research purposes) a text (another's) and creating a framing text (one that comments, evaluates, objects, and so forth).

The special feature of thinking in the human sciences, which involves two planes and two subjects. Textology as the theory and practice of the scientific reproduction of literary texts. The textological subject (textologist) and his particularities.

The problem of the point of view (spatial-temporal position) of the observer in astronomy and physics.

The text as an utterance included in the speech communication (textual chain) of a given sphere. The text as a unique monad that in itself reflects all texts (within the bounds) of a given sphere. The interconnection of all ideas (since all are realized in utterances).

The dialogic relationships among texts and within the text. Their special (not linguistic) nature. Dialogue and dialectics.

The two poles of the text. Each text presupposes a generally understood (that is, conventional within a given collective) system of signs, a language (if only the language of art). If there is no language behind the text, it is not a text, but a natural (not signifying) phenomenon, for example, a complex of natural cries and moans devoid of any linguistic (signifying) repeatability. Of course, each text (both oral and written) includes a significant number of various kinds of natural aspects devoid of signification, which extend beyond the limits of research in the human sciences (linguistic, philological, and so forth), but which are still taken into account (deterioration of a manuscript, poor diction, and so forth). There are not nor can there be any pure texts. In each text, moreover, there are a number of aspects that can be called technical (the technical side of graphics, pronunciation, and so forth).

And so behind each text stands a language system. Everything in the text that is repeated and reproduced, everything repeatable and reproducible, everything that can be given outside a given text (the given) conforms to this language system. But at the same time each text (as an utterance) is individual, unique, and unrepeatable, and herein lies its entire significance (its plan, the purpose for which it was created). This is the aspect of it that pertains to honesty, truth, goodness, beauty, history. With respect to this aspect, everything repeatable and reproducible proves to be material, a means to an end. This notion extends somewhat beyond the bounds of linguistics or philology. The second aspect (pole) inheres in the text itself, but is revealed only in a particular situation and in a chain of texts (in the speech communication of a given area). This pole is linked not with elements (repeatable) in the system of the language (signs), but with other texts (unrepeatable) by special dialogic (and dialectical, when detached from the author) relations.

This second pole is inseparably linked with the aspect of authorship and has nothing to do with natural, random single units; it is realized completely by means of the sign system of the language. It is realized by means of pure context, although natural aspects also enter into it. The relativity of all boundaries (for example, where does one include the timbre of the voice of the reciter, the speaker, and so forth?). A change of functions also effects a change of boundaries. The distinction between phonology and phonetics.[3]

The problem of the semantic (dialectical) and dialogic interrelations among texts within the bounds of a particular sphere. The special problem of historical interrelations among texts. All this in light of the second pole. The problem of the limits of causal explanation. The most important thing is to avoid severance from the text (even if it is only potential, imagined, or inferred).

The science of the spirit.[4] The spirit (both one's own and another's) is not given as a thing (the direct object of the natural sciences); it can only be present through signification, through realization in texts, both for itself and for others. The criticism of self-observation. But there must be a profound, rich, and refined understanding of the text. The theory of the text.

The natural gesture acquires a signifying quality in the actor's performance (as arbitrary, as performative, as something subject to the design of a role).[5]

Natural uniqueness (for example, a fingerprint) and the semantic (signifying) unrepeatability of the text. All that is possible for a fingerprint is mechanical reproduction (in any number of copies); it is possible, of course, to reproduce a text in the same mechanical way (i.e., reprinting), but the reproduction of the text by the subject (a return to it, a repeated reading, a new execution quotation) is a new, unrepeatable event in the life of the text, a new link in the historical chain of speech communication.

Any sign system (i.e., any language), regardless of how small the collective that produces its conventions may be, can always in principle be deciphered, that is, translated into other sign systems (other languages). Consequently, sign systems have a common logic, a potential single language of languages (which, of course, can never become a single concrete language, one of the languages). But the text (as distinct from the language as a system of means) can never be completely translated, for there is no potential single text of texts.

The event of the life of the text, that is, its true essence, always develops *on the boundary between two consciousnesses, two subjects*.

The transcription of thinking in the human sciences is always the transcription of a special kind of dialogue: the complex interrelations between the *text* (the object of study and reflection) and the created, framing *context* (questioning, refuting, and so forth) in which the scholar's cognizing and evaluating thought takes place. This is the meeting of two texts—of the ready-made and the reactive text being created—and, consequently, the meeting of two subjects and two authors.

The text is not a thing, and therefore the second consciousness, the consciousness of the perceiver, can in no way be eliminated or neutralized.

It is possible to proceed toward the first pole, that is, toward language—the language of the author, the language of the genre, the trend, the epoch; toward the national language (linguistics), and, finally, toward a potential language of languages (structuralism, glossematics).[6] It is also possible to proceed toward the second pole—toward the unrepeatable event of the text.

All possible disciplines in the human sciences that evolve from the initial given of the text are located somewhere between these two poles.

Both poles are unconditional: the potential language of languages is unconditional and the unique and unrepeatable text is unconditional.

Any truly creative text is always to some extent a free revelation of the personality, not predetermined by empirical necessity. Therefore, it (in its free nucleus) admits neither of causal explanation nor of scientific prediction. But this, of course, does not exclude the internal necessity, the internal logic of the free nucleus of the text (without which it could not be understood, recognized, or effective).

The problem of the text in the human sciences. The human sciences are sciences about man and his specific nature, and not about a voiceless thing or natural phenomenon. Man in his specific human nature always expresses himself (speaks), that is, he creates a text (if only potential). When man is studied outside a text and independent of it, the science is no longer one of the human sciences (human anatomy, physiology, and so forth).

The problem of the text in textology. The philosophical side of the problem.

The attempt to study the text as "verbal reaction" (behaviorism).[7]

Cybernetics, information theory, statistics, and the problem of the text. The problem of incarnating the text. The boundaries of this incarnation.

A human act is a potential text and can be understood (as a human act and not a physical action) only in the dialogic context of its time (as a rejoinder, as a semantic position, as a system of motives).

"All that is beautiful and sublime"—this is not a phraseological unity in the ordinary sense, but a special kind of intonational or expressive combination of words. This represents style, world view, a human type. It is redolent in contexts; it involves two voices, two subjects (the person who would speak seriously in this way, and the person who parodies him). Taken individually (outside the combination), the words "beautiful" and "sublime" lose their double-voicedness; the second voice enters only in the combination of words, which becomes an utterance (i.e., it acquires a speech subject, without which there can be no second voice). One word can also become double-voiced if it becomes an abbreviated utterance (that is, if it acquires an author). The phraseological unity is created not by the first, but by the second voice.

Language and speech, sentence and utterance. The speaking subject (generalized "natural" individuality) and the author of the utterance. The change of speaking subjects and the change of speakers (authors of the utterance). Language and speech can be identical, since in speech the dialogic boundaries of the utterances are erased. But language and speech communication (as a dialogic exchange of utterances) can never be identical. Two or more sentences can be absolutely identical (when they are superimposed on one another, like two geometrical figures, they coincide); moreover, we must allow that any sentence, even a complex one, in the unlimited speech flow can be repeated an unlimited number of times in completely identical form. But as an utterance (or part of an utterance) no one sentence, even if it has only one word, can ever be repeated: it is always a new utterance (even if it is a quotation).

The question arises as to whether science can deal with such absolutely unrepeatable individualities as utterances, or whether they extend beyond the bounds of generalizing scientific cognition. And the answer is, of course, it *can*. In the first place, every science begins with unrepeatable single phenomena, and science continues to be linked with them throughout. In the second place, science, and above all philosophy, can and should study the specific form and function of this individuality. The need to be clearly aware of a constant corrective to the claim that abstract analysis (linguistics, for example) has completely exhausted the concrete utterance. The study of kinds and forms of dialogic relations among utterances and their typological forms (factors of utterances). The study of extralinguistic and at the same time extrasemantic (artistic, scientific, and so forth) aspects of the utterance. The entire sphere that falls between linguistic and purely semantic analysis. This sphere has disappeared for science.

A sentence can be repeated within the bounds of one and the same utterance (nonarbitrary repetition, self-quotation), but each repetition makes it a new part of the utterance, for its position and function in the entire utterance have changed.

The utterance as a whole is shaped as such by extralinguistic (dialogic) aspects, and it is also related to other utterances. These extralinguistic (dialogic) aspects also pervade the utterance from within.

The speaker's generalized expressions in *language* (personal names, personal forms of verbs, grammatical and lexical forms of expression of modality, and expressions of the speaker's attitude toward his speech) and the speech subject. The author of the utterance.

From the standpoint of the extralinguistic purposes of the utterance, everything linguistic is only a means to an end.

The problem of the author and the forms in which he is expressed in a work. To what degree can one speak about the author's "image"?

We find the author (perceive, understand, sense, and feel him) in any work of art. For example, in a painting we always feel its author (artist), but we never *see* him in the way that we see the images he has depicted. We feel him in everything as a pure depicting origin (depicting subject), but not as a depicted (visible) image. Even in a self-portrait, of course, we do not see its depicting author, but only the artist's depiction. Strictly speaking, the author's image is *contradictio in adjecto*. The so-called author's image is, to be sure, a special type of image, distinct from other images in the work, but it is an *image* and has its own author who created it. The image of the narrator in a story is distinct from the *I*, the image of the hero of an autobiographical work (autobiography, confessions, diaries, memoirs, and so forth), the autobiographical hero, the lyrical hero, and so forth. They are all measured and defined by their relationship to the author as person (as to a special subject of depiction), but they are all depicted images that have their authors, the vehicles of the purely depictive origin. One can speak of a *pure* author as distinct from a partially depicted, designated author who enters as part of the work.

The problem of the author of the most ordinary, standard, everyday utterance. We can create an image of any speaker, we can objectively perceive any work or any speech, but this objective image does not enter into the intent or project of the speaker himself and is not created by him as the author of the utterance.

This does not mean that there are no paths from the pure author to the author as person—they exist, of course, and they exist in the very core, the very depths of man. But this core can never become one of the images of the work itself. The image is in the work as a whole, and to the highest degree, but this core can never become a constituent figural (objective) part of the work. This is not *natura creata* (created nature) or *natura naturata et creans* (nature engendered and creating), but pure *natura creans et non creata* (nature creating and not created).[8]

To what degree are pure, objectless, single-voiced words possible in literature? Is it possible for a word in which the author does not hear another's voice, which includes *only* the author and *all* of the author, to become material for the construction of a literary work? Is not some measure of nonliteralness a necessary condition for any style? Does the author not always stand *outside* the language as material for the work of art? Is not any writer (even the pure lyricist) always a "dramaturge" in the sense that he directs all words to others' voices, including to the image of the author (and to other authorial masks)? Perhaps any literal, single-voiced word is naive and unsuitable for authentic creativity. Any truly creative voice can only be the *second* voice in the discourse. Only the second voice—*pure relationship*—can be completely objectless and not cast a figural, substantive shadow. The writer is a person who is able to work in a language while standing outside language, who has the gift of indirect speaking.

To express oneself means to make oneself an object for another and for oneself ("the actualizing of consciousness"). This is the first step in objectification. But it is also possible to reflect our attitude toward ourselves as objects (second stage of objectification). In this case, our own discourse becomes an object and acquires a second—its own—voice. But this second voice no longer casts (from itself) a shadow, for it expresses pure relationship and all the objectifying, materializing flesh of the word is imparted to the first voice.

We express our relation to the person who would speak in this way. In daily speech this is expressed in slightly humorous or ironic intonation (Leo Tolstoy's Karenin),[9] intonation that expresses surprise, incomprehension, inquiry, doubt, affirmation, refutation, indignation, admiration, and so forth. This is the fairly primitive and very ordinary phenomenon of double-voicedness in daily conversational speech communication, in dialogues and debates on scientific and other ideological subjects. This is a fairly crude and less generalizing double-voicedness that is frequently directly personal: the words of one of the speakers in attendance are repeated with exaggerated accents. Varieties of parodic stylization represent the same crude and less generalizing form. The other's voice is limited, passive, and there is no depth or productivity (creative, enriching) to the interrelations between the voices. In literature—positive and negative characters.

Literal and, one might say, physical double-voicedness is manifest in all of these forms.

The situation is more complex when it comes to the author's voice in drama, where it, to all appearances, is not in the discourse.

To see and comprehend the author of a work means to see and comprehend another, alien consciousness and its world, that is, another subject ("Du"). With *explanation* there is only one consciousness, one subject; with *comprehension* there are two consciousnesses and two subjects. There can be no dialogic relationship with an object, and therefore explanation has no dialogic aspects (except formal, rhetorical ones). Understanding is always dialogic to some degree.

The various types and forms of comprehension. The comprehension of the language of signs, that is, the comprehension (mastery) of a particular sign system (for example, a particular language). The comprehension of a work in an already known, that is, already understood, language. The absence, in practice, of sharp distinctions and transitions from one kind of comprehension to another.

Can one say that the comprehension of a language as a system is objectless and completely devoid of dialogic aspects? To what extent can one speak of the subject of a language as a system? Deciphering an unknown language: substituting possible undetermined speakers, constructing possible utterances in a given language.

Understanding any work in a familiar language (if only our native language) always enriches our understanding of the given language as a system as well.

From the subject of a language to the subjects of literary works. Various transitional stages. The subjects of language styles (of the bureaucrat, the merchant, the scholar, and so forth). The author's masks (the author's images) and the author himself.

The socio-stylistic image of the poor clerk, of the titular counselor (Devushkin, for example).[10] Such an image, although it is produced by methods of self-revelation, is produced as *he* (third person) and not as *thou*. He is objectified and paradigmatic. There are no truly dialogic relations with him.

Bringing the means of depiction close to the subject of depiction as a sign of realism (self-description, voices, social styles; not depiction, but quotation of the heroes as speaking people).

The objective and purely functional elements of any style.

The problem of understanding the utterance. In order to understand, it is first of all necessary to establish the principal and clear-cut boundaries of the utterance. The alternation of speech subjects. The ability to determine the response. The essential responsiveness of any understanding ("Kannitverstan").[11]

When there is a deliberate (conscious) multiplicity of styles, there are always dialogic relations among the styles.[12] One cannot understand these interrelations purely linguistically (or even mechanically).

A purely linguistic (and purely discrete) description and definition of various styles within a single work cannot reveal their semantic (including artistic) interrelations. It is important to understand the total sense of this dialogue of styles from the author's standpoint (not as an image, but as a function). And when one speaks about bringing the means of depiction close to the depicted thing, one understands the depicted thing to be the object and not another subject (*thou*).

The depiction of a thing and the depiction of a person (the speaker in his essence). Realism frequently reifies man, but this is not an approach to him. Naturalism, with its tendency toward a causal explanation of man's acts and thoughts (his semantic position in the world) reifies man even more. The "inductive" approach, which is assumed to be inherent in realism, is, in essence, a reifying causal explanation of man. The voices (in the sense of reified social styles) are thus simply transformed into signs of things (or symptoms of processes); it is no longer possible to respond to them, one can no longer polemicize with them, and dialogic relations with such voices fade away.

The degrees of objectification and subjectification of depicted people (the dialogic nature of the author's relations to them) vary drastically in literature. In this respect, the image of Devushkin differs in principle from other writers' objectified images of poor clerks. And he is polemically pitted against these other images, in which there is no truly dialogic *thou*. Novels usually present completely final arguments summarized from the author's standpoint (if there are arguments at all). Dostoevsky's work contains transcriptions of incomplete and uncompletable arguments. But any novel is generally filled with dialogic overtones (not always with its heroes, of course). After Dostoevsky, polyphony bursts powerfully into all world literature.

With respect to a person, love, hatred, pity, tenderness, and emotions in general are always dialogic in some measure.

In his dialogic treatment (as regards the subjectification of his heroes), Dostoevsky crosses a certain boundary and his dialogic treatment acquires a new (higher) quality.

The objectification of man's image is not pure substantiality. He can be loved, pitied, and so forth, but the main thing is that he can (and should) be understood. In artistic literature (as generally in art) the sheen of subjectification lies even on inanimate things (correlated with man).

Speech understood in an object-oriented way (and such speech necessarily requires understanding—otherwise it would not be speech—but in this understanding the dialogic aspect is weakened) can be included in a chain of causal explanation. Literal speech (purely semantic, functional) remains in an open-ended referential dialogue (e.g., scientific research).

A juxtaposition with utterance-demonstrations in physics.

The text as a subjective reflection of the objective world; the text is an expression of consciousness, something that reflects. When the text becomes the object of our cognition, we can speak about the reflection of a reflection. The understanding of the text is a correct reflection of a reflection. Through another's reflection to the reflected object.

No natural phenomenon has "meaning," only signs (including words) have meaning. Therefore, any study of signs, regardless of the direction in which it may subsequently proceed, necessarily begins with understanding.

The text is the primary given (reality) and the point of departure for any discipline in the human sciences. It is the aggregate of various kinds of knowledge and methods called philology, linguistics, literary scholarship, scientific scholarship, and so forth. Proceeding from the text, they wander in various directions, grasp various bits of nature, social life, states of mind, and history, and combine them—sometimes with causal, sometimes with semantic, ties—and intermix statements with evaluations. From indications of the real object one must proceed to a clear-cut delineation of the objects of scientific research. The real object is social (public) man, who speaks and expresses himself through other means. Is it possible to find any other approach to him and his life (work, struggle, and so forth) than through the signifying text that he has created or is creating? Is it possible to observe and study him as a phenomenon of nature, as a thing? Man's physical action should be understood as a deed, but it is impossible to understand the deed outside its potential (that is, re-created by us) signifying expression (motives, goals, stimuli, degree of awareness, and so forth). It is as though we are causing man to speak (we construct his important testimonies, explanations, confessions, admissions, and we complete the development of possible or actual inner speech, and so forth). Everywhere the actual or possible text and its understanding. Research becomes inquiry and conversation, that is, dialogue. We do not address inquiries to nature and she does not answer us. We put questions to ourselves and we organize observation or experiment in such a way as to obtain an answer. When studying man, we search for and find signs everywhere and we try to grasp their meaning.

We are interested primarily in concrete forms of texts and concrete conditions of the life of texts, their interrelations, and their interactions.

Dialogical relations among utterances that also pervade individual utterances from within fall into the realm of metalinguistics. They differ radically from all possible linguistic relations among elements, both in the language system and in the individual utterance.

The metalinguistic nature of the utterance (speech production).

The semantic ties within a single utterance (although potentially infinite, for example, in the system of science) are referentially logical (in the broad sense of the word), but the semantic ties among various utterances become dialogic (or, in any case, they acquire a dialogic coloring). The ideas are distributed among various voices. The exceptional importance of the voice, the personality.

Linguistic elements are neutral with respect to this division into utterances; they move freely without recognizing the boundaries of the utterance, without recognizing (without respecting) the sovereignty of voices.

But how are the firm boundaries of the utterance determined? By metalinguistic forces.

Extraliterary utterances and their boundaries (rejoinders, letters, diaries, inner speech, and so forth) transferred into a literary work (for example, into a novel). Here their total sense changes. The reverberations of other voices fall on them, and the voice of the author himself enters into them.

Two juxtaposed utterances belonging to different people who know nothing about one another if they only slightly converge on one and the same subject (idea), inevitably enter into dialogic relations with one another. They come into contact with one another on the territory of a common theme, a common idea.

Epigraphy. The problem of the genres of ancient inscriptions. The author and the addressee of the inscriptions. Compulsory patterns. Grave inscriptions ("Rejoice"). The deceased addressing the living passersby. Compulsory standardized forms for evocations, incantations, prayers, and so forth. Forms of eulogies and high praise. Forms of abuse and foul language (ritualistic). The problem of the relationship of the word to the thought and the word to the desire, to the will, to the demand. Ideas about the magicality of the word. The word as action. The entire about-face in the history of the word when it became expression and pure (actionless) information (the communicative function). The sense of one's own and another's in the word. Later, the origin of authorial consciousness.

The author of a literary work (a novel) creates a unified and whole speech work (an utterance). But he creates it from heterogeneous, as it were, alien, utterances. And even direct authorial speech is filled with recognized words of others. Indirect speaking, an attitude toward one's own language as one of the possible languages (and not the only possible and unconditional language).

Finalized, or "closed," individuals in painting (including portraiture). They present man exhaustively; he is already completely there and cannot become other. The faces of people who have already said everything, who have already died [or] may as well have died. The artist concentrates his attention on the finalizing, defining, closing features. We see all of him and expect nothing more (or different). He cannot be reborn, rejuvenated, or transformed—this is his finalizing (ultimate and final) stage.

The author's relation to what he depicts always enters into the image. The author's relationship is a constitutive aspect of the image. This relationship is extremely complex. It must not be reduced to a straightforward evaluation. Such straightforward evaluations destroy the artistic image. They are not to be found even in good satire (Gogol, Shchedrin). To see something for the first time, to realize something for the first time, already means to assume an attitude toward it: it exists neither within itself nor for itself, but for another (already two correlated consciousnesses). Understanding is a very important attitude (understanding is never a tautology or duplication, for it always involves two and a potential third). The condition of not being heard and not being understood (see Thomas Mann).[13] "I don't know" and "that's the way it was, but what difference did it make to me" are important attitudes. The destruction of direct evaluations that accrue to the object and the destruction of attitudes generally creates a new attitude. A special kind of emotional-evaluative attitudes. Their diversity and complexity.

The author cannot be separated from the images and characters, since he enters into these images as an indispensable part of them (images are dual and sometimes double-voiced). But the *image* of the author can be separated from the images of the characters. This image itself, however, is created by the author and is therefore also dual. It is frequently as though the images of characters had been replaced by living people.

The various semantic planes on which the speech of the characters and the authorial speech are located. The characters speak as participants in the depicted life, as it were, from private positions. Their viewpoints are limited in one way or another (they know less than the author does). The author is outside the world depicted (and, in a certain sense, created) by him. He interprets this entire world from higher and qualitatively different positions. Finally, all characters and their speech are objects of an authorial attitude (and authorial speech). But the planes of the characters' speech and that of the authorial speech can intersect, that is, dialogic relations are possible between them. In Dostoevsky, where the characters are ideologists, the author and such heroes (thinker-ideologists) end up on the same plane. The dialogic contexts and situations of the speeches of the characters differ essentially from those of the authorial speech. The speech of the characters participates in the depicted dialogues within the work and does not enter directly into the ideological dialogue of contemporaneity, that is, into the real speech communication in which the work as a whole participates and is communicated (they participate in it only as elements of this whole). Yet the author occupies a position precisely in this real dialogue and is defined by the real situation of the day. As distinct from the real author, the image of the author that is created lacks that direct participation in the real dialogue (he participates in it only through the entire work), but he can participate in the plot of the work and enter into depicted dialogue with the characters (the conversation between the "author" and Onegin). The speech of the depicting (real) author, if it exists, is speech of a fundamentally special type, which cannot exist on the same plane with the speech of the characters. This is precisely what determines the work's ultimate unity and its ultimate semantic instantiation, as it were, its ultimate word.

The images of the author and the images of the characters are determined, according to V. V. Vinogradov, by language-styles, and their differences reduce to differences in languages and styles, that is, to purely linguistic differences. Vinogradov does not reveal the *nonlinguistic interrelations* among them. But, after all, these images (language-styles) in a work do not lie next to one another as linguistic givens; they enter here into complex, dynamic semantic relations of a special type. This type of relations can be defined as dialogic relations. *Dialogic relations* have a specific nature: they can be reduced neither to the purely logical (even if dialectical) nor to the purely linguistic (compositional-syntactic). They are possible only between complete utterances of various speaking subjects (dialogue with oneself is secondary, and, in the majority of cases, already played through). We are not concerning ourselves here with the origin of the term "dialogue" (see Hirzel).[14]

Where there is no word and no language, there can be no dialogic relations; they cannot exist among objects or logical quantities (concepts, judgments, and so forth). Dialogic relations presuppose a language, but they do not reside within the system of a language. They are impossible among elements of a language. The specific nature of dialogic relations requires special study.

The narrow understanding of dialogue as one of the compositional forms of speech (dialogic and monologic speech). One can say that each rejoinder in and of itself is monologic (the absolutely minimal monologue) and each monologue is a rejoinder from a larger dialogue (the speech communication of a certain sphere). Monologue as speech that is addressed to no one and does not presuppose a response. Various possible degrees of monologicity.

Dialogic relations are relations (semantic) among any utterances in speech communication. Any two utterances, if juxtaposed on a semantic plane (not as things and not as linguistic examples), end up in a dialogic relationship. But this is a special form of unintentional dialogicity (for example, the selection of various utterances of various scholars or sages of various eras on a single question).

"Hunger, cold!"—one utterance of a single speaking subject. "Hunger!"—"Cold!"—two dialogically correlated utterances of two different subjects: here dialogic relations appear that did not exist in the former case. The same thing with two developed sentences (think of a cogent example).

When an utterance is used for purposes of linguistic analysis, its dialogic nature is ignored, it is regarded within the system of the language (as its actualization) and not in the larger dialogue of speech communication.

The immense and as yet unstudied diversity of speech genres: from the unpublished spheres of inner speech to artistic works and scientific treatises. The diversity of street genres (see Rabelais), intimate genres, and so forth. In various epochs, in various genres, the emerging of language goes on.

Language and the word are almost everything in human life. But one must not think that this all-embracing and multifaceted reality can be the subject of only one science, linguistics, or that it can be understood through linguistic methods alone. The subject of linguistics is only the material, only the means of speech communication, and not speech communication itself, not utterances in their essence and not the relationships among them (dialogic), not the forms of speech communication, and not speech genres.

Linguistics studies only the relationships among elements within the language system, not the relationships among utterances and not the relations of utterances to reality and to the speaker (author).

With respect to real utterances and real speakers, the system of a language is purely potential. And the meaning of a word, to the extent that it is studied purely linguistically (linguistic semasiology) is determined only with the help of other words of the same language (or another language) and by its relations to them; it acquires a relationship to a concept or an artistic image or to real life only in an utterance and through an utterance. Such is the word as the subject of linguistics (but not the real word as a concrete utterance or part of it, a part and not a means).

Begin with the problem of speech production as the initial reality of speech life. From the everyday rejoinder to the multivolume novel or scientific treatise. The interaction of speech works in various spheres of the speech process. The "literary process," the struggle of opinions in science, the ideological struggle, and so forth. Two speech works, utterances, juxtaposed to one another, enter into a special kind of semantic relationships that we call dialogic. Their special nature. The elements of language within the language system or within the "text" (in the strictly linguistic sense) cannot enter into dialogic relations. Can languages and dialects (territorial, social jargons), language (functional) styles (say, familiar daily speech and scientific language and so forth), enter into these relationships, that is, can they speak with one another and so forth? Only if a nonlinguistic approach is taken toward them, that is, if they are transformed into a "world view" (or some language or speech sense of the world), into a "viewpoint," into "social voices," and so forth.

The artist makes such a transformation when he creates typical or characteristic utterances of typical characters (even if they are not completely embodied and are not named); aesthetic linguistics (the Vossler school, and especially, apparently, Spitzer's latest work) makes such a transformation (on a somewhat different plane). With such transformations the language acquires a unique "author," a speaking subject, a collective bearer of speech (people, nation, occupation, social group, and so forth). Such a transformation always makes a *departure beyond the boundaries of linguistics* (in the strict or precise understanding of it). Are such transformations appropriate? Yes, they are appropriate, but only under strictly defined conditions (for example, in literature, where frequently, especially in the novel, one finds dialogues of "languages" and language-styles), and with a strict and clear methodological intent. Such transformations are not permissible when, on the one hand, one declares that the language as a linguistic system is extraideological (and also impersonal) or, on the other, when the socio-ideological characteristics of languages and styles are smuggled in (to some extent in the work of Viktor Vinogradov). This question is very complex and interesting (for example, to what degree can one speak about the subject of a language, or the speaking subject of a language style, or about the image of the scholar standing behind a scientific language, the image of a bureaucrat behind bureaucratic language, and so forth?).

The unique nature of dialogic relations. The problem of the inner dialogism. The seams of the boundaries between utterances. The problem of the double-voiced word. Understanding as dialogue. Here we are approaching the frontier of the philosophy of language and of thinking in the human sciences in general, virgin land. A new statement of the problem of authorship (the creating individual).

The *given* and the *created* in a speech utterance. An utterance is never just a reflection or an expression of something already existing outside it that is given and final. It always creates something that never existed before, something absolutely new and unrepeatable, and, moreover, it always has some relation to value (the true, the good, the beautiful, and so forth). But something created is always created out of something given (language, an observed phenomenon of reality, an experienced feeling, the speaking subject himself, something finalized in his world view, and so forth). What is given is completely transformed in what is created. An analysis of the simplest everyday dialogue ("What time is it?"—"Seven o'clock"). The more or less complex situation of the question. One must look at the clock. The answer can be true or false, it can be significant, and so forth. In which time zone? The same question asked in outer space, and so forth.

Words and forms as abbreviations or representatives of the utterance, world view, point of view, and so forth, actual or possible. The possibilities and perspectives embedded in the word; they are essentially infinite.

Dialogic boundaries intersect the entire field of living human thought. The monologism of thinking in the human sciences. The linguist is accustomed to perceiving everything in a single closed context (in the system of a language or in the linguistically understood text that is not dialogically correlated to another, responding text), and as a linguist, of course, he is correct. The dialogic nature of our thinking about works, theories, utterances—in general our thinking about people.

Why is quasi-direct speech accepted, while an understanding of it as a double-voiced word is not?[15]

It is much easier to study the *given* in what is created (for example, language, ready-made and general elements of world view, reflected phenomena of reality, and so forth) than to study what is *created*. Frequently the whole of scientific analysis amounts to a disclosure of everything that has been given, already at hand and ready-made before the work has existed (that which is found by the artist and not created by him). It is as if everything given is created anew in what is created, transformed in it. A reduction to that which was previously given and ready-made. An object is ready-made, the linguistic means for its depiction are ready-made, the artist himself is ready-made, and his world view is ready-made. And here with ready-made means, in light of a ready-made world view, the ready-made poet reflects a ready-made object. But in fact the object is created in the process of creativity, as are the poet himself, his world view, and his means of expression.

The word used in quotation marks, that is, felt and used as something alien, and the same word (or some other word) without quotation marks. The infinite gradations in the degree of foreignness (or assimilation) of words, their various distances from the speaker. Words are distributed on various planes and at various distances from the plane of the authorial word.

Not only quasi-direct speech but various forms of hidden, semihidden, and diffused speech of another, and so forth.[16] All this has remained unutilized.

When one begins to hear voices in languages, jargons, and styles, these cease to be potential means of expression and become actual, realized expression; the voice that has mastered them has entered into them. They are called upon to play their own unique and unrepeatable role in speech (creative) communication.

The mutual illumination of languages and styles. The relation toward the *thing* and the relation toward the *meaning* embodied in the work or in some other kind of sign material. The relation to the thing (in its pure thingness) cannot be dialogic (i.e., there can be no conversation, argument, agreement, and so forth). The relation to *meaning* is always dialogic. Even understanding itself is dialogic.

The *reification* of meaning so as to include it in a causal series.

The narrow understanding of dialogism as argument, polemics, or parody. These are the externally most obvious, but crude, forms of dialogism. Confidence in another's word, reverential reception (the authoritative word), apprenticeship, the search for and mandatory nature of deep meaning, *agreement,* its infinite gradations and shadings (but not its logical limitations and not purely referential reservations), the layering of meaning upon meaning, voice upon voice, strengthening through merging (but not identification), the combination of many voices (a corridor of voices) that augments understanding, departure beyond the limits of the understood, and so forth. These special relations can be reduced neither to the purely logical nor to the purely thematic. Here one encounters *integral* positions, integral personalities (the personality does not require extensive disclosure—it can be articulated in a single sound, revealed in a single word), precisely *voices.*

The word (or in general any sign) is interindividual. Everything that is said, expressed, is located outside the "soul" of the speaker and does not belong only to him. The word cannot be assigned to a single speaker. The author (speaker) has his own inalienable right to the word, but the listener also has his rights, and those whose voices are heard in the word before the author comes upon it also have their rights (after all, there are no words that belong to no one). The word is a drama in which three characters participate (it is not a duet, but a trio). It is performed outside the author, and it cannot be introjected into the author.

If we anticipate nothing from the word, if we know ahead of time everything that it can say, it departs from the dialogue and is reified.

Self-objectification (in the lyric, in the confession, and so forth) as self-alienation and, to a certain degree, a surmounting of the self. By objectifying myself (i.e., by placing myself outside) I gain the opportunity to have an authentically dialogic relation with myself.

Only an utterance has a *direct* relationship to reality and to the living, speaking person (subject). In language there are only potential possibilities (schemata) of these relations (pronominal, temporal, and modal forms, lexical means, and so forth). But an utterance is defined not only by its relation to the object and to the speaking subject-author (and its relation to the language as a system of potential possibilities, givens), but—for us most important of all—by its direct relation to other utterances within the limits of a given sphere of communication. It does not *actually* exist outside this relationship (only as a *text*). Only an utterance can be faithful (or unfaithful), sincere, true (false), beautiful, just, and so forth.

The understanding of a language and the understanding of an utterance (including *responsiveness* and, consequently, evaluation).

What interests us is not the psychological aspect of the relationship to others' utterances (and understanding), but its reflection in the structure of the utterance itself.[17]

To what extent can linguistic (pure) definitions of a language and its elements be used for artistic-stylistic analysis? They can serve only as initial terms for description. But the most important thing is not described by them and does not reside within them. For here what matters is not elements (units) of the language system that have become elements of the text, but aspects of the utterance.

The utterance as a *semantic* whole.

The relationship to others' utterances cannot be separated from the relationship to the object (for it is argued about, agreed upon, views converge within it), nor can it be separated from the relationship to the speaker himself. This is a living tripartite unity. But the third element is still not usually taken into account. And even when it has been taken into account (in an analysis of the literary process, the works of journalists, in polemics, in the struggle among scientific opinions), the special nature of relations toward other utterances as utterances, that is, toward semantic wholes, has remained undisclosed and unstudied (these relations have been understood abstractly, thematically and logically, or psychologically, or even mechanically and causally). The special dialogic nature of interrelations of semantic wholes, semantic positions, that is, utterances, has not been understood.

The experimenter constitutes part of the experimental system (in microphysics). One might say, likewise, that the person who participates in understanding constitutes part of the understood utterance, the text (more precisely, utterances and their dialogue enter the text as a new participant). The dialogic meeting of two consciousnesses in the human sciences. The framing of another's utterances with a dialogizing context. For even when we give a causal explanation of another's utterance, by that very gesture we refute it. The reification of others' utterances is a special way (a false way) of refuting them. If the utterance is understood as a mechanical reaction and dialogue as a chain of reactions (as it is in descriptive linguistics or by the behaviorists), then this understanding includes equally both true and false utterances, both works of genius and those lacking talent (the difference will be only in the mechanically understood effects, utility, and so forth). This point of view, which is relatively valid as is the linguistic point of view (even with all the differences between them), does not touch upon the essence of the utterance as a semantic whole, a semantic point of view, a semantic position, and so forth. Every utterance makes a claim to justice, sincerity, beauty, and truthfulness (a model utterance), and so forth. And these values of utterances are defined not by their relation to the language (as a purely linguistic system), but by various forms of relation to reality, to the speaking subject and to other (alien) utterances (particularly to those that evaluate them as sincere, beautiful, and so forth).

Linguistics deals with the text, but not with the work. What it says about the work is smuggled in, and does not follow from purely linguistic analysis. Of course, linguistics itself is usually from the very beginning conglomerate by nature, and saturated with nonlinguistic elements. To simplify the matter somewhat: purely linguistic relations (i.e., the object of linguistics) are relations of sign to sign and to signs at the limits of the language system or text (i.e., systemic or linear relations among signs). The relations of utterances to reality, to the real speaking subject, and to other real utterances—relations that first make the utterances true or false, beautiful, and so forth—can never be the subject of linguistics. Individual signs, the language system, or the text (as a signifying unity) can never be true, false, beautiful, and so forth.

Each large and creative verbal whole is a very complex and multifaceted system of relations. With a creative attitude toward language, there are no voiceless words that belong to no one. Each word contains voices that are sometimes infinitely distant, unnamed, almost impersonal (voices of lexical shadings, of styles, and so forth), almost undetectable, and voices resounding nearby and simultaneously.

Any live, competent, and dispassionate observation from any position, from any viewpoint, always retains its value and its meaning. The one-sided and limited nature of a viewpoint (the position of the observer) can always be corrected, augmented, transformed (transferred) with the help of like observations from others' viewpoints. Bare viewpoints (without living and new observations) are fruitless.

Pushkin's well-known aphorism about lexicon and books.[18]

On the problem of dialogic relations. These relations are profoundly unique and cannot be reduced to logical, linguistic, psychological, mechanical, or any other natural relations. They constitute a special type of *semantic* relations, whose members can be only *complete utterances* (either regarded as complete or potentially complete), behind which stand (and in which are *expressed*) real or potentially real speech subjects, authors of the given utterances. Real dialogue (daily conversation, scientific discussion, political debate, and so forth). The relations among rejoinders of such dialogues are a simpler and more externally visible kind of dialogic relations. But dialogic relations, of course, do not in any way coincide with relations among rejoinders of real dialogue—they are much broader, more diverse, and more complex. Two utterances, separated from one another both in time and in space, knowing nothing of one another, when they are compared semantically, reveal dialogic relations if there is any kind of semantic convergence between them (if only a partially shared theme, point of view, and so forth). Any survey of the history of any scientific question (independent, or included in a scientific work on a given question) also produces dialogic comparisons (utterances, opinions, viewpoints) of the utterances of scientists who did not and could not know anything of one another. Here the shared nature of the problem gives rise to dialogic relations. In artistic literature—"dialogues of the dead" (in Lucian, in the seventeenth century)—there is, in keeping with the specific features of the literature, an imagined situation of a meeting in the hereafter. The opposite example, which is widely used in comedy, is the situation of a dialogue between two deaf people, where the real dialogic contact is understood but where there is no kind of semantic contact between the rejoinders (nor any imaginable contact). Zero-degree dialogic relations. Here the viewpoint of a *third* person is revealed in the dialogue (one who does not participate in the dialogue, but *understands* it). The understanding of an entire utterance is always dialogic.

One cannot, on the other hand, understand dialogic relations simplistically and unilaterally, reducing them to contradiction, conflict, polemics, or disagreement. *Agreement* is very rich in varieties and shadings. Two utterances that are identical in all respects ("Beautiful weather!"—"Beautiful weather!"), if they are really *two* utterances belonging to *different* voices and not one, are linked by dialogic *relations of agreement.* This is a definite dialogic event in the interrelations of the two, and not an echo. For after all, agreement could also be lacking ("No, not very nice weather," and so forth).

Dialogic relations are thus much broader than dialogic speech in the narrow sense of the word. And dialogic relations are always present, even among profoundly monologic speech works.

There can be no dialogic relations among language units, regardless of how we understand them and regardless of the level of the language structure from which we take them (phonemes, morphemes, lexemes, sentences, and so forth). The utterance (as a speech whole) cannot be seen as a unit of the next, higher level or tier of the language structure (above syntax), for it enters into the world of completely different relations (dialogic) that cannot be compared with linguistic relations of other levels. (On a certain plane, only the juxtaposition of the whole utterance to the *word* is possible.) The whole utterance is no longer a unit of language (and not a unit of the "speech flow" or the "speech chain"), but a unit of speech communication that has not mere formal definition, but *contextual meaning* (that is, integrated meaning that relates to value—to truth, beauty, and so forth—and requires a *responsive* understanding, one that includes evaluation). The responsive understanding of a speech whole is always dialogic by nature.

The understanding of entire utterances and dialogic relations among them is always of a dialogic nature (including the understanding of researchers in the human sciences). The person who understands (including the researcher himself) becomes a participant in the dialogue, although on a special level (depending on the area of understanding or research). The analogy of including the experimenter in the experimental system (as a part of it) or the observer in the observed world in microphysics (quantum theory). The observer has no position *outside* the observed world, and his observation enters as a constituent part into the observed object.

This pertains fully to entire utterances and relations among them. They cannot be understood from outside. Understanding itself enters as a dialogic element in the dialogic system and somehow changes its total sense. The person who understands inevitably becomes a *third* party in the dialogue (of course, not in the literal, arithmetical sense, for there can be, in addition to a third, an unlimited number of participants in the dialogue being understood), but the dialogic position of this third party is a quite special one. Any utterance always has an addressee (of various sorts, with varying degrees of proximity, concreteness, awareness, and so forth), whose responsive understanding the author of the speech work seeks and surpasses. This is the second party (again not in the arithmetical sense). But in addition to this addressee (the second party), the author of the utterance, with a greater or lesser awareness, presupposes a higher *superaddressee* (third), whose absolutely just responsive understanding is presumed, either in some metaphysical distance or in distant historical time (the loophole addressee). In various ages and with various understandings of the world, this superaddressee and his ideally true responsive understanding assume various ideological expressions (God, absolute truth, the court of dispassionate human conscience, the people, the court of history, science, and so forth).

The author can never turn over his whole self and his speech work to the complete and *final* will of addressees who are on hand or nearby (after all, even the closest descendants can be mistaken), and always presupposes (with a greater or lesser degree of awareness) some higher instancing of responsive understanding that can distance itself in various directions. Each dialogue takes place as if against the background of the responsive understanding of an invisibly present third party who stands above all the participants in the dialogue (partners). (Cf. the understanding of the Fascist torture chamber or hell in Thomas Mann as absolute *lack of being heard*, as the absolute absence of a *third party*.)[19]

The aforementioned third party is not any mystical or metaphysical being (although, given a certain understanding of the world, he can be expressed as such)—he is a constitutive aspect of the whole utterance, who, under deeper analysis, can be revealed in it. This follows from the nature of the word, which always wants to be *heard,* always seeks responsive understanding, and does not stop at *immediate* understanding but presses on further and further (indefinitely).

For the word (and, consequently, for a human being) there is nothing more terrible than a *lack of response.* Even a word that is known to be false is not absolutely false, and always presupposes an instance that will understand and justify it, even if in the form: "anyone *in my position* would have lied, too."

Karl Marx said that only thought uttered in the word becomes a real thought for another person and only in the same way is it a thought for myself.[20] But this other is not only the immediate other (second addressee); the word moves ever forward in search of responsive understanding.

Being heard as such is already a dialogic relation. The word wants to be heard, understood, responded to, and again to respond to the response, and so forth *ad infinitum.* It enters into a dialogue that does not have a *semantic* end (but for one participant or another it can be physically broken off). This, of course, in no way weakens the purely thematic and investigatory intentions of the word, its concentration on its own object. Both aspects are two sides of one and the same coin; they are inseparably linked. They can be separated only in a word that is known to be false, that is, in one that wishes to deceive (the separation between the referential intention and the intention to be heard and understood).

The word that fears the third party and seeks only temporary recognition (responsive understanding of limited depth) from immediate addressees.

The criterion of *depth* of understanding as one of the highest criteria for cognition in the human sciences. The word, if it is not an acknowledged falsehood, is bottomless. To achieve this depth (and not height and breadth). The microworld of the word.

The utterance (speech work) as an unrepeatable, historically unique individual whole.

This does not exclude, of course, a compositional and stylistic typology of speech works. There exist *speech genres* (everyday, rhetorical, scientific, literary, and so forth). Speech genres are typical models for constructing a speech whole. But these generic models are distinct in principle from *linguistic* models of *sentences.*

Units of language that are studied by linguistics can in principle be reproduced an unlimited number of times in an unlimited number of utterances (including models of sentences that are reproduced). To be sure, the frequency of reproduction differs from various units (the greatest for the phoneme, the least for the phrase). They can be units of a language and perform their function only because of this reproducibility. Regardless of how the relations among these reproducible units are defined (opposition, juxtaposition, contrast, distribution, and so forth), these relations can never be *dialogic*. This would violate their linguistic (language) function.

Units of speech communication—whole utterances—cannot be reproduced (although they can be quoted) and they are related to one another dialogically.

Notes

1. A term in structural linguistics introduced by Louis Hjelmslev, founder of the Copenhagen or so-called Glossematic School. He defines commutation as "mutation between the members of a paradigm," a member being a component and a paradigm being a class within a semiotic system (*Prolegomena to a Theory of Language*, tr. Francis J. Whitfield [Madison: University of Wisconsin Press, 1961], pp. 134–35).

2. In *Anna Karenina*, part 4, chapter 4, Anna accuses Karenin of being cruel during the confrontation in which he announces his decision to divorce her. He responds that she is not aware of what he has suffered. But his tongue becomes twisted and he cannot pronounce the Russian word for "I have suffered" or "endured": *perestradal*. After several attempts he finally lets it suffice to say *pelestral* (which David Magarshack has translated as "shuffered" in the Signet Books edition).

3. A linguistic discipline created by the Russian linguist and member of the Prague Circle N. S. Trubetskoy. See his *Osnovy fonologii* (Fundamentals of phonology) (Prague, 1939; Moscow, 1960). Based on the Saussurean distinction between *langue* and *parole*, Trubetskoy also distinguishes between phonetics—a science of the sounds of speech as a material phenomenon that is studied by methods of natural science—and phonology, the study of the sound of language that performs certain semantic-differentiating functions in the language system.

4. "Science of the spirit" refers to what is known as the *Geisteswissenschaften* in German (i.e., the human sciences). One of the great preoccupations of the Neo-Kantian movement in German universities in the last decades of the nineteenth century was to overcome the growing disparity between the natural (or exact) sciences and the human sciences. The work of the whole Marburg School (Hermann

Cohen, Paul Natorp, Ernst Cassirer) is really a philosophy of science. The most easily assimilated ideas on the relation between the human and exact sciences are found in the work of the Freiburg School that included Wilhelm Windelband (whose 1894 distinction between the homeothetic and idiographic forms of knowledge proved seminal) and his pupil Heinrich Rickert (see his *Science and History*, ed. Arthur Goddard, tr. George Reisman [Princeton: Van Nostrand, 1962]). In "Author and Hero in Aesthetic Activity," Bakhtin distinguishes between spirit (*dukh*), the general compulsion to understand or the drive to meaning shared by all humans, and soul (*dusha*), the features of any particular person that serve to situate him or her in a particular place in existence not occupied by anyone else.

5. Here, and in his very early work, we see another interest Bakhtin shared with Vygotsky: the phenomenology of acting (see "Author and Hero," in *Estetika slovesnogo tvorchestva*, pp. 63–75). Compare Bakhtin's notes with L. S. Vygotsky, "K voprosu o psikhologii tvorchestva aktera" (Concerning the question of psychology in the creative work of actors), in P. M. Jakobson, *Psikhologija stesnicheskikh chustv aktera* (The psychology of actors' feelings on stage) (Moscow: Gosizdat, 1936).

6. See note 1 in this section, above. Glossematics was Hjelmslev's attempt to create a general linguistic theory that would be maximally abstracted from the material of concrete languages: ". . . linguistic theory must be of use for describing and predicting not only any possible text composed in a certain language, but, on the basis of the information that it gives about language in general, any possible text composed in any language whatsoever" (see *Prolegomena to a Theory of Language*, p. 17).

7. See note 3 in "The Problem of Speech Genres." On "verbal reactions" and behaviorism, see also Bakhtin's remarks in V. N. Voloshinov, *Freudianism*, tr. I. R. Titunik (New York: Academic Press, 1976), p. 21, where the relation of verbal reaction to inner speech in Vygotsky is discussed.

8. See note 2 in "From Notes Made in 1970–71."

9. Reference here is to *Anna Karenina*, part 1, chapter 30. " 'Yes, as you see, an affectionate husband, as affectionate as in the first year of marriage, burning with impatience to see you,' he said in his thin voice and that tone which he almost always used with her, a tone of mockery of someone who would actually speak that way."

10. Makar Devushkin is the hero of Dostoevsky's short novel *Poor Folk* (1845).

11. An example from Vasily Zhukovsky's "Two Stories and One More" (1831), the third of which is a poetic rendering of a story by Johann Hebel about a German craftsman who finds himself in Amsterdam without knowing any Dutch; to all his questions he receives the same answer: "Kannitverstan" (I don't understand you). The craftsman assumes after a while that this is a proper name, giving rise in his consciousness to the fantastic figure of Kannitverstan. Vygotsky also uses the example of Kannitverstan in an article Bakhtin quotes in his Freud book: "Consciousness as a Problem in the Psychology of Behavior," in *Psikhologija i Marksizm*, ed. K. Kornilov (Moscow-Leningrad: GIZ, 1925), pp. 179–80.

12. Bakhtin investigated the dialogue of styles in works that deliberately include many styles, using as his example Pushkin's *Eugene Onegin* (see "Discourse in the Novel," in *The Dialogic Imagination*). In "From Notes Made in 1970–71,"

Bakhtin points to major differences in his approach to *Eugene Onegin* from that taken by Yury Lotman in his studies of the same work.

13. See note 19, below.

14. Rudolph Hirzel (1846–1917), a German philologist who wrote *Der Dialog: Ein literarhistorischer Versuch*, 2 vols. (Leipzig, 1895). Also of importance for understanding the *distinctiveness* of Bakhtin's dialogism among other approaches are Gustav Tarde, *L'Opinion et la foule* (Paris, 1901); L. V. Shcherba, "On Dialogic Speech," *Russkija rech* (Petrograd, 1923), vol. 1, pp. 96–194; and Jan Mukarovsky, "Two Studies of Dialogue," in *The Word and Verbal Art*, tr. John Burbank and Peter Steiner (New Haven: Yale University Press, 1977), pp. 81–115.

15. Between the two traditional grammatical categories of *direct speech* (*prjamaja rech*) and *indirect speech* (*kosvennaja rech*), Bakhtin posits an intermediate term, quasi-direct speech (*nesobstvenno-prjamaja rech*). This category is given detailed treatment in chapter 4 of Voloshinov, *Marxism and the Philosophy of Language*, tr. Ladislav Matejka and I. R. Titunik (New York: Academic Press, 1973), pp. 141–59. Quasi-direct speech involves discourse that is formally authorial, but that belongs in its "emotional structure" to a represented character, whose inner speech is transmitted and regulated by the author.

16. The various forms of communicating others' speech in the structures of the Russian language—anticipatory, absentminded, concealed, reified, and substituted direct speech, and, finally, quasi-direct speech (to which a separate, large chapter is devoted)—are described in *Marxism and the Philosophy of Language*.

17. From the outset of his career, Bakhtin was deeply concerned about the dangers of psychologism. The most powerful and subtle of his attacks on psychologism is found in those sections of "Author and Hero in Aesthetic Activity" where he criticizes the so-called Expressionist School of aesthetics, in particular the work of Johann Volkelt (1848–1930) and Theodor Lipps (1851–1914) (see *Estetika slovesnogo tvorchestva*, pp. 58–81).

18. From Pushkin's article "On Man's Duties, an Essay for Silvio Pellico" (1836): ". . . reason is inexhaustible in the *consideration* of concepts, as language is inexhaustible in the *joining* of words. All words are in the lexicon; but the books that are constantly appearing are not a repetition of the lexicon. . . . Taken separately, an *idea* can never offer anything new, but *ideas* can be varied to infinity" (*The Critical Prose of Alexander Pushkin*, tr. Carl Proffer [Bloomington: Indiana University Press, 1969], p. 205).

19. In Mann's *Dr. Faustus*, the devil describes hell as "every compassion, every grace, every sparing, every trace of consideration for the incredulous, imploring objection 'that you verily cannot do so to a soul': it is done, it happens, and indeed without being called to any reckoning in words; in the soundless cellar, far down beneath God's hearing, and happens for all eternity" (*Dr. Faustus*, tr. H. T. Lowe-Porter [London: Penguin Books, 1968], p. 238). The Gestapo and SS torture chambers were very much on Mann's mind as he was writing his novel, for at just that time the most dreadful extermination camps were being liberated and for the first time the full extent of the Nazi horrors was made apparent to all. Mann wrote a special article at this time (first published as "The German Guilt," later as "The Camps") for the newspaper distributed to the Germans in zones occupied by

American troops (see *The Story of a Novel: The Genesis of 'Doktor Faustus,'* tr. Richard and Clara Winston [New York: Knopf, 1961], p. 115).

20. See Karl Marx and Friedrich Engels, *The German Ideology* (Moscow: Progress Publishers, 1964, p. 42): "The production of notions, ideas and consciousness is from the beginning directly interwoven with the material activity and material intercourse of human beings, the language of real life. The production of men's ideas, thinking, their spiritual intercourse, here appears as the direct efflux of their material condition."

From Notes Made in 1970–71

Irony has penetrated all languages of modern times (especially French); it has penetrated into all words and forms (especially syntactic; for example, irony has destroyed the cumbersome "high-flown" periodicity of speech). Irony is everywhere—from the minimal and imperceptible, to the loud, which borders on laughter. Modern man does not proclaim; he speaks. That is, he speaks with reservations. Proclamatory genres have been retained mainly as parodic and semiparodic building blocks for the novel. Pushkin's language is precisely this kind, permeated with irony (to varying degrees), the equivocal language of modern times.

The speaking subjects of high, proclamatory genres—of priests, prophets, preachers, judges, leaders, patriarchal fathers, and so forth—have departed this life. They have all been replaced by the writer, simply the writer, who has fallen heir to their styles. He either stylizes them (i.e., assumes the guise of a prophet, a preacher, and so forth) or parodies them (to one degree or another). He must develop his own style, the style of the writer. For the singer at ancient feasts, the rhapsode, and the tragedian (Dionysian priest), even for the court poet of more recent times, the problem did not yet exist. For them the settings were predetermined: various kinds of festivals, cult rituals, and feasts. Even prenovelistic discourse had a particular setting—festivals of the carnival type. But the writer is deprived of style and setting. Literature has been completely secularized. The novel, deprived of style and setting, is essentially not a genre; it must imitate (rehearse) some extraartistic genre: the everyday story, letters, diaries, and so forth.

A particular nuance of sobriety, simplicity, democratism, and individual freedom inheres in all modern languages. One can say, with certain reservations, that all of them (especially French) have arisen from the popular and profane genres. All of them have been determined to a certain degree by a lengthy and complex process of expunging the other's sacred word, and expunging the sacred and authoritarian word in general, with its indisputability, unconditionality, and unequivocality. Because of its sacrosanct, impenetrable boundaries, this word is inert, and it has limited possibilities of contacts and combinations. This is the word that retards and freezes thought. The word that demands reverent repetition and not further development, corrections, and additions. The word removed from dialogue: it can only be cited amid rejoinders; it cannot itself become a rejoinder among equally privileged rejoinders. This word had spread everywhere, limiting, directing, and retarding both thought and live experience of life. It was during the process of struggling with this word and expelling it (with the help of parodic antibodies) that new languages were also formed. The boundary lines of the other's word. Vestiges in the syntactical structure.

The nature of the sacred (authoritarian) word; the peculiarities of its behavior in the context of speech communication and also in the context of folklore (oral) and literary genres (its inertness, its withdrawal from dialogue, its extremely limited ability to combine in general and especially with profane—not sacred—words, and so forth). These peculiarities, of course, do nothing to define it linguistically. They are metalinguistic. The area of metalinguistics also includes various kinds and degrees of *otherness* of the other's word and various forms of relations to it (stylization, parody, polemics, and so forth) as well as various methods of expunging it from speech life. But all these phenomena and processes, particularly the centuries-long process of expunging the other's sacred word, are also reflected (precipitated) in the linguistic aspect of the language, particularly in the syntactic and lexico-semantic structure of modern languages. Stylistics must be oriented toward a metalinguistic study of large events (events that take many centuries to accomplish) in the speech life of the people. The types of words that embody changes in various cultures and ages (i.e., names, sobriquets, and so forth).

Quietude and sound. The perception of sound (against the background of quietude). *Quietude* and *silence* (the absence of the word). The pause and the beginning of the word. The disturbance of quietude by sound is mechanical and physiological (as a condition of perception); the disturbance of silence by the word is personalistic and intelligible: it is an entirely different world. In quietude nothing makes a sound (or something does not make a sound); in silence nobody *speaks* (or somebody does not speak). Silence is possible only in the human world (and only for a person). Of course, both quietude and silence are always relative.

The conditions for perceiving a sound, the conditions for understanding/recognizing a sign, the conditions for intelligent understanding of the word.

Silence—intelligible sound (a word)—and the pause constitute a special logosphere, a unified and continuous structure, an open (unfinalized) totality.

Understanding-recognition of repeated elements of speech (i.e., language) and intelligent understanding of the unrepeatable utterance. Each element of speech is perceived on two planes: on the plane of the repeatability of the language and on the plane of the unrepeatability of the utterance. Through the utterance, language joins the historical unrepeatability and unfinalized totality of the logosphere.

The word as a means (language) and the word as intelligibility. The intelligizing word belongs to the domain of goals. The word as the final (highest) goal.

The chronotopicity of artistic thinking (especially ancient thinking). A point of view is chronotopic, that is, it includes both the spatial and temporal aspects. Directly related to this is the valorized (hierarchical) viewpoint (relationship to high and low). The chronotope of the depicted event, the chronotope of the narrator and the chronotope of the author (the ultimate authorial instance). Ideal and real space in the fine arts. Easel painting is located outside structured (hierarchically structured) space; it is suspended in air.

The inadmissibility of mono-tony (of serious monotony). The culture of multi-tony. The sphere of serious tone. Irony as a form of silence. Irony (and laughter) as means for transcending a situation, rising above it. Only dogmatic and authoritarian cultures are one-sidedly serious. Violence does not know laughter. Analysis of a serious face (fear or threat). Analysis of a laughing face. The place of pathos. The pathetic element transformed into the maudlin. The sense of anonymous threat in the tone of an announcer who is transmitting important communications. Seriousness burdens us with hopeless situations, but laughter lifts us above them and delivers us from them. Laughter does not encumber man, it liberates him.

The social, choral nature of laughter, its striving to pervade all peoples and the entire world. The doors of laughter are open to one and all. Indignation, anger, and dissatisfaction are always unilateral: they exclude the one toward whom they are directed, and so forth; they evoke reciprocal anger. They divide, while laughter only unites; it cannot divide. Laughter can be combined with profoundly intimate emotionality (Sterne, Jean Paul, and others). Laughter and festivity. The culture of the weekday. Laughter and the kingdom of ends (means are always serious). Everything that is truly great must include an element of laughter. Otherwise it becomes threatening, terrible, or pompous; in any case, it is limited. Laughter lifts the barrier and clears the path.

The joyful, open, festive laugh. The closed, purely negative, satirical laugh. This is not a laughing laugh. The Gogolian laugh is joyful. Laughter and freedom. Laughter and equality. Laughter makes things close and familiar. It is impossible to implant laughter or festivities. A festival is always primordial or anarchic.

Serious tones also sound different in a multitonal culture: resonances of laughing tones fall on them, they lose their exclusivity and uniqueness, they are supplemented by the element of laughter.

The study of culture (or some area of it) at the level of system and at the higher level of organic unity: open, becoming, unresolved and unpredetermined, capable of death and renewal, transcending itself, that is, exceeding its own boundaries. An understanding of the multistyled nature of *Eugene Onegin* (see Lotman) as a recoding (romanticism into realism and so forth) leads to a falling away of that most important *dialogic* aspect and to the transformation of a dialogue of styles into a simple coexistence of various versions of one and the same style.[1] Behind styles lies the integral viewpoint of the integral individual personality. A code presupposes content to be somehow ready-made and presupposes the realization of a choice among various *given* codes.

The utterance (speech product) as a whole enters into an entirely new sphere of speech communication (as a unit of this new sphere), which does not admit of description or definition in the terms and methods of linguistics or—more broadly—semiotics. This sphere is governed by a special law, and its study requires a special methodology and, it should be said outright, a special science (scientific discipline). The utterance as a whole does not admit of definition in terms of linguistics (or semiotics). The term "text" is not at all adequate to the essence of the entire utterance.

There can be no such thing as an isolated utterance. It always presupposes utterances that precede and follow it. No one utterance can be either the first or the last. Each is only a link in the chain, and none can be studied outside this chain. Among utterances there exist relations that cannot be defined in either mechanistic or linguistic categories. They have no analogues.

Abstraction from extratextual aspects, but not from other texts that are related to the given one in the chain of speech communication. Their internal social nature. The meeting of two consciousnesses in the process of understanding and studying the utterance. The personal nature of relations among utterances. The definition of the utterance and its boundaries.

The second consciousness and metalanguage. Metalanguage is not simply a code; it always has a dialogic relationship to the language it describes and analyzes. The positions of the experimenter and the observer in quantum theory. The existence of this active position changes the entire situation and, consequently, the results of the experiment. The event that has an observer, however distant, closed, and passive he may be, is already a different event (see Zosima's "mysterious visitor").[2] The problem of the second consciousness in the human sciences. Questions (questionnaires) that change the consciousness of the individual being questioned.

The inexhaustibility of the second consciousness, that is, consciousness of the person who understands and responds: herein lies a potential infinity of responses, languages, codes. Infinity against infinity.

Benevolent demarcation and only then cooperation. Instead of a disclosure (positive) of the relative (partial) truth of their positions and their viewpoints, they strive—and on this they expend all their efforts—for absolute refutation and destruction of their opponent, for total destruction of the other viewpoint.

Not a single scientific trend (that has not been the work of charlatans) has [illegible] totally, and not one scientific trend has remained in its initial and immutable form. There has not been a single scientific age when only one trend existed (but there has almost always been one dominant trend). This is not a question of mere eclecticism: the merging of all trends into one and only one would be fatal to science (if science were mortal). The more demarcation the better, but benevolent demarcation. Without border disputes. Cooperation. The existence of border zones (new trends and disciplines usually originate in them).

The witness and the judge. When consciousness appeared in the world (in existence) and, perhaps, when biological life appeared (perhaps not only animals, but trees and grass also witness and judge), the world (existence) changed radically. A stone is still stony and the sun still sunny, but the event of existence as a whole (unfinalized) becomes completely different because a new and major character in this event appears for the first time on the scene of earthly existence—the witness and the judge. And the sun, while remaining physically the same, has changed because it has begun to be cognized by the witness and the judge. It has stopped simply being and has started being in itself and for itself (these categories appear for the first time here) as well as for the other, because it has been reflected in the consciousness of the other (the witness and the judge): this has caused it to change radically, to be enriched and transformed. (This has nothing to do with "other existence.")

This cannot be understood as existence (nature) beginning to be conscious of itself in man, beginning to reflect itself. If this were the case, existence would remain the same, it would only begin to replicate itself (it would remain *solitary*, as the world was before the appearance of consciousness—before the witness and the judge). No, something absolutely new has appeared, a *supra-existence* has emerged.[3] And there is no longer just a kernel of existence in this supra-existence; all existence exists in it and for it.

This is analogous to the problem of man's self-awareness. Does the cognizer coincide with the cognized? In other words, does man remain only with himself, that is, remain solitary? Do not all events of human existence here change radically? Such is indeed the case. Something absolutely new appears here: the supraperson, the *supra-I*, that is, the witness and the judge *of the whole* human being, of the whole *I*, and consequently someone who is no longer the person, no longer the *I*, but the *other*. The reflection of the self in the empirical other through whom one must pass in order to reach *I-for-myself* (can this *I-for-myself* be solitary?). The absolute freedom of this *I*. But this freedom cannot change existence, so to speak, materially (nor can it want to)—it can change only the *sense* of existence (to recognize it, to justify it, and so forth); this is the freedom of the witness and the judge. It is expressed in the *word*. Authenticity and truth inhere not in existence itself, but only in an existence that is acknowledged and uttered.

The problem of relative freedom, that is, that freedom which remains in existence and changes the makeup of existence, but not its sense. This freedom changes material existence and can become a force that is detached from sense, a vulgar and naked material force. Creativity is always related to a change of sense and cannot become naked material force.

Let the witness see and know only an insignificant corner of existence, and all existence that is not cognized and not seen by him changes its quality (sense), becoming uncognized, unseen existence, and not simply existence as it was before, that is, without any relationship to the witness.

Everything that pertains to me enters my consciousness, beginning with my name, from the external world through the mouths of others (my mother, and so forth), with their intonation, in their emotional and value-assigning tonality. I realize myself initially through others: from them I receive words, forms, and tonalities for the formation of my initial idea of myself. The elements of infantilism in self-awareness ("Could mama really love such a . . .")[4] sometimes remain until the end of life (perception and the idea of one's self, one's body, face, and past in tender tones). Just as the body is formed initially in the mother's womb (body), a person's consciousness awakens wrapped in another's consciousness. Only later does one begin to be subsumed by neutral words and categories, that is, one is defined as a person irrespective of *I* and *other*.

Three types of relations:

1. Relations among objects, among things, among physical phenomena, among chemical phenomena, causal relations, mathematical relations, logical relations, linguistic relations, and so forth.
2. Relations between subject and object.
3. Relations among subjects—individual, personal relations: dialogic relations among utterances, ethical relations, and so forth. This also includes all kinds of personified semantic ties. Relations among consciousnesses, truths, mutual influences, apprenticeship, love, hate, falsehood, friendship, respect, reverence, trust, mistrust, and so forth.

But if the relations are de-personified (among utterances and styles, with the linguistic approach, and so forth), they change into the first type. On the other hand, it is possible to personify many objectlike relations and transform them into the third type. Reification and personification.

The determination of the subject (of personality) in intersubjective relations: concreteness (name), integrity, answerability, and so forth; inexhaustibility, open-endedness, openness.

Transitions and combinations among the three types of relations. For example, a literary scholar disputes (polemicizes) with the author or the protagonist and at the same time explains him as being completely causally determined (socially, psychologically, and biologically). Both viewpoints are justified, but within certain methodologically recognized limits and without combining them. One cannot forbid a physician to work on cadavers on the grounds that his duty is to treat not dead but living people. Death-dealing analysis is quite justified within certain limits. The better a person understands the degree to which he is externally determined (his substantiality), the closer he comes to understanding and exercising his real freedom.

Pechorin, for all his complex and contradictory nature, seems unified and naive compared to Stavrogin.[5] He had not tasted of the Tree of Knowledge. Before Dostoevsky, no heroes in Russian literature had tasted of the tree of knowledge of good and evil. Therefore, the novel could still contain naive and integral poetry, lyric and poetic landscape. They (the heroes before Dostoevsky) still had access to bits (corners) of earthly paradise from which Dostoevsky's heroes were cast out once and for all.

The narrow historical horizons of our literary scholarship. Enclosure within the most immediate historical epoch. The lack of definition (methodological) of the very category of the epoch. We explain a phenomenon in terms of its own present and the recent past (within the limits of the "epoch"). What we foreground is the *ready-made* and *finalized.* Even in antiquity we single out what is ready-made and finalized, and not what has originated and is developing. We do not study literature's preliterary embryos (in language and ritual). The narrow ("specialists'") understanding of specifics. Possibility and necessity. It is hardly possible to speak about necessity in the human sciences. Here it is scientifically possible only to disclose *possibilities* and the *realization* of one of them. The repeatable and unrepeatability.

Vernadsky on the slow historical formation of basic categories (not only scientific but also artistic).[6] Literature, at its historical stage, came upon what was ready-made: languages were ready-made, the main modes of seeing and thinking were ready-made. They also continued to develop, but slowly (their development cannot be traced within an epoch). The link between literary scholarship and history of culture (culture not as a sum of phenomena, but as a totality). Herein lies Veselovsky's strength (semiotics).[7] Literature is an inseparable part of the totality of culture and cannot be studied outside the total cultural context. It cannot be severed from the rest of culture and related directly (bypassing culture) to socioeconomic or other factors. These factors influence culture as a whole and only through it and in conjunction with it do they affect literature. The literary process is a part of the cultural process and cannot be torn away from it.

Science (and cultural consciousness) of the nineteenth century singled out only a miniature world (and we have narrowed it even more) from the boundless world of literature. This miniature world included almost nothing of the East. The world of culture and literature is essentially as boundless as the universe. We are speaking not about its geographical breadth (this is limited), but about its semantic depths, which are as bottomless as the depths of matter. The infinite diversity of interpretations, images, figurative semantic combinations, materials and their interpretations, and so forth. We have narrowed it terribly by selecting and by modernizing what has been selected. We impoverish the past and do not enrich ourselves. We are suffocating in the captivity of narrow and homogeneous interpretations.

The main lines of the development of literature that have prepared one writer or another, one work or another, throughout the centuries (and in various nations). But we know only the writer, his world view, and his times. *Eugene Onegin* was created during the course of seven years. But the way was being prepared for it and it was becoming possible throughout hundreds (or perhaps thousands) of years. Such great realities of literature as genres are completely underestimated.

The problem of *tone* in literature (laughter, tears, and their derivatives). The problem of typology (the organic unity of motifs and images). The problem of sentimental realism (as distinct from sentimental romanticism; Veselovsky).[8] The significance of tears and sadness for one's world view. The tearful aspect of the world. Compassion. The discovery of this aspect in Shakespeare (complex of motifs). Spiritualists.[9] Sterne. The cult of weakness, unprotectedness, kindness, and so forth—animals, children, weak women, fools and idiots, the flower, everything small, and so forth. The naturalistic world view, pragmatism, utilitarianism, and positivism create a monotonous, gray seriousness. The impoverishment of tones in world literature. Nietzsche and the struggle against compassion. The cult of power and triumph. Compassion debases man, and so forth. Truth cannot triumph and conquer. Elements of sentimentalism in Romain Rolland. Tears (along with laughter) as a liminal situation (when practical action is precluded). Ears (and sentimentalism) are antiofficial. Conventional cheerfulness. Bravado. Bourgeois nuances of sentimentalism. Intellectual weakness, stupidity, and self-satisfied mediocrity (Emma Bovary and compassion for her, animals). Degeneration into mannerism. Sentimentalism in the lyric and in lyrical roles in the novel. Elements of sentimentalism in melodrama. The sentimental idyll. Gogol and sentimentalism. Turgenev. Grigorovich.[10] Sentimental treatment of everyday life. The sentimental apology for family life. The sensitive romance. Compassion, pity, and emotionality. Hypocrisy. Sentimental executioners. Complex combinations of the carnival and sentimentalism (Sterne, Jean Paul, and others). There are certain aspects of life and man that can be interpreted and justified only in terms of sentimentalism. The sentimental aspect cannot be universal or cosmic. It narrows the world, makes it small and isolated. The pathos of the small and the personal. The salon nature of sentimentalism. Alfonse Daudet.[11] The theme of the "poor clerk" in Russian literature. The rejection of the large spatiotemporal historical scopes. Departure into the microworld of simple human experiences. The journey without a journey (Sterne). The reaction to neoclassical heroics and to Enlightenment rationalism. The cult of sensibility. The reaction to large-scale critical realism. Rousseau and Wertherism in Russian literature.

The false tendency toward reducing everything to a single consciousness, toward dissolving in it the other's consciousness (while being understood). The principal advantages of outsideness (spatially, temporally, and nationally). One cannot understand understanding as emotional empathy [*Einfühlung*] as the placement of the self in the other's position (loss of one's own position). This is required only for peripheral aspects of understanding. One cannot understand understanding as a translation from the other's language into one's own language.

To understand a given text as the author himself understood it. But our understanding can and should be better. Powerful and profound creativity is largely unconscious and polysemic. Through understanding it is supplemented by consciousness, and the multiplicity of its meanings is revealed. Thus, understanding supplements the text: it is active and also creative by nature. Creative understanding continues creativity, and multiplies the artistic wealth of humanity. The co-creativity of those who understand.

Understanding and evaluation. Understanding is impossible without evaluation. Understanding cannot be separated from evaluation: they are simultaneous and constitute a unified integral act. The person who understands approaches the work with his own already formed world view, from his own viewpoint, from his own position. These positions determine his evaluation to a certain degree, but they themselves do not always stay the same. They are influenced by the artwork, which always introduces something new. Only when the position is dogmatically inert is there nothing new revealed in the work (the dogmatist gains nothing; he cannot be enriched). The person who understands must not reject the possibility of changing or even abandoning his already prepared viewpoints and positions. In the act of understanding, a struggle occurs that results in mutual change and enrichment.

A meeting with a great human being,[12] as something that determines, obligates, and unites—this is the highest moment of understanding.

Meeting and communication in Karl Jaspers (*Philosophie*, 2 vols. [Berlin, 1932]).[13]

Active agreement/disagreement (if it is not dogmatically predetermined) stimulates and deepens understanding, makes the other's word more resilient and true to itself, and precludes mutual dissolution and confusion. The clear demarcation of two consciousnesses, their counterposition and their interrelations.

Understanding repeatable elements and the unrepeatable whole. Recognizing and encountering the new and unfamiliar. Both of these aspects (recognition of the repeated and discovery of the new) should merge inseparably in the living act of understanding. After all, the unrepeatability of the whole is reflected in each repeatable element that participates in the whole (it is, as it were, repeatably unrepeatable). The exclusive orientation toward recognizing, searching only for the familiar (that which has already been), does not allow the new to reveal itself (i.e., the fundamental, unrepeatable totality). Quite frequently, methods of explanation and interpretation are reduced to this kind of disclosure of the repeatable, to a recognition of the already familiar, and, if the new is grasped at all, it is only in an extremely impoverished and abstract form. Moreover, the individual personality of the creator (speaker), of course, disappears completely. Everything that is repeatable and recognizable is fully dissolved and assimilated solely by the consciousness of the person who understands: in the other's consciousness he can see and understand only his own consciousness. He is in no way enriched. In what belongs to others he recognizes only his own.

I understand the other's word (utterance, speech work) to mean any word of any other person that is spoken or written in his own (i.e., my own native) or in any other language, that is, any word that is *not mine.*[14] In this sense, all words (utterances, speech, and literary works) except my own are the other's words. I live in a world of others' words. And my entire life is an orientation in this world, a reaction to others' words (an infinitely diverse reaction), beginning with my assimilation of them (in the process of initial mastery of speech) and ending with assimilation of the wealth of human culture (expressed in the word or in other semiotic materials). The other's word sets for a person the special task of understanding this word (such a task does not exist with respect to one's own word, or it exists in an entirely different sense). Everything that is expressed in the word collapses into the miniature world of each person's own words (words sensed as his own). This and the immense, boundless world of others' words constitute a primary fact of human consciousness and human life that, like all that is primary and taken for granted, has not yet been adequately studied (consciously perceived). In any case, it has not been consciously perceived in view of its immense and essential significance. The immense significance of this for the personality, for the human *I* (in its unrepeatability). The complex interrelations with the other's word in all spheres of culture and activity fill all of man's life. But neither the word in the cross section of these interrelations nor the *I* of the speaker in that same interrelation has been studied.

All of each individual's words are divided into the categories of his own and others', but the boundaries between them can change, and a tense dialogic struggle takes place on the boundaries. But when language and various areas of ideological creativity are studied, this struggle becomes distant and abstract, for there exists an abstract *position of a third party* that is identified with the "objective position" as such, with the position of some "scientific cognition." The position of the third party is quite justified when one person can assume another's position, when a person is completely replaceable. But it is justified only in those situations, and when solving those problems, where the integral and unrepeatable individuality of the person is not required, that is, when a person, so to speak, is specialized, reflecting only a part of his individuality that is detached from the whole, when he is acting not as *I myself,* but "as an engineer," "as a physicist," and so forth. In the area of abstract scientific cognition and abstract thought, such a replacement of one person with another, that is, abstraction from the *I* and *thou,* is possible (but even here, probably, only up to a certain point). In life as the object of thought (abstract thought), man in general exists and a third party exists, but in the most vital, experienced life only *I, thou,* and *he* exist. And only in this life are such primary realities as *my word* and the *other's word* disclosed (exist). And in general those primary realities that have not yet been the subjects of cognition (abstract, generalizing) therefore go unnoticed by it.

The complex event of encountering and interacting with another's word has been almost completely ignored by the corresponding human sciences (and above all by literary scholarship). Sciences of the spirit; their field of inquiry is not one but two "spirits" (the studied and the person who studies, which must not be merged into one spirit). The real object of study is the interrelation and interaction of "spirits."

The attempt to understand the interaction with another's word by means of psychoanalysis and the "collective unconscious." What psychologists (mainly psychiatrists) disclose existed at one time; it was retained in the unconscious (if only the collective unconscious) and was fixed in the memories of languages, genres, and rituals; from here it penetrates into the speech and dreams (related, consciously recalled) of people (who have a particular psychic constitution and are in a particular state). The role of psychology and of the so-called psychology of culture.

The first task is to understand the work as the author himself understood it, without exceeding the limits of his understanding. This is a very difficult problem and usually requires introducing an immense amount of material.

The second task is to take advantage of one's own position of temporal and cultural outsideness. Inclusion in our (other's for the author) context.

The first stage is understanding (there are two tasks here); the second stage is scholarly study (scientific description, generalization, historical localization).

The distinction between the human and natural sciences. The rejection of the idea of an insurmountable barrier between them. The notion that they are opposed to one another (Dilthey, Rickert) was refuted by subsequent development of the human sciences.[15] The infusion of mathematical and other methods—an irreversible process, but at the same time specific methods, a general trend toward specifics (for example, the axiological approach)—is and should be developing. A strict demarcation between understanding and scientific study.

False science, based on communication that is not experienced, that is, without the initial given of the actual object. The degree of perfection of this given (of the true experience of art). At a low level, scientific analysis is inevitably superficial or even false.

The other's word should be transformed into one's own/other (or other/one's own). Distance (outsideness) and respect. In the process of dialogic communication, the object is transformed into the subject (the other's *I*).

The simultaneity of artistic experience and scientific study. They cannot be separated, but they do not always pass through their various stages and degrees at the same time.

With meaning I give *answers* to questions. Anything that does not answer a question is devoid of sense for us.

It is not only possible to understand a unique and unrepeatable individuality; there can also be individual causality.

The responsive nature of contextual meaning. Meaning always responds to particular questions. Anything that does not respond to something seems meaningless to us; it is removed from dialogue. Contextual meaning and formal definition. Formal definition is removed from dialogue, but it is deliberately and conventionally abstracted from it. It contains potential meaning.

The universalism of contextual meaning, its universality and omnitemporality.

Contextual meaning is potentially infinite, but it can only be actualized when accompanied by another (other's) meaning, if only by a question in the inner speech of the one who understands. Each time it must be accompanied by another contextual meaning in order to reveal new aspects of its own infinite nature (just as the word reveals its meanings only in context). Actual contextual meaning inheres not in one (single) meaning, but only in two meanings that meet and accompany one another. There can be no "contextual meaning in and of itself"—it exists only for another contextual meaning, that is, it exists only in conjunction with it. There cannot be a unified (single) contextual meaning. Therefore, there can be neither a first nor a last meaning; it always exists among other meanings as a link in the chain of meaning, which in its totality is the only thing that can be real. In historical life, this chain continues infinitely, and therefore each individual link in it is renewed again and again, as though it were being reborn.

The impersonal system of sciences (and knowledge in general) and the organic whole of consciousness (or the individual personality).

The problem of the speaker (of the person, the speaking subject, author of the utterance, and so forth). Linguistics knows only the system of language and the text. Yet every utterance, even a standard greeting, has a specific form of an author (and addressee).

Notes in philosophical anthropology.

My image of myself. The nature of one's idea of one's self, of one's *I* as a whole. How it is principally distinguished from my idea of the *other.* The image of *I*, a concept or an experience, a sensation, and so forth. The nature of this image's existence. The composition of this image. (How it accommodates, for example, ideas about my body, about my exterior, my past, and so forth.) What I understand by *I* when I speak and experience: "I live," "I will die," and so forth. ("I am," "I will not be," "I was not") *I-for-myself, I-for-another,* and *another-for-me.* What in me is given to me directly and what is given only through another. Minimum and maximum—primitive self-sensation and complex self-awareness. But the maximum develops that which was already embedded in the minimum. The historical development of self-awareness. It is related to the development of signifying means of expression (language above all). The history of autobiography (Misch).[16] The heterogeneous composition of my image. A person at the mirror. *Not-I* in me, that is, existence in me; something larger than me in me. To what degree is it possible to combine *I* and *other* in one neutral image of a person. Feelings that are possible only toward the other (for example, love), and feelings possible only toward oneself (i.e., self-love, selflessness, and so forth). My temporal and spatial boundaries are not given for me, but the other is entirely given. I enter into the spatial world, but the other has always resided in it. The differences between space and time of *I* and *other*. They exist in living sensation, but abstract thought erases them. Thought creates a unified, general world of man, irrespective of *I* and *other*. In primitive, natural self-sensation, *I* and *other* merge. There is neither egoism nor altruism here.

The *I* hides in the other and in others, it wants to be only an other for others, to enter completely into the world of others as an other, and to cast from itself the burden of being the only *I* (*I-for-myself*) in the world.

Semiotics deals primarily with the transmission of ready-made communication using a ready-made code. But in live speech, strictly speaking, communication is first created in the process of transmission, and there is, in essence, no code. The problem of changing the code in inner speech (Zhinkin).[17]

Dialogue and dialectics. Take a dialogue and remove the voices (the partitioning of voices), remove the intonations (emotional and individualizing ones), carve out abstract concepts and judgments from living words and responses, cram everything into one abstract consciousness—and that's how you get dialectics.

Context and code. A context is potentially unfinalized; a code must be finalized. A code is only a technical means of transmitting information, but it also has cognitive, creative significance. A code is a deliberately established, killed context.

The search for one's own (authorial) voice.[18] To be embodied, to become more clearly defined, to become less, to become more limited, more stupid. Not to remain tangential, to burst into the circle of life, to become one among other people. To cast off reservations, to cast off irony. Gogol also sought the serious word, the serious walk of life: to convince (teach) and, consequently, to convince oneself. Gogol's naiveté, his extreme lack of experience in the *serious*; therefore, it seemed to him that he must surmount laughter. Salvation and transformation of comic heroes. The right to the serious word. There can be no word apart from the speaker, from his position, from his attitude toward the listener, and from the situations that join them (the word of the leader, the priest, and so forth). The word of the private person. The poet. The prose writer. The "writer." The performance of the prophet, leader, teacher, judge, procurator (accuser), advocate (counsel for the defense). The citizen. The journalist. The purely objectlike nature of the scientific word.

Dostoevsky's quests. The journalist. *The Diary of a Writer.* Tendency. The word of the people. The word of the holy fool (Lebyadkin, Myshkin).[19] The word of the monk, the elder, the wanderer (Makar).[20] There is a moral person who is wise and holy. "And meanwhile the hermit in a dark cell" (Pushkin).[21] The murdered tsarevich Dmitry. The tears of the tortured child. A great deal from Pushkin. (Not yet investigated.) The word as something personal. Christ as truth. I ask him.[22] A profound understanding of the personal nature of the word. Dostoevsky's Pushkin speech. Any person's word addressed to any other person. The drawing close of literary language to conversational language makes the problem of the authorial word more acute. Purely object-oriented scientific argumentation in literature can only be parodic to one degree or another. Genres of ancient Russian literature (hagiographies, homilies, and so forth). Genres of medieval literature in general. The unuttered truth in Dostoevsky (Christ's kiss). The problem of silence. Irony as a special kind of substitute for silence. The word removed from life: the word of the idiot, the holy fool, the insane, the child, the dying person, and sometimes women. Delirium, dream, intuition (inspiration), unconsciousness, alogicality [alogism], involuntary behavior, epilepsy, and so forth.

The problem of the image of the author. The primary (not created) and secondary author (the image of the author created by the primary author). The primary—*natura non creata quae creat*; the secondary author—*natura creata quae non creat.* The image of the hero—*natura creata quae non creat.*[23] The primary author cannot be an image. He eludes any figurative representation. When we try to imagine the primary author figuratively, we ourselves are creating his image, that is, we ourselves become the primary author of the image. The creating image (i.e., the primary author) can never enter into any image that he has created. The word of the primary author cannot be *his own* word.

It must be consecrated by something higher and impersonal (by scientific argument, experiment, objective data, inspiration, intuition, authority, and so forth). The primary author, if he expresses a direct word, cannot be simply a *writer.* One can tell nothing from the face of a writer (the writer is transformed into a commentator, a moralist, a scholar, and so forth). Therefore, the primary author clothes himself in *silence.* But this silence can assume various forms of expression, various forms of reduced laughter (irony), allegory, and so forth.

The problem of the writer and his primary authorial position became especially acute in the eighteenth century (because of the decline of authorities and authoritarian forms, and the rejection of authoritarian forms of language).

The form of the simple impersonal story in language that is literary, but close to conversational language. The story does not move far from the heroes and it does not move far from the average reader. The paraphrase of a novel in a letter to the publisher. A paraphrase of the intent. This is not a mask, but an ordinary face of an ordinary person (the face of the primary author cannot be ordinary). Existence itself speaks through the writer, through his mouth (Heidegger).[24]

In painting, the artist sometimes depicts himself (usually at the edge of the picture). The self-portrait. The artist depicts himself as an ordinary person and not as an artist, not as the creator of the picture.

Quests for my own word are in fact quests for a word that is not my own, a word that is more than myself; this is a striving to depart from one's own words, with which nothing essential can be said. I myself can only be a character and not the primary author. The author's quests for his own word are basically quests for genre and style, quests for an authorial position. This is now the most critical problem of contemporary literature, which leads many to reject the genre of the novel altogether, to replace it with a montage of documents, a description of things, to bookishness [*lettrizm*], and, to a certain degree, also to the literature of the absurd. In some sense all these can be defined as various forms of silence. These quests led Dostoevsky to the creation of the polyphonic novel. He could not find the word for the monologic novel. A parallel path led Leo Tolstoy to folk stories (primitivism), to the introduction of biblical quotations (in the final parts of his novels).[25] Another route would be to cause the world to begin speaking and to listen to the word of the world itself (Heidegger).

"Dostoevsky and sentimentalism. An exercise in typological analysis."

Polyphony and rhetoric. Journalism and its genres as modern rhetoric. The rhetorical word and the novelistic word. Persuasiveness that is artistic and rhetorical persuasiveness.

The rhetorical argument and dialogue about current questions (about the whole and in the whole). Victory or mutual understanding. My word and the other's word. The *primary nature* of this juxtaposition. The viewpoint (position) of the third party. The limited goals of the rhetorical word. Rhetorical speech argues from the viewpoint of the third party: profound individual levels do not participate in it. In antiquity the boundaries between rhetorical and artistic literature were drawn in a different way, and they were not clear-cut, for there was no deep individual personality in the modern sense. It (individual personality) originated on the eve of the Middle Ages ("to me myself" of Marcus Aurelius, Epictetus, Augustine, *soliloquia,* and so forth).[26] The boundaries between one's own and the other's word become sharper here (or perhaps they even appear for the first time).

In rhetoric there is the unconditionally innocent and the unconditionally guilty; there is complete victory and destruction of the opponent. In dialogue the destruction of the opponent also destroys that very dialogic sphere where the word lives. In classical antiquity this sphere did not yet exist. This sphere is very fragile and easily destroyed (the slightest violence is sufficient, references to authority, and so forth). Razumikhin discussing lies as a way to truth.[27] The juxtaposition of truth and Christ in Dostoevsky.[28] What I have in mind here is impersonal objective truth, that is, truth from the standpoint of a third party. The court of arbitration is a rhetorical court. Dostoevsky's attitude toward juries. Impartiality and *higher* partiality. The extraordinary refinement of all ethical categories of personality. They lie in the border area between the ethical and the aesthetic.

"Soil" in Dostoevsky as something intermediate (medial) between impersonal and personal. Shatov as a representative of this typical feature.[29] The thirst to become embodied. The majority of articles in *Diary of a Writer* lie in this medial sphere between rhetoric and the personal sphere (i.e., in the sphere of Shatov, "soil," and so forth). This medial sphere in Bobok (the seemly shopkeeper). The real insufficiency of understanding in state, legal, economic, and business spheres and also the objective scientific sphere (the legacy of roman-

The journalist is above all a contemporary. He is obliged to be one. He lives in the sphere of questions that can be resolved in the present day (or in any case in the near future). He participates in a dialogue that can be ended and even finalized, can be translated into action, and can become an empirical force. It is precisely in this sphere that "one's own word" is possible. Outside this sphere "one's own word" is not one's own (the individual personality always transcends itself); "one's own word" cannot be the ultimate word.

The rhetorical word is the word of the acting agent himself or is addressed to acting agents.

The word of the journalist, when introduced into the polyphonic novel, submits to unfinalized and infinite dialogue.

When entering the area of Dostoevsky's journalism, we observe a sharp narrowing of the horizon; the universality of his novels disappears, even though the problems of the hero's personal life are replaced by social and political problems. The heroes lived and acted (and thought) before the entire world (before heaven and earth). Ultimate questions that originated in their small personal and daily lives broke away from their lives and attached themselves to "the divine universal life."[32]

This representation of the hero to all humanity, to all the world, is similar to classical tragedy (and to Shakespeare), but it is also profoundly different from them.

The rhetorical dispute is a dispute in which it is important to gain victory over the opponent, not to approach the truth. This is the lowest form of rhetoric. In all higher forms one can reach solutions to questions that are capable of temporal, historical solutions, but not to ultimate questions (where rhetoric is impossible).

Metalinguistics and the philosophy of the word. Ancient teachings about logos. John.[33] Language, speech, speech communication, utterance. The specific nature of speech communication.

The speaking person. As whom and how (i.e., in what situation) the speaking person appears. Various forms of speech authorship, from the simplest everyday utterances to large literary genres. It is customary to speak about the authorial mask. But in which utterances (speech acts) is there a *face* and not a mask, that is, no authorship? The form of authorship depends on the genre of the utterance. The genre in turn is determined by the subject matter, goal, and situation of the utterance.

ticism) and those spheres whose representatives are liberals (Kaveli and others).[30] The utopian belief in the possibility of a purely interna path for transforming life into paradise. Sobering up. The striving tc curtail ecstasy (epilepsy). "The Drunkards" (sentiments).[31] Marmeladov and Fedor Pavlovich Karamazov.

Dostoevsky and Dickens. Similarities and differences ("Christmas Tales" and "Bobok" and "Dream of the Ridiculous Man"); *Poor Folk, The Insulted and the Injured,* "The Drunkards"—sentimentalism.

The denial of (failure to understand) the sphere of necessity through which freedom must pass (both on the historical and the individual-personal plane), that intermediate sphere that lies between the Grand Inquisitor (with his state power, rhetoric, and authority) and Christ (with his silence and his kiss).

Raskolnikov wanted to become something like a Grand Inquisitor (to take sins and suffering upon himself).

The peculiarities of polyphony. The lack of finalization of the polyphonic dialogue (dialogue about ultimate questions). These dialogues are conducted by unfinalized individual personalities and not by psychological subjects. The somewhat unembodied quality of these personalities (disinterested surplus).

Every great writer participates in such a dialogue; he participates with his creativity as one of the sides in this dialogue. But writers themselves do not create polyphonic novels. Their rejoinders in the dialogue are monologic in form; each has one world of his own while other participants in the dialogue remain with their worlds outside the work. They appear with their own personal worlds and with their own immediate, personal words. But prose writers, especially novelists, have a problem with their own word. This word cannot be simply their own word (from the *I*). The word of the poet, the prophet, the leader, the scientist, and then the word of the "writer." It must be grounded. The need to represent somebody. The scientist has arguments, practical work, experimentation. The poet relies on inspiration and a special *poetic* language. The prose writer does not have this poetic language.

Only a polyphonist like Dostoevsky can sense in the struggle of opinions and ideologies (of various epochs) an incomplete dialogue on ultimate questions (in the framework of great time). Others deal with issues that have been resolved within the epoch.

The form of authorship and the hierarchical place (position) of the speaker (leader, tsar, judge, warrior, priest, teacher, private individual, father, son, husband, wife, brother, and so forth). The corresponding hierarchical position of the addressee of the utterance (the subject, the defendant, the student, the son, and so forth). The one who speaks and the one spoken to. All this determines the genre, tone, and style of the utterance: the word of the leader, the word of the judge, the word of the teacher, the word of the father, and so forth. This determines the form of the authorship. One and the same actual character can assume various authorial forms. In what forms and how is the face of the speaker revealed?

Various *professional* forms of authorship are developing in modern times. The authorial form of the writer has become professional and has broken down into generic subcategories (novelist, lyricist, writer of comedies, of odes, and so forth). Forms of authorship can be usurped or conventional. For example, the novelist can assimilate the tone of the priest, the prophet, the judge, the teacher, the preacher, and so forth. The complex process of development of extrahierarchical generic forms. Authorial forms and particularly the *tone* of these forms, which are essentially traditional and reach back into antiquity. They are renewed in new situations. One cannot *invent* them (just as one cannot invent language).

The immense diversity of speech genres and authorial forms in daily speech communication (entertaining and intimate communications, various kinds of requests and demands, confessions of love, squabbling and abuse, exchanges of courtesies, and so forth). They differ in terms of their hierarchical spheres: the familiar sphere, the official sphere, and their subcategories.

Are there genres of pure *self*-expression (without the traditional authorial form)? Do there exist genres without an addressee?

Gogol. The world without names, in which there are only various kinds of sobriquets and nicknames. The names of things are also sobriquets. Not from the thing to the word, but from the word to the thing; the word gives birth to the thing. It equally justifies both destruction and birth. Praise and abuse. One merges into the other. The boundary between the ordinary and the fantastic is erased: Poprishchin—the Spanish king, Akaky Akakievich—the phantom grabbing the overcoat.[34] The category of absurdity. "From the comical to the great . . ." Festivity measures the mediocrity and the everyday nature of the everyday world. The hyperbolic style. Hyperbole is always festive (including abusive hyperbole).

The turn to prose in an appeal to the familiar and public element. Narezhny.[35] Gogol. Fear and laughter. The thoroughly festive quality of *The Inspector General.* The festivity of Chichikov's arrivals and departures (as a guest). Balls, dinners (masks are transparent). A return to the sources of speech life (praise—abuse) and material life (eating, drinking, the body, and the corporeal life of the organs: blowing one's nose, yawning, dreaming, and so forth). And the troika with bells on it.

The rupture between real life and symbolic ritual. How unnatural this rupture is. Their false juxtaposition. They say: at that time everyone traveled in troikas with bells, that was real everyday life. But the carnivalistic overtone remains everyday in life, and in literature it can be the main tone. Pure everyday life is fiction, a product of the intellect. Human life is always shaped and this shaping is always ritualistic (even if only "aesthetically" so). The artistic image can also rely on this ritualism. Memory and awareness in everyday ritual and in the image.

The reflection in speech of relations among people, and their social hierarchy. The interrelations of speech units. The keen sense of one's own and someone else's in speech life. The exceptional role of tone. The world of abuse and praise (and their derivatives: flattery, toadying, hypocrisy, humiliation, boorishness, caustic remarks, insinuations, and so forth). The almost objectless world that reflects the interrelations of speakers (their sequence according to importance, their hierarchy, and so forth). The least-studied aspect of speech life. This is not the world of tropes, but the world of personal tones and nuances, and it consists not in the relations among things (phenomena, concepts), but in the world of others' personalities. The tone is determined not by the referential content of the utterance and not by the experiences of the speaker, but by the relationship of the speaker to the individual personality of the other speaker (to his rank, his importance, and so forth).

The erasure of boundaries between the terrible and the comical in images of folk culture (and to a certain degree in Gogol). Between the mediocre and the terrible, the ordinary and the miraculous, the small and the grand.

Folk culture under the conditions of the new (Gogolian) epoch. Intervening links. The court. Didactics. Gogol's quest for a justification ("goal," "purpose," "truth") for the comical picture of the world. The "life path," "service," "vocation," and so forth. Truth always judges to a certain degree. But the court of truth is not like the ordinary court.

Pure denial cannot give birth to an image. In the image (even the most negative one) there is always an aspect of the positive (love—admiration). Blok on satire.[36] Stanislavsky on the beauty of play—the actor's depiction of a negative image. Mechanical division is unacceptable: ugliness—a negative character, beauty—a performing actor. The universality of the comic Gogolian world. In his world there are no "positive heroes."

This collection of my essays is unified by one theme in various stages of its development.[37]

The unity of the emerging (developing) idea. Hence a certain *internal* open-endedness of many of my ideas. But I do not wish to turn shortcomings into virtues: in these works there is much external open-endedness, that is, an open-endedness not of the thought itself but of its expression and exposition. Sometimes it is difficult to separate one open-endedness from another. It cannot be assigned to a particular trend (Structuralism). My love for variations and for a diversity of terms for a single phenomenon. The multiplicity of focuses. Bringing distant things closer without indicating the intermediate links.

Notes

1. Reference here is to Lotman's "Khudozhestvennaja struktura Evgenija Onegina" in *Trudy po russkoj i slavjanskoj filologii* 9 (Tartu, 1966), pp. 5–22. Lotman's idea of recoding depends on his conviction that literature is a secondary modeling system. He distinguishes between natural languages, artificial languages ("systems of conventional signs and the rules of their usage, such as those of algebra or chemistry"), and secondary modeling systems, which he defines as "semiotic systems constructed on the basis of a natural language but having a more complex structure. Secondary modelling systems include ritual, all aggregates of social and ideological sign communications, and art, all of which merge into a single complex whole—culture" (Yury Lotman, *Analysis of the Poetic Text*, tr. D. Barton Johnson [Ann Arbor: Ardis, 1976], p. 19).

2. In chapter 2, part 2, of *The Brothers Karamazov* we are told of the visit by a mysterious visitor to Zosima, who fourteen years earlier had murdered a woman he loved, who had refused him. Although no one suspects him of murder (there were no witnesses), the man is tormented by his crime and eventually confesses.

3. Compare these remarks on "supra-existence" with Bakhtin's concept of the *superaddressee* in "The Problem of the Text."

4. From a poem by V. Khodasevich, "In Front of the Mirror" (1924):

I, I, I. What an uncivilized word!
Is that one there really—I?
Could Mama really love such a
Yellow-gray, half-graying
And omniscient person, like a snake?

5. Pechorin is the splenetic hero of Lermontov's *Hero of Our Time* (1841). Stavrogin is the central character of Dostoevsky's novel *The Possessed*.

6. Vladimir Vernadsky (1963–1945), mineralogist and crystallographer, founder of geochemistry and biogeochemistry, central figure in the reorganization of the Academy of Sciences under the Soviets. He was one of Russia's greatest scientists, who made contributions in several different disciplines. He was important for Bakhtin because of his emphasis on the wholeness and connectedness of the cosmos. His Paris lectures in the early 1920s on what he called the biosphere influenced Teilhard de Chardin. Vernadsky was among other things a geographer and historian of science; thus, it is not surprising that he wrote on Kant's activity as a natural scientist (Kant was made a corresponding member of the Petersburg Academy not because he was a philosopher, but because he was author of the *Physical Geography*). Vernadsky was also interested in the ideas of the "philosopher of the Common Task," Nikolay Fedorov (1828–1903), whose doctrine that all is alive also influenced Dostoevsky. The Kantian and Fedorovian implications of Vernadsky's work were not lost on Bakhtin.

7. On Veselovsky, see note 1 to the essay "Response to a Question from the *Novy Mir* Editorial Staff."

8. In the late 1960s, Bakhtin was at work on a book devoted to sentimentalism (in which Dostoevsky played a large role). The work was never finished.

See A. N. Veselovsky, *Poezija chuvstva i serdechnogo voobrazhenija* (St. Petersburg, 1904). Zhukovsky is regarded mainly as a sentimentalist poet in this book, "The only real poet of our age of sensibility" (p. 46).

9. At the end of the thirteenth century, the Spiritualists were the more radical followers of Francis of Assisi who protested strongly against the secularization of the church. Bakhtin apparently has in mind the religious poet Jacopone da Todi (1230–1306), a zealous Spiritualist whose poems, in his native Italian, expressed deep compassion with the sufferings of Christ and the Virgin Mary.

10. Dmitry Grigorovich (1822–99), author of such tales as "The Village" and "Anton-Goremyka," which described the life of the poorer classes with great compassion. He was associated with the journal *The Contemporary;* his style is called in Russian "sentimental naturalism."

11. Alphonse Daudet (1840–97), French novelist of the naturalist school. Bakhtin has in mind here such novels of Parisian salon life as *Le nabob* (1877) and *Les rois en exil* (1879).

12. Compare the description of the "meeting" as one of the most important chronotopic motifs in literature in "Forms of Time and Chronotope in the Novel," in *The Dialogic Imagination*, pp. 97–99, 244.

13. Karl Jaspers (1883–1969)—his basic concept is "encompassing," an essentially religious concept intended to suggest the all-embracing transcendent reality within which human existence is enclosed. Jaspers is deeply aware of the limita-

tions of abstract science (in the human as well as the natural sciences) because they cloud perception of the specific situatedness of human being. Communication is the means by which human beings exercise freedom in their situatedness.

14. The notes on "the other's word" are associated with an article intended for *Voprosy filosofii* (Questions of Philosophy), the major journal for philosophy in the Soviet Union. In "Notes Made in 1970–71," Bakhtin gives two possible titles for the piece: "The Other's Word as the Specific Object of Investigation in the Human Sciences" and "The Problem of the Other's Word (Other's Speech) in Culture and Literature: From Essays on Metalinguistics." He also was considering an epigraph from *Faust*: "Was ihr den Geist der Zeiten nennt . . ." (What they *name* the spirit of the times . . .). Bakhtin was probably quoting from memory, for the correct quote is: "Was ihr den Geist der Zeiten heisst . . ." (What they *call* the spirit of the times . . .).

15. Dilthey developed what he felt were the foundations for a "science of the spirit" (*Geisteswissenschaft*) as distinct from the natural sciences. The method of *Geisteswissenschaft* was to be grounded in understanding, as opposed to causal explanation in the natural sciences. Understanding coincides with our interpretation of significant experience; thus, the means for becoming aware of spirit—Dilthey's hermeneutics—coincide with attempts to understand psychology. Bakhtin discusses his differences with Dilthey in *Marxism and the Philosophy of Language* (pp. 26–28 in English ed.). See also note 4 of "The Problem of the Text."

16. See Georg Misch, *Geschichte der Autobiographie*, 4 vols. (Leipzig-Berlin, 1907; 2nd ed. Bern, 1949), vol. 1, and (Frankfurt a.M., 1955), vols. 2–4. There is an English translation: *A History of Autobiography in Antiquity*, tr. E. W. Dickes, 2 vols. (Cambridge, Mass.: Harvard University Press, 1951).

17. See N. I. Zhinkin, "On Code Translations in Inner Speech," *Voprosy jazykoznanija* (Questions of Linguistics, no. 6) (1964). Zhinkin studied the physiological evidence (subvocal voicing) for inner speech.

18. A projected work on this subject would have relied heavily on Dostoevsky's activity as a journalist, especially in his "Diary of a Writer," in correlation with his activity as a novelist.

19. Lebyadkin is the comic and unscrupulous brother of Stavrogin's wife in *The Possessed*.

Myshkin is the hero of Dostoevsky's novel *The Idiot*.

20. Makar is the hero's father in *A Raw Youth*.

21. A statement by Pimen, a monk and chronicler in Pushkin's drama *Boris Godunov*.

22. See *Problems of Dostoevsky's Poetics*, ed. and tr. Caryl Emerson (Minneapolis: University of Minnesota Press, 1984), pp. 124–25.

23. In a major essay by Duns Scotus (b. 810), *De Divisione Naturae*, the philosopher describes four modes of being: (1) "nature creating and not created," that is, God as the everlasting first cause of all things; (2) "nature created and creating," that is, the Platonic world of ideas, residing in the intellect of God and determining the being of things; (3) "nature created and not creating," that is, the world of individual things; and (4) "nature not created and not creating," again God, but now as the final goal of all things, absorbing them back into himself at the origin of the world dialectical process. Bakhtin metaphorically applies these terms, which

were devised to describe the creative activity of the divinity, to the ontology of human artistic activity. On a par with these are other terms used elsewhere by Bakhtin—*natura naturans* (nature originating) and *natura naturata* (nature originated)—which go back to the lexicon of Latin translations of Averroës (ibn-Rashid), and which were used by the Christian scholastics, but are especially well known because of their role in Spinoza's text. From the 1890s through the 1920s, Spinoza was a fairly influential figure in Russia, important for—among others—Vygotsky.

24. A leading idea in Heidegger's philosophy of art is that the word originates in the depths of existence, and through the poet as "medium" it speaks to the world; the poet "listens attentively" (a concept Heidegger counterposes to the category of "contemplation," which is a more traditional way of thinking in Western philosophy about what the poet does) in existence, especially in the area of its richest expression—language. See *Holzwege* (Frankfurt a.M., 1950) and *Unterwegs zur Sprache* (Pfullingen, 1959).

25. As, for instance, in his last novel, *Resurrection* (1899).

26. On soliloquy, see Bakhtin's *Problems of Dostoevsky's Poetics* (p. 113, in Eng. ed.) and "Forms of Time and the Chronotope in the Novel," in *The Dialogic Imagination*, p. 145.

27. See *Crime and Punishment*, part 2, chapter 4.

28. See the famous letter from Dostoevsky to N. D. Fonvizina of February 1854, in which he says, ". . . if someone were to prove to me that Christ is outside the truth, then I would prefer to remain with Christ than with the truth."

29. Shatov is a major figure in Dostoevsky's novel *The Possessed*.

30. In a famous letter to Dostoevsky, K. D. Kavelin polemicized about the novelist's speech at the unveiling of a statue of Pushkin. See *Vestnik evropy* (The European Herald), no. 11 (1880).

31. A plan for a novel out of which *Crime and Punishment* grew.

32. From Tyutchev's poem "Spring" (1838).

33. John 1 : 1—"In the beginning was the Word . . ."

34. Poprishchin is the main protagonist of Gogol's story "Notes of a Madman," who thinks he is the king of Spain.

Akaky Akakievich is the main protagonist of Gogol's short story "The Overcoat," which concludes with the rumor that Akaky's ghost is stealing coats.

35. V. T. Narezhny (1780–1825), satirist, author of *A Russian Gil Blas* (1814).

36. From an article by the poet Aleksandr Blok, "On Art and Criticism" (1920): "Indeed, if Maupassant had written all this with a sense of satire (if such things exist), he would have written it quite differently; he would always have been showing how Georges Duroi behaved badly. But he shows only how Duroi behaved, giving the reader the opportunity to judge whether it was badly or not. And he, the artist, is 'in love' with Georges Duroi, as Gogol was in love with Khlestyakov [hero of the play *The Inspector General*]."

37. Bakhtin is referring here to a collection of his works from various years that he was working on just before his death. It appeared as *Voprosy literaturi i estetiki*, most pieces from which are included in *The Dialogic Imagination* (the foreword Bakhtin alludes to here was never finished).

Toward a Methodology for the Human Sciences

Understanding. The dismemberment of understanding into individual acts. In actual, real concrete understanding these acts merge inseparably into a unified process, but each individual act has its ideal semantic (content-filled) independence and can be singled out from the concrete empirical act. 1. Psychophysiologically perceiving a physical sign (word, color, spatial form). 2. *Recognizing* it (as familiar or unfamiliar). 3. Understanding its *significance* in the given context (immediate and more remote). 4. Active-dialogic understanding (disagreement/agreement). Inclusion in the dialogic context. The evaluative aspect of understanding and the degree of its depth and universality.

Converting an image into a symbol gives it semantic *depth* and semantic perspective. The dialogic correlation between identity and nonidentity. The image must be understood for what it is and for what it designates. The content of a true symbol, through mediated semantic coupling, is correlated with the idea of worldwide wholeness, the fullness of the cosmic and human universe. The world has contextual meaning. "The image of the world appears miraculously in the word" (Pasternak).[1] Each particular phenomenon is submerged in the primordial elements of the *origins of existence*. As distinct from myth, this is an awareness that one does not coincide with one's own individual meaning.

The symbol has a "warmth of fused mystery" (Averintsev).[2] The aspect of contrasting *one's own* to *another's*. The warmth of love and the coldness of alienation. Contrast and comparison. Any interpretation of a symbol itself remains a symbol, but it is somewhat rationalized, that is, brought somewhat closer to the concept.

A definition of *contextual meaning* in all the profundity and complexity of its essence. Interpretation as the discovery of a path to seeing (contemplating) and supplementing through creative thinking. Anticipation of the further growing context, its relation to the finalized whole, and its relation to the unfinalized context. This meaning (in the unfinalized context) cannot be peaceful and cozy (one cannot curl up comfortably and die within it).

Formal definition and contextual meaning. *Filled-in* recollections and *anticipated* possibilities (understanding in remote contexts). In recollections we also take subsequent events (within the past) into account, that is, we perceive and understand what is remembered in the context of the unfinalized past. In what forms is the whole present in the consciousness (in Plato and in Husserl)?

To what extent can the *contextual meaning* (of an image or symbol) be revealed and commented upon? Only with the aid of another (isomorphous) meaning (of a symbol or image). It cannot be dissolved into concepts. The role of commentary. There can be a *relative* rationalization of the contextual meaning (ordinary scientific analysis) or a deepening with the help of other meanings (philosophical-artistic interpretation). Deepening through expansion of the remote context.

The interpretation of symbolic structures is forced into an infinity of symbolic contextual meanings and therefore it cannot be scientific in the way precise sciences are scientific.

The interpretation of contextual meanings cannot be scientific, but it is profoundly cognitive. It can directly serve practice, practice that deals with things.

". . . it will be necessary to recognize that symbology is not an unscientific, but a *differently scientific* form of knowledge that has its own internal laws and criteria for precision" (S. S. Averintsev).[3]

A work's author is present only in the whole of the work, not in one separate aspect of this whole, and least of all in content that is severed from the whole. He is located in that inseparable aspect of the work where content and form merge inseparably, and we feel his presence most of all in form. Literary scholarship usually looks for him in *content* excised from the whole. This makes it easy to identify him with that author who is a person of a particular time, with a particular biography and a particular world view. Here the image of the author almost merges with the image of a real person.

The true author cannot become an image, for he is the creator of every image, of everything imagistic in the work. Therefore, the so-called image of the author can only be one of the images of a given work (true, a special kind of image). The artist frequently depicts himself in a picture (near the edge of it) and he also draws his self-portrait. But in a self-portrait we *do not see* the author as such (he cannot be seen); in any case, we see him no more than in any of the author's other work. He is revealed most of all in the author's best pictures. The author-creator cannot be created in that sphere in which he himself appears as the creator. This is *natura naturans* and not *natura naturata*.[4] We see the creator only in his creation, and never outside it.

The exact sciences constitute a monologic form of knowledge: the intellect contemplates a *thing* and expounds upon it. There is only one subject here—cognizing (contemplating) and speaking (expounding). In opposition to the subject there is only a *voiceless thing*. Any object of knowledge (including man) can be perceived and cognized as a thing. But a subject as such cannot be perceived and studied as a thing, for as a subject it cannot, while remaining a subject, become voiceless, and, consequently, cognition of it can only be *dialogic*. Dilthey and the problem of understanding.[5] Various ways of *being active* in cognitive activity. The activity of the one who acknowledges a voiceless thing and the activity of one who acknowledges another subject, that is, the *dialogic* activity of the acknowledger. The dialogic activity of the acknowledged subject, and the degrees of this activity. The thing and the personality (subject) as *limits* of cognition. Degrees of thing-ness and personality-ness. The event-potential of dialogic cognition. Meeting. Evaluation as a necessary aspect of dialogic cognition.

The human sciences—sciences of the spirit—philological sciences (as part of and at the same time common to all of them—the word).

Historicity. Immanence. Enclosure of analysis (cognition and understanding) in one given *text*. The problem of the boundaries between text and context. Each word (each sign) of the text exceeds its boundaries. Any understanding is a correlation of a given text with other texts. Commentary. The dialogic nature of this correlation.

The place of philosophy. It begins where precise science ends and a different science begins. It can be defined as the metalanguage of all sciences (and of all kinds of cognition and consciousness).

Understanding as correlation with other texts and reinterpretation, in a new context (in my own context, in a contemporary context, and in a future one). The anticipated context of the future: a sense that I am taking a new step (have progressed). Stages in the dialogic movement of *understanding*: the point of departure, the given text; movement backward, past contexts; movement forward, anticipation (and the beginning) of a future context.

Dialectics was born of dialogue so as to return again to dialogue on a higher level (a dialogue of *personalities*).

The monologism of Hegel's "Phenomenology of the Spirit."

Dilthey's monologism has not been completely surmounted.

Thought about the world and thought in the world. Thought striving to embrace the world and thought experiencing itself in the world (as part of it). An event in the world and participation in it. The world as an event (and not as existence in ready-made form).

The text lives only by coming into contact with another text (with context). Only at the point of this contact between texts does a light flash, illuminating both the posterior and anterior, joining a given text to a dialogue. We emphasize that this contact is a dialogic contact between texts (utterances) and not a mechanical contact of "oppositions," which is possible only within a single text (and not between a text and context) among abstract elements (signs within a text), and is necessary only in the first stage of understanding (understanding formal definition, but not contextual meaning). Behind this contact is a contact of personalities and not of things (at the extreme). If we transform dialogue into one continuous text, that is, erase the divisions between voices (changes of speaking subjects), which is possible at the extreme (Hegel's monological dialectic), then the deep-seated (infinite) contextual meaning disappears (we hit the bottom, reach a standstill).

Complete maximum reification would inevitably lead to the disappearance of the infinitude and bottomlessness of meaning (any meaning).

A thought that, like a fish in an aquarium, knocks against the bottom and the sides and cannot swim farther or deeper. Dogmatic thoughts.

Thought knows only conditional points; thought erodes all previously established points.

The elucidation of a text not by means of other texts (contexts) but with extratextual thinglike (reified) reality. This usually takes place in biographical, vulgar sociological and causal explanations (in the spirit of the natural sciences) and also in depersonalized historicity ("a history without names").[6] True understanding in literature and literary scholarship is always historical and personified. The position and limits of the so-called *realia*. *Things fraught with the word.*

The unity of monologue and the special unity of dialogue.

Pure epic and pure lyric know no provisos. Provisionary speech appears only in the novel.

The influence of extratextual reality in the shaping of the writer's artistic vision and the artistic thought (and the vision and thought of others who create culture).

Extratextual influences are especially important in the early stages of a person's development. These influences are invested in the word (or in other signs), and these words are the words of other people, above all, words from the mother. Then these "others' words" are processed dialogically into "one's own/others' words" with the help of different "others' words" (heard previously) and then in one's own words, so to speak (dropping the quotation marks), which are already creative in nature. The role of meetings, visions, "insights," "revelations," and so forth. See, incidentally: Aleksey Remizov, "Close-cropped eyes. A book of knots and twists of memory."[7] Here, the role of drawings as signs for self-expression. "Klim Samgin" (man as a system of phrases),[8] "The Unsaid" and its special nature and role are interesting from this standpoint. The early stages of verbal cognition. The "unconscious" can become a creative factor only on the threshold of consciousness and of the word (semiverbal/semisignifying consciousness). They are fraught with the word and the potential word. The "unsaid" as a *shifting boundary*, as a "regulative idea" (in the Kantian sense) of creative consciousness.

The process of gradual obliteration of authors as bearers of others' words. Others' words become anonymous and are assimilated (in reworked form, of course); consciousness is *monologized*. Primary dialogic relations to others' words are also obliterated—they are, as it were, taken in, absorbed into assimilated others' words (passing through the stage of "one's own/others' words"). Creative consciousness, when monologized, is supplemented by anonymous authors. This process of monologization is very important. Then this monologized consciousness enters as one single whole into a new dialogue (with the new external voices of others). Monologized creative consciousness frequently joins and personifies others' words, others' voices that have become anonymous, in special symbols: "the voice of life itself," "the voice of nature," "the voice of the people," "the voice of God," and so forth. The role of the *authoritative word* in this process,[9] which usually does not lose its bearer, does not become anonymous.

The striving to reify extraverbal anonymous contexts (to surround oneself with nonverbal life). I only am a creative speaking personality, everything else outside me is only thinglike, material conditions, which as *causes* call forth and define my word. I do not converse with them—I *react* to them mechanically, as a thing reacts to external stimuli.

Such speech phenomena as orders, demands, precepts, prohibitions, promises (oaths), threats, praises, reprimands, abuse, curses, blessings, and so forth comprise a very important part of extracontextual reality. They all are linked with a sharply expressed *intonation* capable of passing (being transferred) to any words or expressions that do not have the direct formal definition of an order, a threat, and so forth.

Tone, released from phonetic and semantic elements of the word (and other signs) is important. Those signs determine the complex *tonality* of our consciousness, which serves as an emotional-evaluative context for our understanding (complete, semantic understanding) of the text we read (or hear) and also, in more complex form, for our creative writing (origination) of a text.

The task consists in forcing the *thinglike* environment, which mechanically influences the personality, to begin to speak, that is, to reveal in it the potential word and tone, to transform it into a semantic context for the thinking, speaking, and acting (as well as creating) personality. In essence any serious and probing self-examination/confession, autobiography, pure lyric, and so forth, does this.[10] Among writers, Dostoevsky, by revealing the actions and thoughts of his main heroes, achieved the greatest profundity in this transformation of the thing into contextual meaning. A thing, as long as it remains a thing, can affect only other things; in order to affect a personality it must reveal its *semantic potential,* become a word, that is, assimilate to a potential verbal-semantic context.

When analyzing Shakespeare's tragedies, we also observe a sequential transformation of all reality that affects the heroes into the semantic context of their actions, thoughts, and experiences: either they are actually words (the words of witches, of a father's ghost, and so forth) or they are events and circumstances translated into the language of the interpretive potential word.[11]

One must emphasize that this is not a direct and pure reduction of everything to a common denominator: the thing remains a thing and the word, a word; they retain their essences and are only augmented by contextual meaning.

One must not forget that "thing" and "personality" are *limits* and not absolute substances. Meaning cannot (and does not wish to) change physical, material, and other phenomena; it cannot act as a material force. And it does not need to do this: it itself is stronger than any force, it changes the total contextual meaning of an event and reality without changing its actual (existential) composition one iota; everything remains as it was but it acquires a completely different contextual meaning (the semantic transformation of existence). Each word of a text is transformed in a new context.

The inclusion of the listener (reader, viewer) in the system (structure) of the work. The author (bearer of the word) and the person who *understands*. The author when creating his work does not intend it for a literary scholar and does not presuppose a specific scholarly *understanding*; he does not aim to create a collective of literary scholars. He does not invite literary scholars to his banquet table.

Contemporary literary scholars (the majority of them Structuralists) usually define a listener who is immanent in the work as an all-understanding, ideal listener. Precisely this kind of listener is postulated in the work. This, of course, is neither an *empirical* listener nor a psychological idea, an image of the listener in the soul of the author. It is an abstract ideological formulation. Counterposed to it is the same kind of abstract ideal author. In this understanding the ideal listener is essentially a mirror image of the author who replicates him. He cannot introduce anything of his own, anything new, into the ideally understood work or into the ideally complete plan of the author. He is in the same time and space as the author or, rather, like the author he is outside time and space (as is any abstract ideal formulation), and therefore he cannot be *an-other* or other for the author, he cannot have any *surplus* that is determined by this otherness. There can be no interaction between the author and this kind of listener, no active dramatic relations, for these are not voices but abstract concepts that are equal to themselves and to one another.[12] Only mechanistic or mathematical, empty tautological abstractions are possible here. There is not a bit of personification.

Content as *new*; form as stereotyped, congealed, old (familiar) content. Form serves as a necessary bridge to new, still unknown content. Form was a familiar and generally understood congealed old world view. In precapitalistic epochs there was a less abrupt, smoother transition between form and content: form was content that had not yet hardened up, was still unfixed, was not hackneyed. Form was linked to the results of general collective creativity, to mythological systems, for example. Form was, as it were, implicit context: the content of a work developed content that was already embedded in the form and did not create it as something new, by some individual-creative initiative. Content, consequently, preceded the work to a certain degree. The author did not invent the content of his work; he only developed that which was already embedded in tradition.

Symbols are the most stable and at the same time the most emotional elements; they pertain to form and not to content.

The strictly semantic aspect of the work, that is, the *formal meaning* of its elements (the first stage of understanding) is in principle accessible to any individual consciousness. But its evaluative-semantic aspect (including symbols) is meaningful only to individuals who are related by some common conditions of life (see the formal definition of the word "symbol")[13]—in the final analysis, by the bonds of brotherhood on a high level. Here we have *assimilation* and, at higher stages, assimilation to higher value (at the extreme, absolute value).

The meaning of emotional-evaluative exclamations in the speech life of peoples. But the expression of emotional-evaluative relations can be explicitly verbal while their *intonation* is, so to speak, implicit. The most essential and stable intonations form the intonational background of a particular social group (nation, class, professional collective, social circle, and so forth). To a certain degree, one can speak by means of intonations alone, making the verbally expressed part of speech relative and replaceable, almost indifferent. How often we use words whose meaning is unnecessary, or repeat the same word or phrase, just in order to have a material bearer for some necessary intonation.

The extratextual intonational-evaluative context can be only partially realized in the reading (performance) of a given text, and the largest part of it, especially in its more essential and profound strata, remains outside the given text as the dialogizing background for its perception. To some degree, the problem of the *social* (extraverbal) conditioning of the work reduces to this.

The text—printed, written, or orally recorded—is not equal to the work as a whole (or to the "aesthetic object"). The work also includes its necessary extratextual context. The work, as it were, is enveloped in the music of the intonational-evaluative context in which it is understood and evaluated (of course, this context changes in the various epochs in which it is perceived, which creates a new resonance in the work).

The mutual understanding of centuries and millennia, of peoples, nations, and cultures, provides a complex unity of all humanity, all human cultures (a complex unity of human culture), and a complex unity of human literature. All this is revealed only on the level of great time. Each image must be understood and evaluated on the level of great time. Analysis usually fusses about in the narrow space of small time, that is, in the space of the present day and the recent past and the imaginable—desired or frightening—future. Emotional-evaluative forms for anticipating the future in language-speech (order, desire, warning, incantation, and so forth), the trivially human attitude toward the future (desire, hope, fear); there is no understanding of evaluative nonpredetermination, unexpectedness, as it were, "surprisingness," absolute innovation, miracle, and so forth. The special nature of the *prophetic* attitude toward the future. Abstraction from the self in ideas about the future (the future without me).

The time of the theatrical spectacle and its laws. Perception of the spectacle in those epochs when religious-cultic and state-ceremonial forms were present and reigned supreme. Everyday etiquette in the theater.

Nature juxtaposed to man. The Sophists, Socrates ("not the trees in the forest, but the people in the cities interest me").[14]

Two limits of thought and practice (deed) or two types of relations (thing and personality). The deeper the personality, that is, the closer to the personality extreme, the less applicable generalizing methods are. Generalization and formalization erase the boundaries between genius and lack of talent.

Experiment and mathematical elaboration. One raises a question and obtains an answer—this is the personal interpretation of the process of natural scientific cognition and of its subject (the experimenter). The history of cognition in terms of its results and the history of cognizing people. See Marc Bloch.[15]

The process of reification and the process of personalization. But personalization is never subjectivization. The limit here is not *I* but *I* in interrelationship with other personalities, that is, *I* and *other*, *I* and *thou*.

Is there anything in the natural sciences that corresponds to "context"? Context is always personalized (infinite dialogue in which there is neither a first nor a last word)—natural sciences have an object system (subjectless).

Our *thought* and our *practice,* not technical but *moral* (that is, our responsible deeds), are accomplished between two limits: attitudes toward the *thing* and attitudes toward the *personality. Reification* and *personification.* Some of our acts (cognitive and moral) strive toward the limit of reification, but never reach it; other acts strive toward the limit of personification, and never reach it completely.

Question and *answer* are not logical relations (categories); they cannot be placed in one consciousness (unified and closed in itself); any response gives rise to a new question. Question and answer presuppose mutual outsideness. If an answer does not give rise to a new question from itself, it falls out of the dialogue and enters systemic cognition, which is essentially impersonal.

The various chronotopes of the questioner and the answerer, and various semantic worlds (*I* and *other*). From the standpoint of a third consciousness and its "neutral" world, where everything is *replaceable,* question and answer are inevitably depersonified.

The difference between *stupidity* (ambivalent) and dullness (monosemantic).

Others' assimilated words ("one's own/others'"), eternally living, and creatively renewed in new contexts; and others' inert, dead words, "word-mummies."

Humboldt's main problem: the multiplicity of languages (the premise and the background of the problem—the unity of the human race).[16] This is in the sphere of languages and their formal structures (phonetic and grammatical). But in the sphere of *speech* (within a single or any language) there arises the problem of one's own and another's word.

1. Reification and personification. The distinction between reification and "alienation." Two limits of thinking; the application of the principle of augmentation.

2. One's own and another's word. Understanding as the transformation of the other's into "one's own/another's." The principle of outsideness. The complex interrelations of the understood and the understanding subjects, of the created and understanding, and of the creatively rejuvenating chronotopes. The importance of reaching, digging down to the creative nucleus of the personality (in the creative nucleus the personality continues to live, that is, it is immortal).

3. Precision and depth in the human sciences. The limit of precision in the natural sciences is identity (a = a). In the human sciences precision is surmounting the otherness of the other without transforming him into purely one's own (any kind of substitution, modernization, nonrecognition of the other, and so forth).

The ancient stage of personification (naive mythological personification). The epoch of reification of nature and man. The contemporary stage of personification of nature (and man), but without loss of reification. See V. V. Kozhinov's article on nature in Prishvin.[17] In this stage, personification is not mythic, and yet it is not hostile to the mythic, and frequently utilizes its language (transformation into the language of symbols).

4. Contexts of understanding. The problem of *remote contexts*. The eternal renewal of meanings in all new contexts. *Small time* (the present day, the recent past, and the foreseeable [desired] future) and great time—infinite and unfinalized dialogue in which no meaning dies. The living in nature (organic). Everything inorganic is drawn into life in the process of exchange (only in abstraction can things be juxtaposed by taking them separately from life).

My attitude toward Formalism: a different understanding of specification; ignoring content leads to "material aesthetics" (criticism of this in my article of 1924);[18] not "making" but creativity (only an "item" is obtained from material); the lack of understanding of historicity and change (a mechanical perception of change). The positive significance of formalism (new problems and new aspects of art); what is new always assumes one-sided and extreme forms in the early, more creative stages of its development.

My attitude toward structuralism: I am against enclosure in a text. Mechanical categories: "opposition," "change of codes" (the many styles of *Eugene Onegin* in Lotman's interpretation and in my interpretation).[19] Sequential formalization and depersonalization: all relations are logical (in the broad sense of the word). But I hear *voices* in everything and dialogic relations among them. I also perceive the principle of augmentation dialogically. High evaluations of structuralism. The problem of "precision" and "depth." Depth of penetration into the *object* (thinglike) and depth of penetration into the *subject* (personal).

Structuralism has only one subject—the subject of the research himself. Things are transformed into *concepts* (a different degree of abstraction); the subject can never become a concept (he himself speaks and responds). Contextual meaning is personalistic; it always includes a question, an address, and the anticipation of a response, it always includes two (as a dialogic minimum). This personalism is not psychological, but semantic.

There is neither a first nor a last word and there are no limits to the dialogic context (it extends into the boundless past and the boundless future). Even *past* meanings, that is, those born in the dialogue of past centuries, can never be stable (finalized, ended once and for all)—they will always change (be renewed) in the process of subsequent, future development of the dialogue. At any moment in the development of the dialogue there are immense, boundless masses of forgotten contextual meanings, but at certain moments of the dialogue's subsequent development along the way they are recalled and invigorated in renewed form (in a new context). Nothing is absolutely dead: every meaning will have its homecoming festival. The problem of *great time*.

Notes

1. Taken from Pasternak's poem "August" from his 1946–53 period (when he was at work on *Dr. Zhivago*). This line appears in the last stanza of the poem, which is part of a quotation from the poet's "former, clairvoyant voice":

> Farewell, spread of the wings out-straightened
> The free stubbornness of pure flight,
> The word that gives the world its image,
> Creation: miracles and light.

As translated in Vladimir Markov and Merrill Sparks, *Modern Russian Poetry* (New York: Bobbs-Merrill Co., 1967) p. 607.

2. See S. S. Averintsev, "The Symbol," in *Kratkaja literaturnaja entsiklopedija* (Moscow, 1972), vol. 7, column 827.
3. Ibid., column 828.
4. See note 23 to "From Notes Made in 1970–71."
5. See note 15 to "From Notes Made in 1970–71."
6. Reference here is to attempts by such figures as Alois Riegl and, above all, Edward Hanslick (1825–1904) to conceive art as perfectly immanent: the history of music, for instance, was a function only of a logic internal to music and had very little to do with composers themselves. See Edward Hanslick, *The Beautiful in Music*, tr. Gustav Cohen (Indianapolis: Bobbs-Merrill Co., 1957). Bakhtin was an acute student of philosophical attempts to found new bases for aesthetics, and his earlier works are peppered with commentary on them. See "Author and Hero in Aesthetic Activity," and *The Formal Method in Literary Scholarship* (pp. 50ff. in Eng. ed.).
7. Reference is to *Podstrizhennymi glazami: Kniga uzlov i zakrut pamjat* (Paris, 1951).

8. The eponymous hero of Maksim Gorky's novel *Zhizn Klima Samgina* (1927–36).

9. Cf. "Discourse in the Novel" in *The Dialogic Imagination*, pp. 342ff.

10. See the analysis of these forms in Bakhtin's early work, where he concentrates on the way authors relate to their heroes; of particular relevance is the chapter on "The Semantic Whole of the Hero" in the forthcoming translation of "Author and Hero" by Vadim Liapunov included in *The Architectonics of Responsibility* (Austin: University of Texas Press, forthcoming).

11. In the spring of 1970, Bakhtin wrote an internal review for the future publishers of a book on Shakespeare by his good friend L. E. Pinsky (*Shekspir* [Moscow, 1971]). In the review, a copy of which is in the Bakhtin archives, he said among other things:

> The stage of the Shakespearean theater is the entire world (*Theatrum mundi*). This is what gives that special significance . . . to each image, each action, and each word in Shakespeare's tragedies, which has never again returned to European drama (after Shakespeare, everything in drama became trivial). . . . This peculiarity of Shakespeare's . . . is a direct legacy of the medieval theater and forms of public spectacles, determining the evaluative-cosmic coloring of above and below . . . the main thing is the perception (or, more precisely, the living sense unaccompanied by any clear awareness) of all action in the theater as some kind of special symbolic ritual.

12. Compare similar ideas in Bakhtin's earlier work (V. N. Voloshinov, "Discourse in Life and Discourse in Art," tr. I. R. Titunik, in *Freudianism: A Marxist Critique* [New York: Academic Press, 1976], p. 112):

> Nothing is more perilous for aesthetics than to ignore the autonomous role of the listener. A very commonly held opinion has it that the listener is to be regarded as equal to the author, excepting the latter's technical performance, and that the position of a competent listener is supposed to be a simple reproduction of the author's position. In actual fact this is not so. Indeed, the opposite may sooner be said to be true: the listener never equals the author. The listener has *his own independent place* in the event of the artistic creation; he must occupy a special, and, what is more, a *two*-sided position in it—with respect to the author and with respect to the hero—and it is this position that has determinative effect on the style of the utterance.

13. See Averintsev, "The Symbol," column 827.

14. In the "Phaedrus," Socrates says, "it is true I rarely venture outside my gates, and I hope that you will excuse me when you hear the reason, which is that I am a lover of knowledge, and the men who dwell in the city are my teachers, and not the trees of the country" (*The Dialogues of Plato*, tr. B. Jowett, 3rd ed. [London: Oxford University Press, 1892], vol. 1, p. 435).

15. See *The Historian's Craft*, tr. Peter Putnam (New York: Random House, 1953).

16. See Wilhelm von Humboldt, *Linguistic Variability and Intellectual Development*, tr. George C. Buck and Frithjof A. Raven (Coral Gables: University of Miami Press, 1971), esp. pp. 1–21.

17. See Vadim Kozhinov, "Not Competition, but Co-Creation," *Literaturnaja gazeta*, 31 October 1983.

18. A translation of this essay ("The Problem of Content, Material, and Form in Artistic Creativity") by Kenneth Brostrom will appear in *The Architectonics of Responsibility*.

19. See note 1 to "From Notes Made in 1970–71."

Index